# MARTIN BUBER

## *The Hidden Dialogue*

### DAN AVNON

ROWMAN & LITTLEFIELD PUBLISHERS, INC.
*Lanham • Boulder • New York • Oxford*

ROWMAN & LITTLEFIELD PUBLISHERS, INC.

Published in the United States of America
by Rowman & Littlefield Publishers, Inc.
4720 Boston Way, Lanham, Maryland 20706

12 Hid's Copse Road
Cummor Hill, Oxford OX2 9JJ, England

Copyright © 1998 by Rowman & Littlefield Publishers, Inc.

Cover photograph copyright © R. M. Kneller

British Library Cataloguing in Publication Information Available

**Library of Congress Cataloging-in-Publication Data**

Avnon, Dan.
    Martin Buber : the hidden dialogue / Dan Avnon.
      p.   cm.
    Includes bibliographical references and index.
    ISBN 0-8476-8687-6 (alk. paper). — ISBN 0-8476-8688-4 (pbk. :
alk. paper)
    1. Buber, Martin, 1878–1965.  I. Title.
B3213.B84A96  1998
    181'.06—dc21
                                        97-41158
                                          CIP

ISBN 0-8476-8687-6 (cloth : alk. paper)
ISBN 0-8476-8688-4 (pbk. : alk. paper)

Printed in the United States of America

♾ ™ The paper used in this publication meets the minimum requirements of
American National Standard for Information Sciences—Permanence of Paper
for Printed Library Materials, ANSI Z39.48–1984.

*For Tal,* עזר כנגדי

# CONTENTS

# PREFACE

A Coolidge fellowship from the Association for Religion in Intellectual Life (ARIL) enabled me to begin work on this book in Cambridge, Massachusetts, during the summer of 1995. I thank ARIL for their generosity and hospitality. I developed the ideas and methodology guiding this book while teaching "Buber" courses at the Hebrew University of Jerusalem between the years 1993 and 1996. Many thanks to the participants in those classes, whose interest and critical questioning sustained my commitment to this project and enriched my understanding.

I am greatly indebted to my friends and colleagues who read earlier drafts of the manuscript and were generous in offering supportive criticism and helpful suggestions: Jill Frank, Hanna Pitkin, David Ricci, and Ronen Shamir. Special thanks to Hanna Pitkin, who was the first to suggest to me that I may have a Buber book "in me" a couple of years before I came to the same conclusion. Thanks to Shlomo Avineri, Shmuel Noah Eisenstadt, Maurice Friedman, Ilana Pardes, and Zeev Sternhell for their encouragement and advice. Thanks also to Sheila Sachar, for helping me with the typing, to Ayelet Levi, for her research assistance, and to Judy Copeland, an excellent copyeditor. Finally, thank you to the team at Rowman and Littlefield—Steve Wrinn, Robin Adler, Lynn Weber, and Serena Leigh—whose efficient and friendly support is highly appreciated.

My greatest gratitude is to my family: Tal, Aviv, and Adar. Tal knows why she is mentioned here and why I dedicate the book to her. The kids may be surprised to find their names here. But if they read these lines and want to know why they made it to these opening pages, they can come and ask me.

Since this book is based on interpretations of Buberian texts written in, or translated from German into, Hebrew, I have checked the existing English translations against the Hebrew versions. When I found an English translation lacking, I provided my own translation. That is why in many cases quotations from Buber's books and essays are supported by two references: one to the English version and the other to the Hebrew version. When the first source cited is the Hebrew version, it means that that quotation is based on my own English translation. When only an English translation is cited, it means either that the Hebrew version is irrelevant in that particular instance or that the existing translation is in my opinion adequate.

I gratefully acknowledge the permission granted to me by Sage Publications to reprint parts of my article, "The 'Living Center' of Martin Buber's Political Theory," *Political Theory* 21:1 (February 1993), 55–77. Selections from *Tales of the Hasidim* by Martin Buber, translated by Olga Marx, copyright 1947, 1948, copyright renewed 1975 by Schocken Books, Inc., are reprinted by permission of Schocken Books, distributed by Pantheon Books, a division of Random House, Inc. I thank Ralph M. Kneller for permission to use his photograph of Martin Buber.

# 1

# INTRODUCTION

The title of this book, *Martin Buber: The Hidden Dialogue*, alludes to a number of propositions. First, it refers to the proposition that Buber included in his writings certain key words and biblical phrases that enshrine a hidden meaning. When reading his texts with an awareness of these key words, we discover a hidden subtext that clarifies difficult passages and affords coherence to dissonant writings. Buber's works therefore include an implicit narrative that is deciphered only through an understanding of key words used in his texts. Thus, the title refers to my making explicit a story that is written in Buber's hermeneutic code.

Second, the hidden dialogue refers to the authority behind Buber's texts, the source that inspired his way of writing: the Hebrew Bible. I shall demonstrate how Buber's writings emulate the hermeneutic rules that guided the work of the final redactor of the Hebrew scripture. From this perspective, my reading of Buber is also an exposition of a story that Buber learned from the Hebrew Bible, a story that he never put together in one coherent work.

Third, the title refers to Buber's conviction that we lack self-knowledge, and that what we consider to be "I" is in fact only a partial representation of our whole selves. To know ourselves more completely necessitates an awareness of an element of our being that is attentive both to our unique singularity *and* to our being inseparable from the one, unified creation. Such awareness of self is ordinarily absent from the everyday experience of life. (It is worth noting that Buber raised this issue half a century before the emergence of New Age parlance.)

Fourth, the title refers to Buber's belief that at all times and in all cultures there are people who are aware of the possibility of knowing self in a manner qualitatively different from the purely biographical or psychological perspective. Such persons consciously cultivate a quality of attention necessary to sustain the "dialogue" between the human species (referred to as *Adam*, which corresponds to the English "human being") and the life energy (referred to in a symbolic way as *Elohim*, a word usually translated as "God"). Because of the unconventional nature of these people's knowledge and understanding, the actions of such "hidden doers" are often absent from conventional chronicles of social and historical development.

The four meanings of the hidden dialogue reflect different dimensions of Buber's philosophy: to seek and bring to light a new-found relation to self and to being. "To bring to light" in this context means to exemplify in conduct and deed the trust and openness to the other that come with the transformed attitude to being. (The word "light" derives from Jewish sources, and Buber uses it as a metaphor for the moment of insightful understanding that *precedes* mental interpretation.) Such a revised ontology rejects the prevalent assumption that the intellect is the only reliable organ for making sense of reality. One may call Buber's alternative a teaching of the heart, a notion that I shall explain in chapter 3.

Having mentioned Buber's critique of what has come to be known as Western "logocentrism" (the term was developed after his death), I would like to add an introductory comment about this aspect of his work. Buber seeks to correct two assumptions that constitute the basis of modern philosophy: the Cartesian assumption that the only experience that enables me to be certain that I exist is the sensation of thinking ("I think, therefore I am"); and the Kantian assumption that the world as we know it is ordered according to categories and postulates that exist a priori in our consciousness. Buber acknowledges that both assumptions do indeed determine our commonplace relation to self (as a thinking being) and to the world (as a reflection of our inner "thought-world"). He also accepts the fact that such use of the intellect is necessary as a means to discriminate between the endless impressions and sensations that we receive, experience, and organize into objectified forms. He understands the necessity of the economizing order that is established through translating "reality" into terms of objects (what is "out there") and subject (what is "in me").[1]

However, the trouble with this dominant ontology and the sense of "order" that it establishes is that it causes us to forget that prior to activating the ability to objectify reality, there is a reality that has been objectified. For example, when we call a person by her name, and refer to her by the name with which we have designated her, we unconsciously distance ourselves from the reality that precedes the name. We do not notice the human being: its glance, its changing moods, its sorrow and joy, its body language, the tenor of its voice, the quality of its presence. Erroneously assuming that the name introduces us to the named, we meet the name, the word, rather than the being itself. We meet a construct of our thought and proceed to relate to things we encounter through the mediation of our thought. This misplaced use of the intellect and of its modes of communication (language, the movement of thought and its organization around fixed structures and categories, and speech) constitutes a barrier between ourselves and the reality that we encounter. In the background of a world mediated by thought is an original position, that in which what is to be seen prior to the construct of thought is revealed.

These introductory comments are supported by Buber's own testimony about the ultimate significance of his teachings. Asked at the end of his days to respond to critiques of his philosophy, Buber readily admitted that he had not attempted to articulate a fixed system of thought: "The thinking, the teaching had to be determined by the task of pointing. Only what was connected with the pointing to what was to be pointed to was admissible. . . . I must say it once again: I have no teaching. I only point to something. I point to reality. I point to something in reality that had not or had too little been seen."[2] This passage directs attention to Buber's basic intention when writing: he sought innovative ways to sensitize his readers to the reality for which forms of linguistic communication serve as indicators. I believe that Buber's theory of society and of politics is inseparable from his choice of literary styles, and I shall devote considerable attention to the relation between form and content in his work. Buber struggled with the paradox of using words in a manner that would transcend language, as vehicles of *seeing* and of *listening*; *seeing* and *listening* in the sense of a direct relation to what is present, an attitude to being that is prior to, and unmediated by, language.

❀

Buber believed that each person is a unique expression of the generic Adam and that the generic Adam is present in each of its human forms. This belief is expressed in the title of the last Hebrew collection of Buber's essays, *Pnei Adam* (The Faces of Adam), published in 1962. This collection includes essays on philosophy, philosophical anthropology, ethics, and religion. They address what Buber perceived as a common misunderstanding about the essential nature of being human and indicate alternative ways of looking at how to live a good life and how to seek individual perfection.

The collection opens with the question "What is the Human Being [*Adam*]?" This question is part of a larger essay called "The Problem of the Human Being: A Study in its Chronology." The study begins by pointing to modern philosophy's inadequate treatment of the most elementary of existential questions: "what am I?" This opening is characteristic of Buber's teachings. To fully understand the "problem" of Adam, one must first understand what Adam is. The "problem" can then be characterized in terms of the deviation of the human (Adam) from its essential nature. To know what one may be means first knowing what one is. To know what one is requires both *seeing* how one's "self" is conditioned by convention (and, as such, is oriented to life as it is ordinarily experienced) *and* discovering the greater reality within which all selves exist (thus situating the self in the greater context of creation).

What is the experience indicated by the terms "*seeing*" and "*listening*"?[3] I will deal with these questions in greater detail later, but at this juncture it is worth noting two of Buber's many responses. First, *seeing* is "[the] opening [of] one's eyes without turning aside and without adapting the gaze to prior prejudice and preconceived thoughts." Buber seems to suggest that by putting aside one's mental and cultural preconceptions, "one will *see* [reality], and this *seeing* will surely influence him to the extent that he will begin to think for himself about what he had *seen* and perhaps may even begin to act according to the implications of such thinking."[4] Buber's experience taught him that such an open attitude to self and world leads one to the discovery of the "fundamental relation of his soul to the world: [to] his responsibility."[5] To understand that thought and cultural conditioning are an obstacle to *seeing* is thus a central concern of Buber's philosophy, and it is the first step to realizing one's role in the world.

Second, an initial understanding of the meaning of *listening* in Buber's parlance is communicated in the following Hasidic saying: "I shall teach you the best way to say Torah. You must cease to be aware of yourselves. You must be nothing but an ear that hears what the universe of the word is constantly saying within you. The moment you start hearing what you yourself are saying, you must stop."[6] To hear the "universe of the word" necessitates a quality of *listening* that can distinguish between the ordinary, automatic movement of thought and the "words" that are prior to this reactive characteristic of thinking. Hence the advice to direct awareness to the latent and ever-present "saying" that is "within you." Such refocusing of attention assumes prior recognition of such a distinction, between an "I" shaped by convention and an "I" that is attentive to the voice of creation. Hence the concluding imperative: "The moment you start hearing what you yourself are saying, you must stop."

To *see* necessitates study of self (as does *listening* to the primal "saying"). Such self-study involves being aware of obstacles that stand in the way of one's ability to relate without preconceptions. However, self-study is not a solitary endeavor. In Buber's writings, self-knowledge is necessarily intertwined with knowledge of others. For example, "love" is experienced in relation to that which is loved; one enters into love. That entrance is created when one's being is open to an other. Love therefore exists in between the person and the object of its desire. This understanding of the nature of emotions lies at the heart of Buber's emphasis on the centrality of interhuman relationships.

The reality of the "space" that is in between persons is the focus of Buber's philosophy. That is why one of the collections of Hebrew essays that precede *Pnei Adam* is called *Besod Siach* (In the Secret of Dialogue).[7] Even though the goal of his teaching is the single Adam, the way towards his model of human perfection entails human relationship and dialogue. In this collection, Buber expounds the philosophy of dialogue, the philosophy of I and You, for which he is famous. The root of this philosophy is the belief that self-perfection is attainable only in the context of one's relation to others. This relation "exists in the form of dialogue."

An additional element makes dialogue inclusive and complete: self-knowledge is possible only "if the relation between man and creation is understood to be also a dialogical relation."[8] Dialogue therefore includes all spheres of relation: relation to self, relation to other(s), and relation to all forms of created being. Dialogue is at the heart of Buber's mature writings, and is the conceptual linchpin of his teachings.

*Besod Siach* was published in 1959 at the height of the cold war, a period characterized by the replacement of dialogue with ideology. Ideology is a form of political thought that is eminently antidialogical. It accentuates difference, it assumes superiority over alternative forms of political thought, and it seeks to impose itself on others. In the same way he approaches the "problem" of Adam, Buber begins his investigation of ideology's antidialogical character by examining prevailing assumptions about the purpose of political association and revealing how this translates into modern forms of social and political organization. Through studying the concrete social and political effects of modern ontology, Buber shows how blind trust in well-ordered words precludes an awareness of one's responsibility to the realities that exist prior to the words that label them.[9]

The Hebrew collection of Buber's writings on Judaic heritage, also published in 1959, is called *Te'udah Veyeud* (Testimony and Mission). These writings include essays on the nature of Judaism: its history, the purpose of its continued historical existence as a community of faith, the significance of the Jewish return to the ancient land of Israel, and the responsibility of this tradition and its bearers to the life of Adam. Ultimately, these essays attempt to introduce the reader to a paradox: that "God" is beyond the grasp of human beings ("who are absolutely incommensurable with him") and "that he faces them."[10] Stated differently, this paradox refers to the fact that if I exist I am part of "being," yet if I experience a "relation to being," then I live in relation to what I am part of. Can I have a "relation" to what I am a part of? To know both these things at the same time—that what is distant is also present—constitutes a complete dialogical relation.

In Buber's reading of Judaic tradition, the Hebrew Bible transmits in allusive form the possibility to experience this apparent paradox. In addition, the Hebrew Bible teaches its community of faith its mission: to establish "in the end of times" (at the end of the present historical epoch) a form of community that will exemplify in social practice the way to live the paradox: to be Adam, with a relation to being that includes self, others, and all that is. And to do so by acting justly.

Why did I choose to illustrate Buber's philosophy with an overview of the titles of his Hebrew collections of essays? And why did I start with the most recent and move backward? First, I find the sequence significant: the *end* (*Pnei Adam*, which opened the survey) is oriented to any person, to any *Adam*. The *way* is universal. It includes others and addresses philosophies and cultures of diverse societies and historical periods. The *beginning* is in Buber's interpretation of his particular culture and community and develops in relation to the historical contingencies of his life and times. The way is present in the distance between beginning and end. The three elements—end, way, and beginning—are inseparable. As such, my reading of Buber presents a complete teaching. This is contrary to many interpretations of Buber's work, which tend to emphasize one aspect of his teachings and consequently lose sight of the whole.[11]

Second, by presenting Buber's titles from the most recent to the earliest, I demonstrate my belief that as he grew older, Buber became increasingly clear as to the rationale that guided his quest and as to the lessons he had learned on the way. This book will focus on these lessons, rather than on the twists and turns that led up to them.

Third, by quoting the Hebrew titles, I draw the reader's attention to the significance of Hebrew in my interpretation of Buber's intentions and deeds. Buber began writing in Hebrew in 1938. He was sixty years old at the time and had just arrived in Palestine. Prior to this he had written in German. I argue in this book that Buber's Hebrew writings (including translations of his essays and books written originally in German) represent a new maturity of thought and best reflect his most essential teachings.

Fourth, the reader will discover that Hebrew words applied in a seemingly arbitrary fashion in this introduction are in fact loaded with meaning. The words *Adam, Sod, Te'udah,* and *Yeud*, elaborated upon in later chapters, are all part of Buber's lexicon of significant terms. It is my intention to acquaint readers with their implicit meanings beyond their common usage.

Finally, this preliminary survey points to the fact that Buber's philosophy has an intrinsic social value: self-study and self-knowledge materialize in the context of relationships. In Buber's vision, communities of mutual support on the path to refined self-knowledge,[12] such as those idealized in his revision of biblical stories and Hasidic tales, will become the basic social unit of a future civilization of dialogue. The unique characteristic of such communities is not their social structure, but rather the effect of the relationships that they foster. Buber's revision of hasidic lore illustrates how dialogical centers of community (in the Hasidic case, the *zaddikim*, or "just persons") transform commonplace events and relationships into opportunities for self-study and for the subsequent opening of self to the greater reality of being.[13] This effect (the "opening") is referred to in Buber's philosophical and political works as the "Between," a refined essence that permeates the social sphere when a person's attitude to being originates in a transformed relation to self and others.[14]

A Buberian community is thus composed of members who know that their everyday relationships are opportunities to perfect both self and community. We all live ordinary lives, and from a Buberian perspective, this implies that every encounter is an opportunity to be present to what is. This approach emphasizes the commonplace and attempts to establish the relevance of community for any person. An additional aspect of Buber's teaching is that while an ideal community is usually bounded by territory or culture, the notion of community also alludes to a shared attitude to being that does not necessitate a common formal framework.[15]

The subtext that I shall reconstruct from a hermeneutic reading of Buber's texts is difficult to present in scholarly form. The story assumes familiarity with the two ontological sources of Western culture—the Bible (revelation) and classical philosophy (reason)—and occasionally sets out propositions that seem audacious.[16]

In chapter 4, for example, I reconstruct Buber's interpretation of the biblical creation story. The logic of Buber's presentation leads to the conclusion that the Hebrew words *Adam* and *Elohim* signify the human potential for self-perfecting through the conscious direction of awareness toward an immanent source of energy indicated by the word *Elohim*. The essence derived from the fusion of *Adam* and *Elohim*—a meeting of awareness and a fine source of *energia*—creates a certain texture in the space surrounding human life; the air is infused with an essence that is vital for the sustenance and growth of life. This interpretation of biblical imagery as representative of mental and emotive states is one way of understanding Buber's dialogical social philosophy. It is predicated on the assumption that people's attitudes to being determine the quality of their social space—an alternative way of understanding Buber's notion of the Between.[17]

Buber's audacity is not limited to his writings about the Bible. He is equally innovative in his philosophical writings. Buber's increasingly focused critique of contemporary ontology stems from his understanding of the origins of linguistic communication in a prelinguistic relation to being. My reconstruction of Buber's philosophy of language may be presented as follows: When one is attentive to the origins of thought, to the encounter with reality that is granted communicative form through the arising of thought, one discerns a primal relation to events that exists as wordless attention. This original relation activates an innate desire to share understanding with like-minded beings. The innate desire to relate is formed into language; words become thought, and thought becomes speech (or text).

Thus, in Buber's understanding, language—the external form of the movement of thought—is thrice removed from the original relation to reality. This is the basis for his critique of philosophical perspectives that are grounded in Cartesian assumptions about the nature of thought. In claiming a nonlinguistic relation to being (to "what is") that is the essential origin of thought, Buber challenges the Cartesian assumption that the self is basically a construct of thought ("I think, therefore I am"). From this discussion of the origins of language and speech in prelinguistic insight, one can see why Buber's thesis is difficult to translate into written form. According to his logic, the written word is at least once removed from its origin in thought, and language, the vehicle of thought, is itself far removed from the original relation that precedes its arising.

Buber's understanding of the basis of the "social self" and of the origin of language as a prelinguistic desire to share insight form the ontological basis of his writings on interhuman relationships and community. In later chapters, I shall look at how this understanding determines, and manifests itself in, his political theory and practice, including, for example, his consistent objection to founding an independent Jewish nation-state (he prefers a binational federative union of Jewish and Arab communities) and his all-encompassing vision of a global "community of communities." To state it simply, Buber's social criticism and political activities are inseparable from their roots in his biblical interpretation and philosophical contemplation.

One final example of the audacious nature of Buber's propositions has to do with his unconventional presentation of the "secret" that Judaism transmits in the course of preserving and continually reinterpreting its heritage. Buber considered that the task of ancient Judaism and of modern Zionism was to sustain within history the essential ahistorical relation to being that he associated with "the primal voice of the Hebrew Bible" and with the "essential insight of philosophical contemplation." I show that this understanding determined his studies of historical events and personalities. These studies encompass Buber's view of the *past* (his discussions of the prophet Isaiah, of the messiah Jesus, and of the founder of Hasidism, the Ba'al Shem) and of the *present* (the Holocaust, the founding of the State of Israel, and the Jewish-Arab conflict) and in addition determine his vision of the *future* (his notion that Zionism should create a paradigm of social conduct that would be a viable alternative to conventional forms of social and political order). This level of my analysis of Buber's intentions explains the complex roots of Buber's political vision of a global civilization of dialogue, a "community of communities" that would emerge as a constructive reaction to the failure of the modern nation-state to create social relationships supportive of the emergence of the Between.

Buber's unconventional attitude to history merits attention here. The story that I reconstruct presents Buber's assumption that what we ordinarily refer to as "history" is inherently limited by the ontology that developed through immoderate trust in fixed structures of thought as the basis of certainty about the movement of life. Buber suggests that from the beginning of the present epoch, dubbed the Axial Age by Karl Jaspers,[18] historical consciousness has gradually become the dominant way of relating to reality. This ontological form reinforces the human type that it assumes, based on a view of human nature as violent and unruly, inherently inclined to domination and wrongdoing. Buber's alternative does not refute the historical basis for belief in the fundamental evil intrinsic in human nature. He seeks rather to subvert the Hobbesian assumption that the lack of trust and readiness to resort to violence that characterize human conduct are proof that this conduct is "natural." He presents his case indirectly, by undermining the ontology that accepts "historical accounts" as reliable explanations and descriptions of the nature and purpose of human existence.

Chapter 4 discusses Buber's alternative relation to history and his parallel attitude towards text: history, like the written word, is but a facade that masks, rather than reflects, reality. Hence his notion of "the hidden history," analogous to the subtext in a body of writing. The hidden history is the chronicle of an ongoing relation to being that exists in diverse cultural forms and is characterized by the agent's ability to relate directly to being, without the a priori mediation of thought.

This perspective does not conform to conventional ideas of history, which assume our past to be a chronicle of events related to one another in a sequential and causal pattern. We relate to ourselves (as individuals and as collectives) in a manner that assumes past events that lead to present circumstances. This commonplace attitude seems to Buber limited (in terms of understanding our origins) and hence limiting (in terms of realizing our ends). Buber thus draws an analogy between individual and collective forms of self-conception, between identification with biography and identification with history. The conventional conception of historical order replicates the post-Cartesian understanding of self as a linear continuity that progresses from past to future, between birth and death. The individual sense of being and of personal progress is affirmed by identification with the linear movement of thought and with the contents that it conveys. Analogous to this understanding of, and identification with, self, history is ordered in such a fashion as to correspond with and reinforce the logic of individual reasoning about self and existence. Consequently, if historical events seem to be incongruent and out of sync with one another—a judgment that is based on the degree of conformity of events to preconceived notions about what should materialize—we tend to think that there is a missing detail that would explain our discomfort. Such a reaction to apparent dissonance between what we encounter and what we expect (on the basis of past experience) is familiar from our personal lives too. This kind of relation to self and to history leads us to assume that if something is wrong in our personal or communal development, it can be rectified by "fixing" our past in a way that makes the present more coherent and bearable. Having drawn our attention to this practice, Buber asks us to reconsider our approach.

Up to this point, I have presented the logic that guides my reading of Buber's works, with particular emphasis on selected aspects of his philosophy and of the role of relationships within this philosophy. I would now like to add some comments about the traditions of interpretation that guide his work (and mine). I want to draw attention to Buber's intentions and his interpretive enterprise in two complementary contexts: as part of the Jewish tradition of interpretation and as a study written in a period of considerable "postmodern" confusion about the limits of "legitimate" interpretation.[19]

I begin with the Jewish context. An accepted tradition in Judaism assumes that the Torah stands on two foundations: the Halacha (the written commandments and their body of interpretation) and the Aggadah (the oral tradition of legends, anecdotes and sayings "of the wise"). The Halacha focuses its attention on the transmitted text, attempting to be as precise as possible, whereas the Aggadah enables one to speak one's heart, using poetic and allusive language.[20] Gerald Bruns notes that although the text's words are binding as law (Halacha), they are not always understandable, engendering a tension between the written and the spoken word of the Torah: recorded in the text, the prophetic word "has something unwritable about it."[21] Ambiguity regarding the exact nature of the prophetic voice is a primary source of the dialogue within Judaism about the meaning inherent in the canonical texts and is one of the foundations of the aggadic tradition, which offers an alternative perspective on the nature of textual authority. The aggadic tradition views the Torah as a dynamic entity, its teaching open to diverse interpretation. In this tradition, the interpreter replaces the prophet as an authority on biblical text.[22]

The tension between disparate understandings of the nature and intention of the Torah, and between the interpretations considered permissible and legitimate, is therefore part and parcel of the tradition. This tension is apparent in the frequent attempts made to rationalize Judaism (a development that, for our purposes, may be considered part of the halachic stream of interpretation) and in the counterarguments that seek to reinforce that dimension of Judaism which cannot be reduced to rational discourse—the Kabbalah (the esoteric or "mystical" stream within Judaism, a development that in the context of this discussion, may be considered an aspect of the aggadic tradition). For example, Moshe Idel attributes the development of an exoteric form of the Kabbalah to this dialectic. Idel asks why the Kabbalah developed at the same time and in the same place—late-twelfth century Provence—as the controversy regarding the teachings of Maimonides (1135–1204). He suggests that the Kabbalah of Nachmanides (1194–1270) developed as a form of reaction to the attempt by Maimonides to replace the mystical tradition with a philosophical system of textual interpretation, thereby subordinating Jewish esotericism to the principles of philosophical inquiry. Nachmanides' response to this redirection of tradition was not a direct attack on the new method but rather a continuing effort to construct an alternative based on ancient materials.[23] The revival of tradition based on a renewed interpretation of ancient texts in response to the changing dialectic between halachic and aggadic modes of interpretation is thus part of the ongoing dialogue within Judaism. Attempts to resolve, once and for all, the creative tension between the written and the oral traditions inevitably give rise to counterreactions.

In his attempts to transform discourse to meet needs of the day, Buber was an active participant in the ongoing dialogue within Judaism. However, while clearly following Jewish interpretive practices, Buber departed from established custom in one significant way: traditional forms of Jewish renewal assume a theological basis, while Buber's interpretation of the "voice" required no prior theology. His work can be read as an increasingly focused attempt to resensitize his and future generations to the decisive experience that precedes any fixed, authoritative textual interpretation. As such, his work is anarchical and challenges Jewish orthodoxy.

How are we to consider my reading of Buber in a non-Jewish context? Existing paradigms of reading may be organized into three groups, according to categories devised by Umberto Eco (in his role as professor of semiotics): *reader oriented* (the only reliable reading of a text is a misreading, and the chain of responses that a text elicits is ultimately its reliable interpretation); *author oriented* (the only valid interpretation aims at finding the author's original intention); and—the category preferred by Eco—*text oriented* (there is an intention of the text, which may or may not cohere with the author's intention).[24] My work is of the third variety, supported by the second.

It is difficult to define abstractly what is meant by "intention of the text."[25] However, in this instance—a reading of Buber's texts—the author sets limits to interpretation by furnishing the reader with a code for reading the nonliteral senses contained within his texts:[26] Buber spelled out how one should read the Hebrew Bible, and applied the same principles to his own writings. Some critics may protest that there is no empirical ground for assuming that Buber applied to his own writings principles that had guided the biblical redactor, and that my hermeneutic assumptions are based on conjecture. Happily, I am supported in my hypothesis by the author of the texts I reconstruct. At the end of his days, Buber was explicit in stating his intentions. In his essay "Replies to My Critics," he directs his critics to certain biblical verses as keys to understanding his intentions. "It is entirely incomprehensible to me how one can interpret my statement [here Buber refers to a quote from his Hasidic works] . . . I have ever again pointed to what it means when a man steps forth arbitrarily out of the hiddenness of the 'quiver' in which God has sunk him like a 'polished arrow' (Isaiah 49:2)."[27] In this quote Buber draws a direct relation between his writings on Hasidism and a verse from the Book of Isaiah. The meaning he attributes to the verse becomes clear only if the critic reads it in the context of Buber's many texts and recognizes its importance as a guiding verse.[28] I will elucidate this meaning in chapter 4 and subsequent chapters.

Although my book focuses on the intention of the text (rather than of the author), I do not eliminate Buber from my discussion. In chapter 2 I refer to the relation between Buber's intellectual (and biographical) development and his conscious inclusion of guiding words in his texts. Neither do I claim that the interpretation I present is the only viable one. Indeed, my own experience of reading Buber's works reveals that the same texts may elicit manifold interpretations and that these are not necessarily mutually exclusive.

For example, when I first read Buber's Hasidic tales, I was primarily interested in them as illustrating concepts central to his social and political vision. On second reading, I noticed that as well as conveying the texture of the dialogical moment, these Hasidic legends served as a means of presenting potentially offensive scriptural exegesis in an apparently innocuous and inoffensive form. Both interpretations are valid and are supported by the text and its intentions. However, the second reading of the Hasidic legends was based on the assumption that these exegetical gems were part of a greater literary strategy, a code of writing that was carried through all Buber's mature texts. My second reading therefore included an understanding of the nature of dialogue and of Buber's way of writing about this subject that was absent from my first reading. In sum, I experienced the transition from being what Eco terms a "Model naive reader" of a first interpretive level (interpretation based

on the linear text) to being a "Model smart reader"[29] of a second interpretive level (where the text is open to additional critical interpretation
by a "Model reader" who has been constructed by the text). The
second-interpretive-level Model reader is the one who uncovers "the
brilliant narrative strategy by which the first-level naive reader has been
designed."[30]

These comments notwithstanding, the only way to check a conjecture about a text's intention is to verify it against the text as a whole. Eco
summarizes this point: "Any interpretation given of a certain portion of
a text can be accepted if it is confirmed and must be rejected if it is
challenged by another portion of the same text. *In this sense the internal
textual coherence controls the otherwise uncontrollable drives of the reader* [my
italics—D.A.]."[31] This is what I do in my book. The idea is an old one
and central to texts that fall into the category referred to in contemporary scholarship as ancient hermeneutics.[32] However, we are justifiably
wary of modern attempts to reproduce ancient techniques of writing.
Accordingly, we should ask: How do we know that Avnon is not over-
interpreting Buber? Do Buber's texts have an intention that is subject to
"controllable" interpretation? *Martin Buber: The Hidden Dialogue*, as a
coherent whole, is the ultimate response to this question.

I would like to end this introduction with an anecdote that is more
telling than additional analysis. Not long ago I invited a friend, an expert
on Henri Bergson's philosophy, to read Buber's article[33] about Bergson's
notion of intuition and then to share his impressions of Buber's presentation of Bergson's philosophy with the participants of a Buber seminar
that I taught at the Hebrew University.

In that article, Buber writes that there are two apparently different
I's: one is original, and its existence and being "is immersed in the free
flow of being, in its moving difference"; the other is oriented to goals
and fixated around some purpose determined by the mind. The "I" of
the second kind is an objecification of the first. It operates in the social
world and is formed by the demands of society. The first "I" is not
formed into a fixed image or function, and its power lies in its ability to
accept facts without immediately forging them into the mold of necessity. The second "I" is formed according to predetermined thoughts
and relates to the other accordingly. Buber writes that had our intuitive

attention been able to grasp the undivided presence, "we would have known ourselves absolutely."[34]

My friend read this article, and after a week he called me. "If I have to read one other text of Buber's, what would you recommend to me?"

I replied, "*The Way of Man according to the Teachings of Hasidism.*"[35]

After another week, my friend showed up at the seminar. "Buber is split between his commitment to two conflicting voices. As such, he is a servant of two masters," he declared.

"???" The blank stares of my students and me indicated our bewilderment.

"I read the article as you requested, and I was struck by a deep tension that underlies the essay. It is a tension not between conflicting ideas but rather between two conflicting voices. One voice reacts to Bergson's philosophy from within Bergson's discourse. That external layer of the text was easy for me to read and critique. I'll go on to that in a moment. However, present in the text is an additional voice that is struggling to be heard. That voice seems to be aware of the limits of the philosophical language he is using and analyzing, but is hesitant and weak, enabling the predominant voice to override its doubts.

"So, parallel to the philosophical discourse explicit on the text's surface, a second voice seems to be critical of the philosophical enterprise that he himself is undertaking by writing that essay. The man is split between the voices—the voice of conventional thinking and writing and the voice that despairs of this mode of communication. It's as if analysis of Bergson stands in the way of that other voice and its vocalization. Overall, it is obvious to me that the Buber who writes this essay is reluctant to let go of scholarly and academic discourse yet at the same times wishes to write differently."

After a moment's reflection, he continued: "What I am left with is the attraction to the latent voice that I sense present between the lines. That voice intrigues me. Reading Buber's Hasidic text confirmed my intuition: there one hears more clearly echoes of the other voice."

My friend, whose interest in Bergson stemmed from genuine interest in the forms of knowledge that Bergson had attempted to communicate, did not fret over what he considered Buber's misrepresentation of some of Bergson's positions. After prompting debate among my students about the meaning of "intuition" and presenting his interpretation of Buber's article, my friend left. Later he asked me: "What is the matter with this Buber of yours? I can feel that he is extremely honest in his questioning, yet at the same time somewhat weak and accommodating in his response to the questions he raises. Why doesn't he simply state his own position? Why present his ideas by writing through Bergson, and so obliquely, too?"

Buber was indeed a servant of two voices, of two masters. One voice sought to participate in the ordinary discourse—philosophical, literary, political and scholarly—prevailing in his time. That voice was grounded in the texts of the day and addressed contemporary philosophical and political concerns. As such, this was the voice of Buber's "socially constructed self": the part of "self" that constructs its identity in response to other persons' expectations and that continually adapts itself to the discourse and responses of others. It is a "self" we all experience in our everyday lives and relationships. Yet in the case of Buber, one intuits that there was an additional, latent voice in the background. This book aims to draw attention to the effects of *seeing* the other, latent voice and of *listening* to it, with particular emphasis on the personal, social, and cultural dimensions and implications of such awareness.

# 2

# BIOGRAPHY: FROM MYSTICISM TO DIALOGUE TO ATTENTIVE SILENCE

B uber wrote with great attention to every word and turn of phrase and was careful to publish pieces that, on the one hand, were complete in themselves yet, on the other, were parts of his greater literary and philosophical whole. The fact that Buber was meticulous in his choice of words will become clear in later chapters as we shall discover how he used key words and phrases to correlate apparently disparate essays and texts so as to facilitate deeper understanding of his writings. Yet this chapter, dealing with his biography and development, looks beyond textual sources to the comments of colleagues and friends. For example, Avraham Shapira notes that he once approached Buber and asked him if difficult passages in his works were simply variations on a theme or if, in fact, they were distinct in terms of nuance and intention. Showing Buber some apparently similar passages from different works, Shapira commented that while the passages were linguistically rich, they did not seem substantially different in terms of central concepts or principles. Buber answered succinctly: "I have a habit of using my tongue accurately." He then went on to show Shapira that every expression represented a specific distinction.[1]

Similarly, the executors of Buber's formidable literary estate found an abundance of drafts of letters, written and rewritten, with very few original manuscripts that were complete and ready to be printed or sent. Ernst Simon writes that the numerous drafts "testify not only to the extraordinary industriousness of a person who was busy beyond imagination but also to one of [Buber's] defining traits: the 'responsibility to the word,' which even when it is written is a form of speech intended for a specific person."[2]

I open my discussion of Buber's biography with comments about his self-conscious attention to the written and spoken word because this book is based on the assumption that Buber's texts indeed stand as artifacts that do not need biographical explanation in order to be read and interpreted. Buber considered his writings to be careful representations of the truths he encountered, and they should be read accordingly. This is not to suggest that intellectual, historical, religious, or cultural contexts are irrelevant to issues raised in his writings. They are clearly indispensable. However, in studying a thinker whose primary intention was to open the minds and hearts of his readers to the reality that *precedes* intellectual or historical influences, it is important to study that "additional" reality. This primary intention of Buber's called for minimizing his presence in the text as a person with a particular biography and agenda. Buber realized that when the biographical circumstances of the author assume importance to the text, the reader loses sight of the relevance of the words themselves to his or her own life and experience.

Commensurate with this insight, Buber kept his personal life to himself. He thought that inordinate focus on biographical details interfered with his readers' ability to comprehend the intention and implications of his works. It is therefore not surprising to find in Buber's letters and essays a skeptical attitude to those who attempted to interpret his writings by applying superficial psychological explanations based on his life-circumstances. Maurice Friedman records that shortly before his death Buber remarked to a psychologist friend, "No one will ever write this man's biography!"[3] To ensure that this really would be the case, Buber directed the executor of his literary estate to refrain from publishing personal material included in his correspondence.[4] One might add that unlike Rousseau (who abandoned his children in orphanages) or Nietzsche (who ended his life mentally deranged), Buber seems to have been well balanced and had no dark secrets. He was married happily for some sixty years, with children and grandchildren; his primary vices seem to have been pride, a sweet tooth, and a stingy streak.[5]

Buber's reticence about personal details that might be used to interpret his works is evident in a letter he wrote in 1952 to a graduate student who kept pestering him for information about his childhood: "I am not interested in the world being interested in my person. I want to influence the world, but I do not want it to feel being influenced by 'me.' " He added that "in order to see what a writer (or speaker) has to show you there is no need to know more about his personal qualities or his personal life than what his sayings, his works themselves tell you." In this respect, he felt blessed with a "gift" of perception and communication shared by such great writers as Shakespeare, Plato and Homer.[6] When interpreting works of this magnitude, the texts speak for themselves.

The fact that this book analyzes the significance of Buber's work based strictly on his writings (thus following Buber's own logic in this matter) does not mean I regard Buber as having been devoid of ego. He, too, had a facade and mannerisms and modes of behavior that reflected his personality.[7] For example, he liked chocolate, and did not always share the delicacies that he kept in the drawer of his table.[8] He was rather spoiled. When his wife brought him his tea, he did not always ask his guests if they, too, wanted a drink. This particularly annoyed the young men and women who came to see him after a night of military duty in 1948 war-time Jerusalem.[9] In addition, many of his contemporaries write that he had a vain streak, that he was proud of his intense eyes and his flowing "rabbinical" beard.[10]

Ultimately, it is not Buber's weaknesses, but rather *the* insight (not *his* insight) about the nature of what is that granted his work direction and meaning. Later chapters will deal exclusively with this insight. They will explain my understanding of Nobel laureate S. Y. Agnon's comment that Buber was a person whose work was not understood by his generation because they "did not see the light within him; they did not take the time to fathom his words."[11] Thus, chapters 3 through 7 will direct attention to the "light" that Buber's words (texts) both hide and reveal. This primary focus notwithstanding, the present chapter deals with the facade. It summarizes external events that position Buber in historical and temporal context, briefly introduces his primary works and stages of intellectual development, and touches on a number of issues that serve as a background for the ensuing exegesis of Buber's texts. This survey is a necessary element of this book and is commensurate with the understanding that the book seeks to communicate; to encounter the "two-foldedness" of being necessarily implies *inclusion* of the facade.

We begin, therefore, with the facade.

## EXTERNAL EVENTS

Martin Buber was born in Vienna in 1878. His parents separated when he was three years old, and his mother disappeared, leaving him to the care of his father.[12] (She reappeared briefly when Buber was into his thirties, already married and the father of a son and a daughter.) With the dissolution of his parents' marriage, Buber was raised in the home of his grandparents in an estate near Lvov (Lemberg), then the capital city of Austrian Galicia. Buber writes that "they were both people of high rank, noble persons in the exact sense of the term. . . . They were both disinclined to talk over the affairs of their existence."[13]

His grandparents were also disinclined to talk to young Martin about the affairs of *his* existence: "Of what had taken place between my parents, nothing, of course, was spoken in my presence." Four-year-old Martin learned of the finality of his mother's disappearance in a chance conversation that he had with a girl who was taking care of him. Leaning with him over the railing of a balcony, Buber recalls, the girl said: "No, she will never come back." This was a decisive moment in the development of his sensitivity to spoken words and their ability to communicate truth. He adds: "All that I have learned about genuine meeting in the course of my life had its first origin in that hour on the balcony."[14]

What does this rather obscure comment mean? It seems that there is a double lesson embodied in this childhood memory: (1) the pain and tragedy of unfulfilled relationships and (2) the reward and opportunity immanent in direct encounters with what is. Buber writes that following the incident on the balcony, he made up the word *Vergegnung* (mismeeting, or misencounter) to designate "the failure of real meeting between persons," referring perhaps both to his mother's inability to be a mother (and hence for him to be her son) and to his grandparents' inability to present him with basic facts central to his existence. The lasting impact of the episode on the balcony lay in its teaching Buber the power and impact of words truthfully spoken, even those that present a painful reality. In the long run, it was the power of the words spoken by the girl, not the loss felt by the child deprived of a mother, that left its mark on his soul. In this respect, Buber seems to identify with the experience of Plato, whose meetings with Socrates were of far more significance than his childhood recollections of his parent. Hence Buber's rhetorical question: "If we knew what in [Plato's] infancy he felt about his parents would it help us to grasp the development of his thought as much as the fact of his meeting a man called Socrates or even the fact of his meeting a man called Dion helps us to grasp it?"[15]

Until the age of ten, Buber was raised at home by his grandparents and by private tutors. From his grandfather Solomon Buber, a dedicated scholar and skilled editor of rabbinic works, he learned the Jewish sources; and from his grandmother Adele, sensitivity to language, texts, and German culture.[16] Buber describes his grandfather as "a genuine philologist, who is to be thanked for the first . . . critical edition of a special class of Hebrew literature: the Midrashim—a unique mixture of interpretation of the Bible, wise sayings, and rich saga." We shall see in later chapters that in basing his interpretation of the Jewish heritage on midrashic and legendary sources, Buber was following the tradition of his grandfather. His grandmother instilled in her grandson "a respect for the authentic word that cannot be paraphrased. . . . I learned before the age of fourteen (at the same time that I moved into the house of my father and stepmother) what it really means to express something." Buber sums up his grandparents' influence on his later development in the following words: "My grandfather was . . . a 'lover of the word,' but my grandmother's love for the genuine word affected me even more strongly than his: because this love was so direct and so devoted."[17] It is significant to note that Buber had a knack for languages. In addition to German (the tongue spoken at home), Yiddish (the tongue of the Hasidic community of Lvov), and Polish (the tongue of the gymnasium that he joined at the age of ten), he was fluent as a child in Greek, Latin, French, and Hebrew.

At the age of thirteen he was called to read from the Torah at the synagogue, as is customary for Jewish boys (bar mitzvah). Contrary to custom, Buber chose on this occasion to deliver an interpretation of a poem by Schiller, and not an interpretation of the Torah, Talmud, or some other traditional text. Within a year of his bar mitzvah, Buber stopped observing Jewish rituals, a decision symbolized by his ceasing to lay phylacteries (*tefillin*).[18] This early aversion to orthodox, halachic Judaism was to remain with Buber until the end of his days, much to the chagrin of mainstream Jews.

❀

In 1896, Buber enrolled in the University of Vienna, taking a wide variety of courses in classical studies, philology, philosophy, psychology, art, theater, literature, economics, and psychiatry both there and at the University of Leipzig. In 1898 and again in 1899, Buber traveled to Berlin to take courses with Wilhelm Dilthey and Georg Simmel. Both teachers exerted a strong influence on the development of Buber's hermeneutic theories.[19]

In 1904 Buber submitted his doctoral dissertation, *Toward the History of the Problem of Individuation: Nicholas of Cusa and Jakob Boehme*. Grete Schaeder provides an excellent overview of Buber's interpretation of these thinkers. For our purposes it is significant to note Schaeder's summary of how Buber interpreted Boehme's metaphor for God's presence in every element of creation:

> Buber cited Boehme's image of the organ where every pipe emits a characteristic tone, and yet there is but *one* stream of air in all the pipes. For Boehme, as for Nicholas of Cusa, God is wholly in every thing, and hence each thing must bear all things latent within itself. Creation is not a process that has ended, a closed circle. God remains the dynamic principle of individuation in nature, the "eternally creative power," so that here as well "everything is in the process of creation."[20]

In this early work, we can discern seeds of Buber's later understanding of the unity and interconnectedness of all creation. By considering the uniqueness of every created thing through the metaphor of an organ whose separate pipes emit a characteristic tone that manifests the same stream of air, one is led to consider both the particular and the universal that coexist in one unified being. Buber's dissertation is therefore one way of anticipating his later concern with addressing the "twofoldedness" of being.[21]

During this period, a meeting with Theodor Herzl, the impressive founder of the Zionist movement, led Buber to rediscover his Judaism. After meeting Herzl in 1898 (one year after the first Zionist congress in Basel), Buber was convinced that Zionism constituted a Jewish entry into history, a movement that would renew both Jews and Judaism. At this point (Buber was barely twenty), he considered Zionism primarily a cultural (not a political) movement, aimed at creating a *kulturpolitik*, a rediscovery of the original, primal, spiritual sources of Judaism, of cultural roots that went deeper than contemporary Judaism's cultural forms.[22] His early commitment to Zionism is evident in the fact that in 1902 he worked with Herzl as editor of the Zionist organ *Die Welt.*

This relationship did not last long. Herzl's domineering personality, coupled with the bourgeois (and non-Jewish) vision of Zionism articulated in his novel *Altneuland,* led to a row with Buber and other members of the "Democratic Faction" of the Zionist movement. Buber resigned his formal position and joined the increasingly small number of in-house critics of Zionism's immoderate emphasis on political accomplishments at the expense of what he and others considered Zionism's primary task—cultural and spiritual renewal.[23]

Buber turned to study and writing, actively supported by his wife, Paula Winkler, a gentile from Munich whom he had married in 1899 (she converted to Judaism). In 1902, he founded, together with Berthold Feiwel, a Jewish publishing house in Berlin oriented to granting Jewish works a form commensurate with the aesthetic norms of German culture.[24] Buber, however, chose to publish his works with respectable German publishers, an indication of his desire to reach a wide audience (and perhaps, as some skeptical critics may say, of his need to be acknowledged by the gentiles).

Buber's literary projects were extremely innovative and far-ranging in scope. Between 1906 and 1908, he published studies of the two most prominent figures in the Hasidic movement, the Ba'al Shem and Rabbi Nachman of Bratslav, the first of a long series of pioneering studies about hasidism.[25] In addition, he initiated in 1907 a forty-volume series of sociological studies, *Die Gesellschaft* (Society), which included such classics as Georg Simmel's *Die Religion,* Ferdinand Toennies' *Die Sitte* (Custom), Franz Oppenheimer's *Der Staat* (The State), and Gustav Landauer's *Die Revolution.*[26] Buber also edited an unusual collection of personal descriptions of mystic ecstasy from diverse cultural traditions and historical ages, *Ecstatic Confessions,* published in 1909. His first attempt at a comprehensive philosophical statement, *Daniel: Dialogues on Realization* (1913), was written as a series of dialogues between a man on a spiritual quest and five of his friends.

During the summers of 1909–1911 Buber traveled to Prague, where he delivered lectures on Judaism to a group of young Jewish intellectuals, members of the Jewish student society of Prague University, called the Bar Kochva Verein (Bar Cochba Association). In these addresses, he sought to establish the rebirth of Jewish spirituality as the goal of Zionism.[27] These lectures presented an alternative vision to political Zionism's emphasis on physical insecurity as the primary raison d'etre of Jewish nationalism. Buber began to develop a notion of Judaism as a tradition that seeks to bring into social existence a form of communal life that is aware of the mutuality and responsibility that comes with the realization that all life is a reflection of one eternal creative source. In these lectures, one notes Buber's distancing himself from his early emphasis on cultural revival as the goal of Zionism, replacing cultural revival with the idea of a creative and unifying community of self-aware members, each of whom assumes personal responsibility for redeeming self and the world.

The first of the three lectures ended with a story that reflected this newfound approach to Judaism and to the ultimate goal of Zionism:

> When I was a child I read an old Jewish tale I could not understand. It said no more than this: "Outside the gates of Rome there sits a leprous beggar, waiting. He is the Messiah." Then I came upon an old man whom I asked: "What is he waiting for?" And the old man gave me an answer I did not understand at the time, an answer I learned to understand only much later. He said: "He waits for you."[28]

The last lecture ended with a similar moral, this time by reference to the words of Isaiah: "We read in Isaiah: 'the voice cries: In the wilderness prepare the path of the Lord!'(40:3). To be prepared means to prepare."[29] This call for active personal realization of the age-old mission of Judaism, reflecting a novel combination of adherence to a tradition that is to be radically renewed and emphasis on the communal dimension of an individual's desire to create a good, peaceful, and hopeful future, was exactly what these emancipated young Jews were seeking.[30] Firing their imagination with a vision of Judaism that is not Orthodox yet nonetheless faithful to the tradition's ancient mission, Buber became a spiritual guide for many members of this group, including among others Max Brod, Franz Kafka, Hugo Bergman, and Hans Kohn.[31]

This record of Buber's writings in the years prior to the First World War is by no means comprehensive. It merely gives us a sense of Buber's deep commitment to the study of human life in all of its manifestations:

religious, social, spiritual, and historical. In addition, his devotion to his particular community was not exclusive; he was equally interested in the lives and traditions of others. This ability to delve deeply into his own cultural and national tradition while remaining involved in the concerns of others is another step toward the development of his original notions of dialogue and inclusion.

The outbreak of the First World War signaled to Buber the renewal of the *Volk*. In a letter to Hans Kohn (a member of the Bar Cochba group), he even expressed disappointment that he would not be able to take part in battle.[32] He thought that the war was a sign of the long-awaited release of the "hidden sparks" of creation. He wrote that even though Jews were fighting one another, the experience would enable them to find greater self-awareness and would give rise to the creation of a new community.[33] He lived to regret this erroneous judgment. From later collected editions of his essays, he removed writings that espoused this view. Thus, he writes in the foreword to *Pointing the Way*: "In this selection of my essays from the years 1909 to 1954, I have, with *one* exception, included only those that, in the main, I can also stand behind today."[34] I shall return to this episode shortly, when analyzing the stages of Buber's development.

In 1921 Buber delivered what turned out to be a prophetic speech to the twelfth Zionist congress. Focusing on the question of the Zionist attitude to the Arab populace of Palestine, Buber sought to reconceptualize Zionist nationalism in terms that would correspond to his understanding of the role of Zionism. The bottom line was simple: Jewish "election" was not tested in conditions of exile and lack of power. Rather, the election of Israel was tested in "normal" conditions, in Palestine. And the ultimate test was in Jewish relations to the Arab inhabitants of the land. Buber called for an understanding of the negative dynamics that would ensue if the Jewish immigrants developed a form of nationalism that excluded the Arabs from participation in Palestine's development. He warned that the Arabs would be forced into developing an opposing nationalism and thus would become Zionism's enemies. This speech contributed to a diminishing of Buber's influence within the Zionist movement, for he was considered unrealistic, one who shied away from the "real" political demands of settling the land. In his last appearance before a Zionist congress, in 1929, he again attempted to raise the Arab question but was once again ineffective. After his failure to persuade the 1929 Zionist congress to consider the Arab question as central to the realization of the Zionist dream, Buber decided to stop participating in these forums.[35]

In 1923, Buber published his most famous book, *I and Thou*. In this book, he formulated his understanding that the modern crisis of humanity was an ontological crisis that resulted in a growing distancing between the modern "individual" from its self and a corresponding distancing of man from man and of man from creation. During this period, he also began to translate the Hebrew Bible into German (with his friend Franz Rosenzweig, who died in 1929). The collaboration with Rosenzweig was an extraordinary event in terms of interpersonal relationship. Rosenzweig was paralyzed, dying of an incurable disease. Buber writes that his proposal to Rosenzweig that they engage in this project "touched not only [Rosenzweig's] soul but also the very sources of his life. And from those sources [Rosenzweig's] answer came: 'Well, let's give it a try.' "[36] Buber's experience translating the Bible gave rise to numerous essays and book-length exegetical works such as *The Kingship of God*, published in 1932. At the same time he continued to develop his philosophy of dialogue and to engage in complementary studies on community, society, education, and philosophy.

While Buber's influence on the political leadership and direction of the Zionist movement declined, his influence in non-Jewish circles grew. He became an important spokesman for German Jewry in theological debates with Christians and was an active participant in conferences that dealt with the challenges of education in the period of turmoil that characterized 1920s Europe.

When Hitler came to power in 1933, Buber realized that this represented a danger that went beyond mere politics. He wrote in 1933, on the eve of the Day of Atonement (Yom Kippur), of "an hour of great tribulation," of "darkness." He castigated those who continued to manage their affairs as if "nothing ha[d] happened."[37] His immediate response was to establish a network of centers for Jewish adult education, aimed at teaching the Jewish heritage, and at enhancing Jewish self-understanding and solidarity.

In 1938, after on-off negotiation with the Hebrew University dating back to the 1920s, Buber accepted an offer to teach in Jerusalem, where a group of prominent faculty members, including Gershom Scho-

lem, Hugo Bergman (both former students of Buber), and Judah Magnes, had managed to create a special position for him as professor of
sociology of culture (the professors of Jewish and biblical studies had
vetoed his appointment as professor of biblical studies).[38] He was sixty
years old at the time and was criticized by some of his followers and
colleagues for not earlier having demonstrated his commitment to the
Zionist cause that his teachings so eloquently preached.[39] This criticism
is understandable if we consider the fact that in 1902 he had co-authored
a manifesto outlining the goals and mission of a Jewish university and,
in addition, recall that his brand of Zionism called for personal responsibility toward the realization of the idea of Zion.[40]

This criticism notwithstanding, Buber's arrival in Palestine was an
event welcomed by his friends and followers. The words of S. Y. Agnon
serve as testimony to the impact Buber's presence had on the intellectual
elite of Jerusalem. In a letter to Buber in December 1938, Agnon wrote:
"I am doing something contrary to my ordinary habit, but my heart tells
me to act, so I act. For the past two days I have been contemplating
your lecture about the characteristic of the spirit of Israel, and shall not
exaggerate if I say that neither I nor Jerusalem have heard such a lecture
for many years. . . . Your lecture opened for me a channel to understanding some of your other books."[41]

In addition to having an impact on friends and colleagues in Jerusalem's intellectual milieu, Buber was influential in the more left-wing
kibbutzim, by virtue of the fact that there were groups of "Buberians"
who attempted to realize Buber's teachings in these communal settings.
These groups comprised young Jews who had come under Buber's influence in Europe and had emigrated to Palestine to realize his teachings
in the novel form of the communal life being developed in the kibbutz.

During the years of the Second World War, Buber completed many
studies that he had worked on in previous decades, and published a
steady flow of books and articles on political, philosophical, and biblical
themes. Most of these works will be introduced in due course.[42]

At this juncture, I wish to focus on two works: one strictly philosophical, the other dealing with political theory. The former, "What Is
Man [*Adam*]?" a presentation of Buber's philosophical anthropology, is
written in the form of a critique of a wide range of Western philosophers, from Aristotle to Pascal, Kant, Heidegger, Hegel, Marx, and others. This treatise is based on Buber's inaugural lectures at the Hebrew

University.[43] The latter, published in 1947 and entitled *Paths in Utopia*, is of all his studies the most easily defined as a work of political theory. Addressing the works of utopian socialists such as Count Saint-Simon, Charles Fourier, Robert Owen, Pierre-Joseph Proudhon, Gustav Landauer, Karl Marx, and others, Buber presents a novel interpretation of the meaning and importance of the utopian element in socialism. Basic to *Paths in Utopia* is the idea that a new form of community will evolve out of local groups and that this evolution will be the regenerative force of a new society. The evolution will occur in response to concrete political and social circumstances yet will be guided by the understanding of the deep meaning of fellowship, of fraternity. Buber posits decentralization of power and political structure as a critique of, and an alternative to, the Marxist-Leninist belief in centralized forms of political association, be they political parties or centralized states.

As well as writing books and articles, Buber was an active member of political groups that advocated peaceful coexistence with the Arabs of Palestine, namely Brit Shalom (Covenant of Peace, founded in Jerusalem in 1926) and Ichud (Unity, founded in 1942). He represented Ichud before the 1946 Anglo-American commission, urging them to adopt a binational solution to the conflict between Jews and Arabs in Palestine. Buber delivered his testimony before the commission despite the boycott of these meetings decreed by the leaders of the Jewish community.[44] His recommendation that the Allied Powers develop a political framework that would address on equal terms the needs of both peoples—Jews and Palestinian Arabs—was interpreted correctly as indicative of his opposition to the establishment of an independent Jewish state. This served to yet further marginalize Buber, who was perceived as a naive utopian, one who represented only a tiny fraction of the Jewish intellectual and socialist elite in Palestine.

Buber did not limit his involvement to social and political criticism. He was an active educator; in addition to his responsibilities at the Hebrew University, in 1949 he founded the Israeli Institute for Adult Education, which trained teachers to teach Hebrew to the new immigrants in the camps.[45] When asked by S. N. Eisenstadt, who had been his student and then succeeded him as chair of the department of sociology at the Hebrew University, why he devoted so much energy to adult education, Buber answered: "This is very important in order that we can converse together and dream together." Eisenstadt did not fathom the importance of sharing a common dream, articulated in the same tongue, until much later, when observing processes of disintegration in Israel and in the "postmodern" world.[46]

In the last two decades of his life, Buber continued to express unorthodox views about national and international affairs. He raised a storm of controversy in Israel and in the Jewish world when he traveled in the early 1950s to Germany to accept literary prizes from representatives of the nation responsible for the Holocaust and the destruction of European Jewry.[47] His independent spirit was evident in a series of additional unpopular actions and political positions. One obvious example was his persistent criticism of the military rule imposed on Israeli Arabs. A further example was his testimony in court on behalf of Aharon Cohen, a left-wing Israeli intellectual charged with spying for the Soviet Union. Convinced that the charges leveled at Cohen were false and that Cohen's explanation of the activities leading to his arrest were accurate representations of the facts, Buber took the stand in Cohen's defense. It is worth noting the rationale behind Buber's testimony, which was based on his insistence that Aharon Cohen "says what he thinks" and was therefore incapable of fabricating explanations for his actions (as the prosecution had claimed):

> Since my youth I have been studying human beings, and my entire philosophical thinking is based on my knowledge of their nature. Knowing human nature means knowing people, and this is the only way to learn something about mankind as a whole. I mention this in order to show that I have some experience in knowing people, and I was extremely impressed by Aharon Cohen. . . . I am not talking about abstract things. I consider myself an expert on these matters. What we are discussing is not abstract or vague in the slightest.[48]

Despite the testimony of Buber and others, Cohen was convicted of being a "foreign agent" and spent two years in prison prior to being pardoned.

A final example of Buber's unorthodox and uncompromising adherence to his truth was his critique of David Ben-Gurion's decision to bring to trial in Jerusalem the Nazi criminal Adolf Eichmann. Buber believed that rather than the victims, an international tribunal ought to judge Eichmann. When Eichmann was nevertheless tried in Jerusalem and sentenced to death, Buber publicly stated his opinion that the sentence ought to be commuted to life. He had a number of reasons for advocating this position. On ethical grounds, he argued that the commandment "thou shalt not kill" applied equally to individuals and to states. Maurice Friedman writes that when *Time* magazine quoted Buber's reference to Rabbi Mendel of Kotsk, "What the Torah teaches us is this: none but God can command us to destroy a man," Buber wrote a letter to the magazine, pointing to the significant sequel to this saying that *Time* had omitted: "and if the very smallest angel comes after the commandment has been given and cautions us: 'Lay not thy hand upon . . .' we must obey him." Friedman adds that Buber also stated to *Newsweek*: "The death sentence has not diminished crime—on the contrary, all this exasperates the souls of men. . . . Killing awakens killing." On more practical grounds, Buber feared that Eichmann's execution would be interpreted by the next generation of Germans as an act of symbolic justice relieving them of the burden of guilt that he thought should weigh on their consciences. On this issue, he was criticized not only in Israel but also by prominent Jewish intellectuals elsewhere, including Hannah Arendt.[49]

Traveling to Germany during the years that association with Germany was considered sacrilege, defending the rights of Israeli Arabs when they were considered the dangerous "other," testifying in the court of law and publicly defending an "enemy of the state" (Cohen), and challenging the wisdom of trying and then executing Eichmann—all testify to Buber's deeply felt convictions and to his ability to speak his mind, even when in a minority of one.

During this period Buber was already well established and enjoyed international recognition as a prominent and influential philosopher. He was invited to speak before major scholarly and intellectual audiences and was granted numerous awards in recognition of his work and deeds. However, in his own country, his was a minor voice, heard only by those predisposed to listen, and mostly ignored or criticized and ridiculed by those who opposed his politics. His primary influence during these last years of his life was upon young people, mostly from the kibbutzim. In meetings with the younger generation, he found comfort and solace. These conversations always began with Buber inviting his guests or audience to open the dialogue, and he would respond.[50] In one of the last conversations recorded, Buber spoke of the kind of future that could exist if appropriate effort were made, and predicted a religious and spiritual revival that would take place in Israel during the generation of his great-great-grandchildren (i.e., the 1990s).[51] The spirit of this prediction is evident in a message he sent with Aubrey Hodes to a Reform congregation whose invitation he declined due to his ill health: "Please tell them they are doing something very important in Jewish religious life. This is the kind of pioneering we need now: spiritual pioneering."[52]

Buber died in 1965.

## THE THREE STAGES OF BUBER'S DEVELOPMENT

Most interpreters of Buber's life and work divide his life into two periods, "mystical" and "dialogical," referring to 1923, the year of publication of *I and Thou*, as the watershed year.[53] Although I initially accepted this division,[54] a more thorough reading of Buber's texts led me to believe that there were in fact three stages in the development of his life and work. The third stage reflects Buber's deepening insight into the nature of language and is linked to changes in his personal life and in the political history of the twentieth century. The second, "dialogical" period undergoes a transmutation in the years 1938–1945, after which there is a subtle, yet decisive, shift in emphasis in Buber's comprehension of the enormity of the crisis of contemporary humanity. In this third period of Buber's development, there is a concurrent deepening of his reflections on the role of interpersonal relations in bringing about a "new epoch."[55] Dialogue remains central yet develops more clearly along the lines of a deeper understanding of the eternal, "silent" background of being and of dialogue.

The following pages briefly outline the three periods, with several goals in mind. First, these details contribute to providing the necessary background for discussion in later chapters. Second, it appears that the third stage of Buber's development represents a shift toward a deeper understanding of the appropriate function of language and of its forms of communication: thought, speech, and texts. This later, mature insight can be appreciated more fully when seen in the context of his earlier thoughts, which go through a process of subtle refinement. In this respect, I adopt an Augustinian understanding of the importance of highlighting past occurrences as milestones to present insight. Third, through observing the process by which a person (Buber) arrives at his final insight, we become sensitive to the epistemological and ontological issues that are encountered in meeting the limits of thought as one attempts to order existence in terms of historical narrratives and the latent assumptions about "reality" that these narratives reflect and perpetuate.

To conclude, the division of Buber's life into three periods serves as a background for an understanding of his gradual awakening to the paradoxical insight into the origins of language in an experience that precedes thought. Contemplation of that insight and its relevance to historical, social and political existence—*my existence*—is ultimately the focus, heart, and raison d'etre of this book.

### Mysticism (1897–1923)

It is a well-documented fact that from his early teens, Buber was enamored of mystical contemplation. At the time, the experience appeared to offer respite from the burden and demands of thoughts. As Buber matured, he realized that his inclination towards mysticism and otherworldly concerns prevented him at times from perceiving the needs of others and clouded his understanding of immediate historical events.

The decade between 1914 and 1923 marks Buber's rejection of *Erlebnis* (lived or inner experience) philosophy and mystical ecstasies and his articulation of the alternative philosophy of I and You, the philosophy of dialogue.[56] This shift in perspective was granted final form in 1923, with the publication of *I and Thou*, where he rejected the early emphasis on the virtues of solitary contemplation and replaced it with emphasis on the interhuman as where reality is experienced and where one's innate potential is realized.[57] Consequently, following *I and Thou*, Buber's writing about the role of language and speech, the modes of communication central to the interhuman dimension of human existence, became clearer and more direct.[58]

Buber's early interest in a person's ability to transcend profane conceptions of reality, commonly referred to as his "mysticism," was enhanced and maintained by his concurrent attraction to the legends and lives of specific persons who seemed to have attained such higher reality. In *Ecstatic Confessions* Buber asserted that the ecstatic experience knows no intermediate stage between experience of the ordinary world and the

"deliverance to fullness." In fact, Buber went farther than merely rejecting the notion of an intermediary stage linking the two states of experience: whoever *experiences* the oneness of "I" and the world, said Buber,
"*knows* nothing of I and the world." Experience eliminates knowing;
the immediacy of experience does away with the mediacy of thought.
Accordingly, at this stage of his development, Buber considered the return from the ecstatic experience to ordinary thoughtful perception of
the world a "monstrous contradiction" between two incongruent states
of being. He depicted this return and its attendant reversion to everyday
obligations and responsibilities as an unfortunate "falling back" that is
the lot of the mystic.[59]

This depiction of the mystic is, at the very least, asocial. Indeed, he
wrote of solitude in the following terms: "solitude, absolute solitude;
the solitude of that which is without limits. . . . [O]ne no longer has
others *outside* oneself, no longer has any communion with them or anything in common with them."[60] This interpretation of the ecstatic experience led Buber to the conclusion that mysticism negates community.
He thus suggested that mysticism "does not struggle with any organized
community, nor does it set itself up as a countercommunity, as a sect
would. Rather mysticism negates community, precisely because for it
there is only one real relation [*Beziehung*], the relation to God."[61]

Although concerned with the experience of ecstasy, and thus with
the highly personal nature of this phenomenon, Buber seemed equally
intrigued by the inability to transmit the experience of the *unio mystica*
in ways other than the direct meeting with a person who can guide the
seeker of such experiences to his goal. Buber—who, after all, was engaged in literary projects that dealt with these aspects of human experience—devoted considerable attention to the question of the function of
texts in imparting (what for him seemed to be) humanity's most profound recollections. How can one communicate the apparently incom-
municable? How can one write of the liminal moment that marks the
transition from ordinary descriptions of what is?

Buber realized that myths and legends, allusive in their way of reference, self-contained and complete in their way of describing single moments in terms of parables that signify complex situations, are the literary
form most suitable for transmitting a single person's encounter with
forces beyond analytic description. At its best, the Jewish myth communicates the understanding that "corporeal reality is divine, but it must be

realized in its divinity by him who truly lives it."[62] Jewish myths thus are of two kinds: those that tell the tale of God's deeds ("corporeal reality is divine") and those that transmit the legend of particular persons' perfect realization of the relation between creation and created being.

At this stage of his development, Buber divided the world into the select, "unified" few who can understand the message communicated by the myth and the majority of "simple" persons who inevitably distort it. The select few perceive beyond the form of myth and understand the deep significance of the words of the central person of the parable; "simple" persons do not understand the parable and have no immediate relation to the experience to which it points.

Buber's early elitist attitude to the communicability of certain truths is reflected in his choice of metaphors. For the "simple," the myth is a *prism* rather than a clear glass. Prisms break up the ray of light and, in its place, project incomplete, fragmented beams of the original whole. The "simple" readers' or listeners' understanding of the profound meaning of the myth is similarly distorted and incomplete. Buber drops, and even repudiates, this distinction in the mature works of the second period of his development. "I experience [*erfahre*] something," says Buber in *I and Thou*, "and all this is not changed by adding 'mysterious' experiences to 'manifest' ones." In fact, "those who experience do not participate in the world. For the experience is 'in them' and not between them and the world."[63]

One of the goals of Buber's later, mature conception of community was therefore to demystify the facts he once found so difficult to communicate, and to bring them to the attention of all members of the human community. However, while developing a radically different understanding of the communicability of the truths embodied in the myth and being of the "central person" who was privy to the ecstatic experience, Buber retained throughout his life an intense belief in the proposition that all "truths" reflect the indivisible unity of being. That all forms of creation are reflections of one eternal energy (that we call "life") he considered the essential element of being. This assumption regarding being, creation and self underlies Buber's understanding the meaning and purpose of creation and of humanity's place in it.[64] The unity of being was therefore the one fact he accepted intuitively and unreservedly throughout his life, from his early years to his death.

It is impossible to completely reconstruct the circumstances leading to a person's replacing one kind of understanding with another. However, there are events that indicate the kind of experience that raises doubt in one's mind as to the veracity of deeply ingrained convictions. In the case of Buber's transition from an emphasis on the primacy of solitary ecstasy to an appreciation of the function of communal dialogue, three events suggest the kind of circumstance likely to bring about such change. Each of the events occurred in the historical context created by the First World War. Each exemplifies the nature of the shock of self-recognition that led Buber to discard some of his earlier convictions and to revise others.

First, Buber claims that during a meeting he held in July 1914, he experienced at first hand his self-delusion on the subject of the supremacy of the ecstatic moment. One day, after a morning of mystic rapture, Buber was visited by a young man unknown to him. Although friendly, Buber was not attentive or present to the person's needs. He did not listen to unspoken words, to the existential dimension of the person's presence. Two months later, Buber learned that the young man had come to see him not for an ordinary conversation but in order to make a decision and that soon after, he had died at the front in the First World War. He had died, Buber wrote, out of "that kind of despair that may be defined partially as 'no longer opposing one's death.' " A decade later, Buber referred to this incident as a "conversion," insofar as it revealed to him the illegitimacy of the division of his life into the "everyday" and the "beyond."[65] Had Buber been fully present to the person facing him, perhaps the latter would have seen a way out of his despair.

Second, the highly personal nature of Buber's testimony about his "conversion" ought to be considered in the context of his initial support of German nationalism in 1914. That Buber saw any merit in Germany's embarking on a European war shocked many of his close friends, including the anarchist Gustav Landauer, who chastised Buber for his enthusiasm in a letter written in May 1916. Convincing evidence of the impact of Landauer's letter on Buber's subsequent *volte face* has been advanced by Paul Mendes-Flohr, "not only as regards [Buber's] attitude toward the war, but also with respect to the a-social orientation of his thought."[66]

Third, *Erlebnis* philosophy was being criticized by a growing number of members of Buber's milieu.[67] As recorded by Susan Handelman, both Walter Benjamin and Gershom Scholem "strongly opposed any

cult of pure immediate experience, including Buber's *Erlebnismystik* theology, which proclaimed the superiority of intuitive ecstatic experience
over truths mediated through language."[68] The reaction of Buber's acquaintances to his "mysticism" may be inferred from Walter Benjamin's
antipathy towards him. Benjamin was to harbor "long standing, insurmountable mistrust of that man [Buber]," based on Benjamin's recollection of the image of the early, mystically inclined Buber.

Buber's transition from mysticism to dialogue thus came about as a
confluence of influences that he could not reject: the shock of recognition that his psychological identification with the virtues of ecstasy had
become a barrier between himself and other humans, honest criticism
by a close friend, and the sense of rejection by acquaintances whose
opinions he valued.

### Dialogue (1923–1938)

With Buber's new attitude to being, his early understanding of the
relation between exceptionally sensitive "central persons" and community was reversed. In *I and Thou* (1923), the central person is referred
to not as a master of ecstatic experiences but as the "living center of
community." This person's experience of the absolute is presented as
inseparable from his commitment to social renewal; his primary responsibility is one of establishing conditions conducive to the development
of interpersonal dialogical relationships.

During this period, Buber's philosophy also included a new understanding of the greater reality experienced in the ecstatic moment. First
and foremost, *emphasis was placed on reality rather than on its experience.* In
other words, Buber at this stage was more concerned with convincing
his readers and listeners that there was more to reality than ordinarily
observed, than with recounting inner experiences that seemed to con-
firm this statement. Hence, Buber no longer explained the structure of
social interaction by referring to the psyches of the separate persons. He
now claimed that I and You, the poles of a dialogical relationship, had
neither meaning nor independent existence apart from the relationship
into which they entered.[69]

The shift in emphasis included a new understanding of the nature
of *social* reality. The social context was now perceived as paramount.
Buber depicted the forms of social life generated by the separate poles of

a relationship as having an objective, independent existence. These forms, the "betweenness" of that relationship, became for Buber a total reality that enables a "full comprehension and presentation of what passes between two persons when they stand in dialogue with each other."[70] He attempted to capture the essence of this conception of the interpersonal by devising the "basic words" I–You and I–It.

"Basic words" are a linguistic construct created by Buber as a way of pointing to the quality of experience that this combination of words seeks to connote. Basic words are read as one unit: I–You or I–It. They indicate the state of one's inner being; they express the quality of interpersonal space that is created by the quality of one's inner reality; they establish a mode of existence.[71] The notion of basic words emphasizes the importance of attending to the attitude that underlies one's speech and the energies that define one's presence rather than the words that one utters.

The "I" indicated by the basic word I–You is not the same as the "I" of the basic word I–It. The "I" of I–You indicates a quality of presence that considers self and other as elements of one, inclusive reality: *when* one addresses the other from an inclusive state of being that is present to the unity of creation and of being, *then* the interpersonal is permeated by an I–You mode of existence. This "I" is not sensed as singular; it is the "I" of being present to being. Such a relation to being, connoted by the basic word I–You, constitutes a movement toward relation (a key Buberian word, *Beziehung*) and establishes in the interpersonal sphere a quality of relation that Buber refers to as the Between. To reiterate, the concept of the Between belongs to the sphere of the I–You relation.[72]

In contradistinction, in an I–It attitude to being, the person tends to distance himself from the other, to create in the interpersonal a quality of relationship characterized by the person's desire to distinguish him- or herself by accentuating differences, by emphasizing the uniqueness of "I" in contrast to the other. The "I" of I–It indicates a separation of self from what it encounters. By emphasizing difference, the "I" of I–It experiences a sensation of apparent singularity—of being alive by virtue of being unique; of being unique by accentuating difference; of being different as a welcome separation from the other present in the situation; of having a psychological distance ("I") that gives rise to a sense of being special in opposition to what is. The psychological sensation associated with "I" as a subjective center of being is the root of separation between persons, and the process of thinking and reacting to thoughts is a basic element of this psychological construct (in Buber's discourse, this inner "reality" is called "monologism").

Stated otherwise, in his dialogical period, Buber developed the proposition that the sensation of "I" is inseparable from the quality of one's presence in any given situation; presence to self and to other are inseparable. Such presence is not a permanent sensation but rather is in continual flux. In actual experience, every person senses self in many different ways. At times, self is sensed as the open flow of presence connoted by the "I" of the basic word I–You; at other times, one is self-absorbed and oblivious to the presence of others, a state connoted by the "I" of the basic word I–It.

Buber's mature work attempts to draw attention to the sensation that underlies this distinction and to evoke a recognition of the importance of the I–You relation in the life of persons and communities. To be in a state of I–You relation to others is associated in Buber's work with a quiet attention that silently listens and observes prior to reacting to the demands of a particular situation. However, this is a rare sensation, more often than not experienced in passing, without the subject having really reflected on the qualitative change of presence he or she has just experienced. The I–You relation to being is therefore not depicted as a permanent transformation of self. It appears as an effect of prior dispositions yet cannot be "invited" in the way that words can be willfully extracted from the memory and uttered in public.

Hence, in contrast to his earlier position, in his "dialogical" stage Buber seeks the greater reality of existence not in a person's inner life but rather in the context of the interpersonal, "in the great phenomena of [man's] connection with an otherness which is constituted as otherness by the event of 'distancing.' "[73] The act of reversing the psychological movement referred to as "distancing" is the "entering into relation." Such movement toward relation constitutes the Between, that invisible, yet present quality that permeates the social sphere of relationships. The primary reality of the I–You dialogue lies not in either of the subjects or poles of the relation but in the relation itself.[74] One may summarize this point by suggesting that the difference between the I–You and the I–It relation to being is embedded in the hyphen. The hyphen of I–You indicates relation; the hyphen of I–It indicates separation. Considered in contrast to Buber's earlier understanding, the basic word I–You does not indicate that it is the property of some superior person who has forever overcome the self-centered attitude to being that is indicated by the basic word I–It.

During this period of Buber's development, his understanding of the meaning and significance of myths underwent metamorphosis similar to that of his understanding of the meaning and significance of interpersonal relationships. During his mystical period, Buber had pictured the myth as a mode of communication that might serve opposing purposes; for some, it revealed deeper truths, yet others, the majority, misunderstood the myth and misrepresented it in support of their distorted perception of truth. The potential to misuse myths led Buber to conclude that all in all, given the base interpretations that organized religions, throughout history, had derived from them, myths could damage the life of the spirit.[75] In his dialogical works, Buber developed a new conception of myths and legends that would enable readers to appreciate the fullness of the moments that these essentially oral forms of remembrance attempted to convey when presented in literary form. He revised his earlier interpretation by replacing the emphasis on the ecstatic element in myth with an emphasis on direct meeting with reality.[76] The Hasidic legends of his dialogical period (many of them revisions of those he had used in his earlier, "mystical" period) depict the Hasidic masters as they relate to persons and, through this relation, attempt to create a community of understanding of the truth that cannot be articulated clearly in linear, systematic forms of discourse. One reason why Buber stripped Hasidic tales of their magical elements when he retold them, was his hope that this would help readers gain access to the dialogical moments illustrated in the lives of the great masters of Hasidism.[77] He hoped to make the truth conveyed by myth accessible to every reader, including "simple" persons. The following Hasidic saying conveys his newfound attitude: "In every man there is something precious, which is in no one else. And so we should honor each for what is hidden within him, for what only he has, and none of his companions."[78]

Buber's transition from mysticism to dialogue did not imply a rejection of his commitment to the idea of human perfection represented in the deeds and lives of mythical "central" persons. He simply attributed a new social value to this kind of person. Whereas in his earlier period, the experience that set the unique person apart materialized *"free of the other,"*[79] in the dialogical period it is precisely the *meeting with the other* that creates the conditions within which a person's cleaving to the absolute can take place. That is why, in the dialogical stage, Buber's writings, while emphasizing that in its highest moments dialogue transcends content and thought, nevertheless acknowledge that an element of communication "however inward, seems to belong to its essence." Dialogue "is not completed in some 'mystical' event, but in one that is in the precise sense factual, thoroughly dovetailed into the common human world and the concrete time sequence."[80]

Considering the person as a thinking subject, Buber observes that "there seems to cling to thought something of the life of monologue to which communication takes a secondary place. Thought *seems* to arise in monologue." However, he realizes that to situate the origin of thought in the internal thought process of the thinking subject is to admit that monologue is the source of dialogue, whereas his concept of dialogue sets out to establish the opposite proposition, that "the character of monologue does not belong to the insight into a basic relation with which cognitive thought begins."[81]

What, then, *is* the basic relation that does not originate in the separation of the thinking subject from the concrete person (a separation that establishes and stabilizes a thought-world of its own, a world reflexively experienced as "self," the ground of the I–It relation to being)? The answer is to be sought in Buber's complex and sensitive writings about the silence that forms the background to thought and to being.[82] This is an issue that I shall address repeatedly from a variety of perspectives found in Buber's writings. At this point, I shall refer briefly to the two meanings of silence: silence as the transcendence of thought and silence as not-speaking.[83] The first is an awareness momentarily released from the service of thought, while the second is a concentration of awareness around a thought that is not released as speech yet continues to "exist" as suppressed speech. The first is the silence of the dialogical person; the second, the silence of the monological person.

### Attentive Silence (1938–1965)

The saliency of silence in Buber's writings on dialogue serves as the transition to the third stage of his deepening insight into the paradoxical quality of thought and of language. In this stage, attentive silence emerges more clearly as the basis of dialogue. Growing out of his experience as a translator and biblical scholar, Buber's biblical interpretations of the 1930s and 1940s constitute an attempt to come closer to the original events and personal experiences that gave rise to the text about God, or, in his words, to "the dialogue between *Elohim* and *Adam*."[84] These writings are a vehicle for Buber's study of the eternal, silent, creative background of being. His writings about dialogue, community, and philosophy are grounded in these detailed studies and draw on their findings. (Because of the significance Buber attaches to the distinction between YHVH and *Elohim*—the two names of the biblical deity—I shall hereafter use in my analysis one or the other term rather than the word "God." My choice of names, whether *Elohim* or YHVH, or God, will be based on Buber's Hebrew texts and on my understanding of the meaning that Buber attributes to these appellations.)

According to Buber, to merely think, talk, or write about *Elohim* may be intellectually stimulating, but it is not part of the original text's intention. In the Hebrew Bible, says Buber, "there is no pondering; [the Bible] does not deal with the essence of *Elohim* but with its manifestation to mankind."[85] The text invites the attentive reader to relate to creation ("its manifestation to mankind"), not to thoughts about the creator. For Buber, this approach turns reading the Bible into a form of dialogue with the text and the original voices that it communicates, a dialogue *with* the text rather than a learned discourse *about* its central hero. This text-oriented approach to translation and interpretation, rather than focusing on the intentions of the author or on the predispositions of the reader, treats the text as a complete, whole work that reveals the limits of its own interpretation. In this respect, Buber anticipated the distinction drawn by Umberto Eco among author-oriented, reader-oriented, and text-oriented interpretations of texts.[86] Buber demarcated the limits of biblical interpretation by pointing to the rhythm and code of writing that is characteristic of the Hebrew Scripture as a whole. Buber discerned in the hermeneutical underpinnings of the Hebrew Bible the assumption that the encounter with the presence of that which is designated by the words *Elohim* or YHVH cannot be reduced to ordinary language; hence the need of the biblical redactor to develop a certain way of writing that alludes indirectly to the experience of encountering this other reality.[87]

In later chapters, I shall dwell at length on the decisive impact of translating the Hebrew Bible on Buber's ontology and on his way of writing. Central to my interpretation of Buber's intentions is the claim that in the mature period of his life, he developed a certain form of writing that stemmed from his study of the way the Bible was written. By "unraveling" that element of Buber's writings, I shall point to layers of thought hitherto unobserved by commentators. At this juncture, I wish to highlight one proposition: that while Buber was dealing with political events and philosophical questions, he was concurrently struggling to hear the hidden voice contained within the lines of the Hebrew Bible. If we consider his lifework in retrospective, from grave to cradle, we may venture the proposition that Buber's biblical, philosophical, and political writings and activities are united in that they all reflect his attraction and gradual opening to the voice of being as he detected it in the great works of the Hebrew tradition. I reflect upon this attraction and opening from the perspective of the end of Buber's days ("from grave to cradle") because I discern in Buber's later years an unusual growth in wisdom and insight. As I wish this book to benefit from Buber's final understandings, I focus my analysis on his later works.

An additional fact to be considered regarding Buber's transition to the third period of his maturity is that of the Second World War, and the destruction of European Jewry in the death camps of the Third Reich. Although he lived in Germany between 1933 and 1938, and witnessed the use of the German state in the service of evil, Buber did not—could not—imagine the enormity of that evil. However, he did realize that the political assault on Jewish life necessitated a radical response. This issue will be discussed more thoroughly in the final chapter.

In conclusion, we may note that in the third, most insightful period of Buber's development, themes considered in our review of Buber's earlier stages of development underwent transmutation following a refocusing of his intention. His writing became more clearly attentive to the mystery of historical existence in an age of senseless violence. Buber's sensitivity to the difficulty of writing about the incomprehensible transpired in his works as an inquiry that is at once more focused yet—curiously—indirect and open-ended. Stories and legends became the indirect manner of communicating a vision of community; the central person of community became a "hidden presence," acting in the shadow of "hidden" history, unnoticed by those whose attention was absorbed by events unfolding on the stage of "apparent" history. Support of attempts to create small communities (such as kibbutzim) was tempered by sensitivity to the need to determine the goal of such communities prior to their establishment; the founding of the Jewish state, the culmination of decades of Zionist activity, became for Buber an enigma to be resolved by study of the origins of Zionism and by the attempt to relate historical circumstances to Judaism's original mission.

The writings of this period reveal a visionary view of the dual existence of man. This vision goes beyond the earlier emphasis on the "twofold relation to being," mentioned in the opening line of *I and Thou* and correctly celebrated as the leitmotif of that work and of that philosophy. Now, Buber sought to bring to the fore the quest for the "still quiet voice" that is present in the hidden being of man and is a characteristic of the eclipsed *Elohim*. Realizing the hiddenness of that voice from the experience of modern man, Buber directed his attention to seeking the appropriate literary form that would reopen the dialogue between the person and himself, between the person and the other, and between the person and the essential life force. In his studies of biblical hermeneutics and Hasidic masters, Buber sought the original insight that gave rise to biblical dialogue and to Hasidic community. This layer of Buber's writing has been granted insufficient attention and has been as misunderstood as was the man himself.

## SUMMARY AND TRANSITION

Toward the end of his days, Buber wrote that as he matured, his primary goal was to communicate the nature of "the service" (the responsibility) that results from the encounter with the absolute. This goal determined the way in which he wrote about the Jewish tradition: *indirectly*, by interpretation of the Torah, from the perspective of "the predicament of humanity and of Israel at this hour,"[88] and *directly*, by retelling moments in the lives of those persons whose hidden deeds exemplified the nature of the service. In this respect, writes Buber, he was not bringing something original to the world; he was simply granting textual form to reality as he encountered it.

> Since I have matured to a life from my own experiences . . . I have stood under the duty to insert the framework of the decisive experiences that I had at that time into the human inheritance of thought,

but not as "my" experiences, rather as an insight valid and important for others and even for other kinds of men. . . . My philosophy serves, yes, it serves, but it does not serve a series of revealed propositions. It serves an experienced, a perceived attitude that it has been established to make communicable.[89]

This passage explains, in part, how in addition to being a Jewish thinker, Buber was a universal philosopher, whose writings address any culture or tradition. The insight he sought to communicate was embedded in his own cultural heritage, but he saw its traces in texts of diverse traditions, Eastern and Western alike. Like Plato before him, Buber was critical of sophists who in the guise of philosophy think without contemplating the origins and functions of thought. This kind of thinker ends up as a master of words but does not understand the realities those words reflect and address. In this respect, Buber anticipated the postmodern reaction to modern, Cartesian forms of Western philosophy. "Postmodern" thinkers realize that words and thoughts are indeed merely words and thoughts, subject to deconstruction by alternative words and thoughts. However, unlike these critics of modernity, Buber was not enamored of deconstructive forms of intellectual discourse. In his maturity, he realized that even though thought and counterthoughts (or text and countertexts) do indeed create an apparently endless cycle of opinion that external criteria cannot stem, thought is nevertheless a faculty that serves to communicate what is. By sticking to the conviction that there are absolute realities that can be discerned and addressed by man, Buber represented an attitude that opposes the idea that the only reality is that which is determined by narratives and texts. His later philosophy thus points at the faculty of thinking as a potential that used appropriately, communicates an insight that is prior to thought and is, in fact, the ground of thought's arising. Hence, Buber's critique of Western philosophy endeavors to undermine the assumption attributed to Descartes, that thought is the ultimate experience of presence in the face of being. The following chapters explain this proposition and demonstrate its relevance to the cultural and existential problems of the late twentieth century.

One may sum up this biographical and developmental introduction by advancing a deceptively simple theory: the crisis of humankind is a crisis of thought—not of the content of thought but of the misguided

relationship of contemporary persons to the subjective process of thinking. It is primarily a crisis of *how* we relate to thinking, not of *what* we
think. We shall see that the answer to "how" we think contains the key
to how to create the Between. Also, by looking at this dimension of
Buber's work, we shall see how personal self-perfection and communal
self-perfection are inseparable.

Later chapters will deal with some important questions: What is the
nature of the insight that Buber sought to communicate? Why does
Buber cite silence as the ground of dialogue? How does the voice of
silence correlate with a philosophy of dialogue? And how do these understandings coalesce into a social and political theory? We begin at the
heart of Buber's philosophy: his interpretation of the Bible as it relates
to a person born in the twentieth century.

## 3

# BIBLE: THE HIDDEN HERMENEUTICS

Intermittently, Buber devoted almost forty years to the translation of the Hebrew Bible into German.[1] The translation was based on Buber's discovery of a number of hermeneutic principles that had guided the work of the final redactor of the Scripture. The most important principle was that of the *leitwort* (the guiding word). The guiding-word principle postulates that the author of the biblical text uses certain words in a manner that seeks to arouse the reader's attention to possible interpretive connections between disparate passages in the biblical text. These guiding words constitute a hermeneutic code of reading, a literary strategy that points to hidden levels of meaning that open up and are revealed to the attentive reader. Such a reading is an intertextual type of hermeneutics, one that explores the significance of an obscure, controversial text by means of another, or less obscure, text.[2] In the words of Steven Kepnes, the guiding-word technique "became a principle for translation and, as with the other techniques, a principle of interpretation."[3] This hermeneutic principle lies at the core of Martin Buber's studies of the Bible and is considered one of his most significant contributions to modern scholarly discourse about the Bible.

Focus on the *leitwort* stems from prior assumptions about the nature and origins of the Hebrew Bible. For Buber, as for all Jews who consider the Bible representative of refined wisdom, this text is a record of an original (i.e., from the origin) voice heard by prophets. Buber's reading of the Hebrew Bible is thus characterized by his attempt to retain the original spokenness of the words recorded in the text. Buber's biblical hermeneutics become, in the words of Michael Fishbane, a "training for human listening," a hearing that is attentive to the very careful choice of words of the text.[4] Working against those who postulate that the text

49

represents distinctly different authors—such as the distinction between J (the "Jahwist") and E (the "Elohist")—Buber and Franz Rosenzweig sought to reproduce "R," that is, "the unitary consciousness of the book." In the words of Rosenzweig: "We . . . translate the Torah as one book. For us . . . it is the work of a single mind. We do not know who the mind was; we cannot believe that it was Moses. We name that mind among ourselves . . . R. We, however, take this R to stand not for Redactor but for *rabbenu* [our rabbi]. For whoever he was, and whatever text lay before him, he is our teacher, and his theology is our teaching."[5] Reflecting on Rosenzweig's words, Buber affirms: "It was something we had in common, then, that Rosenzweig expressed in his significantly witty remark that we took R to stand not for 'Redactor' but for 'Rabbenu.' "[6]

The translator into Hebrew of many of Buber's German writings about the Bible, Yehoshua Amir, adds to this background the observation that Buber considered his works in biblical translation and interpretation a necessary corrective to academic tendencies to read the Hebrew Bible as primarily a source for aesthetic impressions and inspiration. Buber considered such a reading of the Hebrew Bible "the most dangerous distortion of the dialogue."[7] Amir writes that since Buber wrote against the dissolution of the one biblical text into fragments attributed to diverse historical personalities who had authored apparently separate literary units (and hence had created a text that is susceptible to potentially conflicting perspectives and "truths"), Buber's development of the guiding word principle was an attempt to grant scientific validity to his assumption that the Hebrew Bible includes discrete, hidden links between apparently incongruent verses and books. These links prove the essential unity of the work of "R." The proof of this theory of reading is in the reading itself. This is a proposition difficult to defend in systematic discourse. The proof (or refutation) is in the experience; sensitive reading of the Bible serves as testimony that such reading is experienced as described, manifested in the *reading*, not in the words read; in the "how" to relate, not in the "what" that is related.[8] The "how" and the "what" of relating to the Hebrew Bible are inseparable; still the "how" precedes the "what." Buber's approach is a text-oriented theory of interpretation, where, in the words of Umberto Eco, there is an intention of the text, which may or may not cohere with a biographical author's apparent "intention."[9]

Buber's discoveries in the field of biblical hermeneutics will be further elaborated subsequently.[10] Before commencing such exposition, however, a short note about the significance of Buber's development of the guiding-word theory for our understanding of his own works is in place. Based on a reading of Buber's texts, I propose that in the mature period of his writing, Buber incorporated into his own works—including into essays about philosophical, social, and political concerns—hermeneutic principles that he had attributed to the redactor of the Hebrew Bible. Reading Buber's writings under the assumption that they, too, include guiding words enables us to appreciate the essential unity of his own works, a perspective lacking in many existing interpretations of Buber's literary legacy.[11]

In this chapter, I present the principles that underlie the notion of the guiding word and point to the presence of such words in Buber's own writings. We shall begin with an exegesis of a Buberian essay about the way one ought to read the Bible. Following this exegesis, I shall engage in a "hermeneutic of Buber's hermeneutics," revealing the presence of these principles in his nonbiblical works. The analysis and interpretation of the hidden dialogue that Buber conducts with the reader of his own texts draw attention to several ideas that he evidently found difficult to communicate in a direct, exoteric manner. These ideas are the locus of this book.

With these background observations in mind, let us examine Buber's use of written words to direct wordless attention to hidden aspects of what is (i.e., of being) and of social realities, beginning with his reading of the principles guiding the writing of the Hebrew Bible. For full appreciation of the hidden nature of Buber's writings about the Bible, however, one should begin with a preliminary overview of the hermeneutic principles that Buber (and Franz Rosenzweig) attributed to "R."[12]

## THE ORAL ORIGINS OF THE WRITTEN TEXT

The Buber-Rosenzweig translation of the Bible was first and foremost an attempt to preserve the original character of the Bible as one book, "no matter out of how many and varied fragments it has grown."[13] It is evident that the translation was undertaken as part of

Buber's attempt to attain greater clarity in his own relating to being, to the silence that precedes human creativity and activity. The mystery of hearing the original voice was for him the gateway to the mystery of understanding. In this respect, Buber and Rosenzweig followed ancient Hebrew tradition: whatever was the source, whoever was the "first" hearer, Jewish tradition assumes that the spoken word was first heard and only later granted the visual form of a text.[14] Yet unlike in Jewish orthodoxy, Buber writes that he and Rosenzweig shared the realization that "one believes not *in* the Bible but *through* it, and throughout it."[15] In other words, the importance of the text is not in its existence as a totemic object sanctioned by rabbinic authority but in the opportunity it offers to open oneself to insight that is not subjective. To write that one believes "through" the Bible implies that this text "speaks" to a reader who is able to "hear." In Buber's terminology, such moments of insight are termed "dialogical."

While sharing a common perspective about the significance of the Bible's original orality, Rosenzweig and Buber disagreed about the authoritative status of biblical commandments. Rosenzweig thought that to be an observing Jew was a necessary part of the relation to the deity.[16] In contrast, Buber thought that the experience of hearing is more significant than the content heard, and did not think that observance of commandments is necessary for attaining such "hearing." Buber's dismissing attitude to commandments, stemming in part from his deeply felt antipathy toward religious institutions and dogmas, was the primary reason why Orthodox Jews considered him heretical and dangerous.

The basic assumption guiding the Buber-Rosenzweig translation was that the unity of the written Torah and the oral Torah is experienced in relating to the text as "the read Torah,"[17] an attitude that enables one to experience the "unitary consciousness of the book."[18] They believed that the apparent distinction between the oral and the written sources of the Hebrew Bible disappears in the existential act of reading, in the meeting of reader and text. Faithful to their preliminary assumptions, Buber and Rosenzweig distinguished between two names for this text: *miqra'* (מקרא), a Hebrew word that derives from a Hebrew verb-stem (Q\R\A) connoting both "to call out" and "to read" and can be translated as "calling out"[19] or "the calling" (i.e., "what is spoken");[20] and *Schrift*, the German word for "Scripture" (or "what is written").[21] Their translation sought to retain this distinction, to enable the reader of the

German translation to experience the precedence of the spoken word over its written representation. They therefore attempted to preserve the spoken quality of Hebrew *miqra'* as they translated it into the written form of German *Schrift*. This precision in their choice of names was not mere pedantry; their purpose was to enable future generations of German readers to experience the immediate encounter with the text. In the words of Buber: "We the translators of Scripture have a [modest] task: to take care that a human ear which the voice reaches from any passage of the Scripture be able to receive that voice more easily and more clearly." Buber adds Rosenzweig's telling comment: "*Schrift* [writing, Scripture] is poison, holy *Schrift* included. Only when it is translated back into orality does it suit my stomach."[22]

Emphasis on the text's orality led Buber to pay attention to the repetition of Hebrew words and sounds.[23] This attention accords with Jewish tradition, which considers that every letter and every word in the Bible has been carefully chosen and that no word or sound is coincidental or unintentional, including instances in which the text may seem unnecessarily repetitive or obscure. Rosenzweig shared Buber's conviction that their translation should retain repetitions that abound in the original Hebrew. He wrote that by hearing the repetition, the reader may be freed from the "fetters of the written word"; to translate into German the "hearing" of the word and thus to retain the potential impact of hearing on the receiving organ (the reader), "drastic measures" were necessary. "Martin Buber," he added, "found those measures." By replacing logical punctuation with oral punctuation (determined by the breaths that punctuate the act of reading), Buber enabled "the bond of tongue [to be] loosened by the eye."[24]

By reading out loud, the readers' attention is directed to subtle forms of repetition and discovers that R attempted "to direct our organic attention to the meaning of the story that is to appear to us," inviting us to experience the "original and concrete sensory meanings." The Bible's use of similar or recurring sounds usually reflects some indirect lesson. Buber refered to this as "the formal secret of biblical style," which he had "discovered in translating."[25] This understanding of the text's intention is the basis for Buber's division of the German translation into breath-units and his consequent attempt to retain in that work the rhythm he had discerned in the Hebrew original.

## THE GUIDING WORDS OF THE WRITTEN TEXT

The guiding-word principle includes two elements: repetition of sounds and repetition of rare words or word-roots. Buber writes that this technique "underscores the lesson of a passage by repetition of sounds, and by repetition in diverse passages of the same rare words or word-roots it allows each passage to comment on and supplement the lessons of the others."[26] Up to this point, we have focused on the importance of hearing the written word as spoken. Yet for our purposes, it is more significant to point to the second principle guiding R's work: the use of Hebrew etymology and plays on words stemming from the same root as indirect indications of hidden connections between apparently unrelated passages.

Underlying the discovery of the guiding word as a code for reading the Bible is Buber's assumption that repetition of the same word-stem in a dissonant manner or of uncommon words in diverse biblical contexts is not merely coincidental. He believed that such irregularities were inserted into the Bible intentionally to serve as discrete invitations to the reader to pause and contemplate the intention indicated by the presence of *leitwörten*. Words thus inserted guide the reader and direct his or her attention to meaning inherent in the text, written between its lines, so to speak. Hence the transformation of an "ordinary" word into its additional function as a "guiding" word.[27] The hermeneutic principle of the guiding word ensures that the Bible will serve its purpose as a conveyor of multiple meanings, meanings that reveal themselves in direct relation to the reader's sensitivity and openness to biblical text.[28] Buber referred to this way of reading as "the excavation of the Hebraic content of the individual word."[29]

Why should the Bible include a discrete level of meaning available only to an attentive reader? Basically, the Bible attempts to replicate (or to anticipate) "reality." Just as one's meeting with reality is mediated by focused attention on this or that element, so too does the surface of the Bible present one conspicuous element of a tale or event. Similarly, just as one may see in simple events complex, hidden backgrounds, so too does the biblical text enable one to read its complex, yet hidden, background. R's task was extraordinarily complex: to point to particular aspects of reality by using words that convey a sense of visual description, while attempting to ensure that attention to select aspects of the text's intention would not cause a gullible reader to erroneously consider attention focused on a detail or event recorded in the text to be a substitute for the encompassing unity of which it constitutes, indeed, but a detail.[30]

The guiding-word principle is thus crucial to developing a sensitivity to the way language mediates between reality and its comprehension by the human subject (or, phrased differently, a sensitivity to the relation between ontology and epistemology). Prior to the intervention of language, reality exists as an undivided whole. Segmentation of reality into separate components serves an objective human necessity, to distinguish among elements of the unified, one, whole, eternal "is." However, to consider this segmentation a permanent "reality" goes against the original unity of which the segment is but a part. That is why attentive reading of the Scripture reveals that words function as conveyors of meaning in their particular context (and in this respect, Buber anticipates the modern philosophy of Wittgenstein) but that they may also convey meaning that is elucidated only when considered in relation to other passages in the text (and here Buber is firmly embedded in Jewish midrashic—oral interpretation—traditions of reading).

We may summarize the discussion of Buber's understanding of the Bible's hermeneutics by suggesting that the first principle guiding the reading of the Bible is its orality. When reading the *miqra'* out loud, one hears certain repetitions that provide clues to meaning that may otherwise be overlooked. The forms of repetition included in biblical words and verses give rise to the presence of the *leitwort* (the guiding word).[31] This is the second principle. The guiding (or "leading") words are "keywords or theme words, [that] have the function of stressing what is important, of enhancing the real meaning of the text or passage."[32] For Buber, *leitwörten* appear in two primary forms: (1) words written in diverse biblical contexts yet related by a common Hebrew verb stem, as well as (2) uncommon words that attract the reader's attention because of their singularity. In both cases, a word becomes a *leitwort* by virtue of the reader's sensitivity to its hermeneutic function.

## THE SIGNIFICANCE OF REPETITIVE USE OF THE VERB-STEM P\T\CH (TO OPEN)

This section presents the first of my interpretations of Buber's works that substantiate the claim that Buber's writings include guiding words.

In addition to justifying the hermeneutic assumptions that guide my reading of Buber's texts, in this section the story hidden within Buber's own texts begins to unfold.

In 1936, Buber published *Die Schrift und ihre Verdeutschung*, a series of essays about the Bible, its translation and its interpretation, rendered into English by Lawrence Rosenwald with Everett Fox as *Scripture and Translation*. The opening essay, entitled "People Today and the Jewish Bible: From a Lecture Series," addresses, among other topics, the importance of attention to the repetition of verb-stems in biblical texts.[33] One may safely assume that if Buber uses derivatives of the same word-stem in such an essay, the reader must pause and contemplate the possible significance of such repetition for understanding the essay itself. This approach guides the following reading of Buber's essay.

In perusing the Hebrew version of "People Today," the reader is struck by the repetitive use of derivatives of the verb-stem פתח, *patach* (P\T\CH—"to open"). More than twenty words stemming from the root *patach* appear in the first ten pages. With a transition in the essay's theme, the word disappears in the next eight pages, only to reemerge in the essay's concluding paragraph. This unevenness creates a sense of dissonance that calls for closer investigation.

The first appearance of the root *patach* refers to *peetchon halev leemunah* (the opening of the heart to faith), which is followed immediately by reference to *p'teechat lev* (opening the heart).[34] A state of openheartedness creates an opening to a relation to being that is indicated by the word "faith," which characterizes one who is present in the face of the reality for which the words of the Bible serve as indicators.

The verb-stem *patach* continues to appear in related forms: the words *petach, peetchon, patooach,* and *p'teechat* all refer to an inner opening to a state of existence in which ordinary ways of thinking about the world are suspended and a direct perception of reality is received. We thus encounter allusions to the possibility of an "open gate" to an open heart;[35] to an "opening of an opening to the Bible";[36] to possible ways of "opening for us this opening" to "revelation";[37] and to the relation between "the opening of one of our generation to the actuality of revelation" and the possibility of his "opening to the reality of creation."[38] This layer of the text unfolds in parallel to a discussion of cultural and mental dispositions that, when internalized, *prevent* an "openhearted" reading of the Bible.[39] In other words, the surface of the text explains what is wrong with how we relate to being; the guiding word directs attention to the alternatives Buber considers present, yet hidden from ordinary perception.

Note the multiple layers of meaning inherent in such a form of writing; the words that explicitly communicate dissatisfaction with existing ways of thinking also serve as indicators of forms of relation that subvert conventional patterns of thought. The subtext, whose existence comes to light only by attention to the role of guiding words present in the text's surface, subverts its surface by constantly drawing the reader's attention toward the importance of listening to the manner of relation indicated by derivatives of the stem "to open." While denouncing the "muddle" of events referred to as "history" and criticizing dogmatic reliance on linear trains of thought (coupled with modern oblivion to the most basic existential questions) as inadequate to the task of conveying meaning to multidimensional reality, Buber constantly inserts words that draw the attentive reader to contemplate what the alternative to convention might be. The reader notes the "bumps" on the surface of the text and listens.

After ten pages, about halfway through the essay, Buber shifts his attention from a discussion of the appropriate attitude to reading the Bible to an exemplary exegesis of select biblical passages. This transition is mediated by an explanation of the importance of pondering the repetition of the same word in separate contexts. At the focus of this explanation, one finds the word *neeftach* (is opened, revealed):

> You pause and listen to this repetition, to what it says. This is the way of *Torah bamiqra* [i.e., instruction, teaching, in the scripture], which frequently does not interpret the substance of the virtue discussed but rather enables it to open of itself [*shetehe neeftachat me'eleha*], not in the language of secret or allegory but in this significant repetition, perceptible to every reader and every hearer who listens with the heart.[40]

We read in this transitional passage that Buber suggests that engagement in biblical interpretation does not result solely in verbal understanding but also may create an unmediated "knowing," experienced as an opening of the text to the reader. The "opening of the text" is commensurate with the "opening of the [reader's] heart." As soon as the importance of opening the heart is established, the verb-stem *patach* recedes to the background of the text. It reappears only once before the essay's concluding paragraph, where Buber says that by calling for Bible reading, he is calling for the "open-heartedness" (*b'feetchon lev*) of faith.[41] This is a realization of the oneness that is the root of biblical reality, of *miqra* as reality (*miqra b'cheenat m'tseeoot*).[42]

Our examination of Buber's method of reading the Bible appears to have uncovered the themes he sought to emphasize through his insertion and subsequent sudden withdrawal of derivatives of the verb-stem "to open." Yet sensitivity to the importance of "opening" the heart to the Bible underscores the centrality of an additional word that dominates Buber's text: לב, *lev* (heart). The repetitive use of the root *patach* has directed our attention to repeated mention of the word *lev*, which appears scores of times in the essay, many more times than the word "open" in its various manifestations. *What* is opened? The heart. It seems that for Buber, the "heart" is a point of reception of unmediated impressions. The guiding word "to open" thus serves an additional intention, to sensitize the reader to a quality of attention and relation designated by the word *lev*. Hence, there is repeated emphasis on the importance of "opening the heart" to a sensation of presence that is qualitatively different from the sensation of "reality" attained when listening primarily through the mediation of preconceived structures of thought. He who listens with the "heart" accepts external impressions directly, without prior mediation of the intellect.[43]

Thus, reading of Buber's "People Today and the Jewish Bible" along the principles of reading that this essay suggests for readers of the Hebrew Bible reveals that the essay itself includes guiding words. We therefore become attentive to a layer of Buber's text that otherwise might be overlooked. This reading helps us understand the rationale underlying the use of guiding words: inclusion of guiding words is based on the assumption that the extra effort required of the reader—to recognize the repetitive use of verb-stems and to contemplate its significance—creates an elevated type of attention that enhances the reader's sensibility and creates a possibility that the text may "open up" to him. In this respect, Buber's form of writing is well within the mainstream of the Jewish oral tradition of biblical interpretation (midrash). The words *petach* or *peticha* (opening, or an opening) abound in midrashic texts, indicating the intention of the student of midrash to find, in the words of Irving Jacobs, "the 'exegetical opening' within the plain meaning of the text as the Rabbis perceive it, through which they could extract or introduce their desired message, or create thematic links."[44] In the case of Buber, attention to derivatives of the verb-stem P\T\CH draws our attention to the notion of *lev* (heart). This word will reappear in this book as a central element in Buber's lexicon of significant words.

## THE SIGNIFICANCE OF THE UNCOMMON WORD *LIMMUD*

So far, we have followed the hermeneutic path indicated by the repetitive use of verb-stem. We now move to contemplate an additional form of the guiding-word principle, the appearance of an uncommon word in diverse biblical contexts. The analysis will begin with examination of a certain word—*limmud*—that Buber uses as a guiding word to prove the unity of the Book of Isaiah. After explaining the meaning of the original biblical verses whose careful use of this particular word attracts the reader's attention, I shall demonstrate how Buber uses these very same biblical verses in his own writing. The key to this interpretation is Buber's book *The Prophetic Faith*. I shall point out how attention to Buber's use of Isaiah's guiding words in the opening sentence of *The Prophetic Faith* opens the Buberian text to additional, implicit meaning if one reads side-by-side those passages within it that make explicit reference to the guiding words of the opening sentence.

In addition to further substantiating the claim that Buber's works include guiding words, the following exegesis will also begin to construct the story that Buber wished to tell. Here we shall encounter Buber's understanding of the presence and purpose of hidden circles of prophets who exist in the shadows of the biblical text and are also present as the background of Buber's interpretation of the prophetic teaching.

### *Isaiah, Jeremiah, and the* Limmudim

In his essay about the unity of the Book of Isaiah, Buber's explicit goal is to challenge learned interpretations of the mission of Isaiah that are based solely on historical or literary analysis of the Book of Isaiah. Those interpretations dwell on the fact that this biblical book represents the words of two prophets. Advocates of such interpretations often apply their scholarly skills to direct attention to differences between the two historical "Isaiahs" and then go on to compare and contrast differences between the figures they reconstruct from the biblical text. Buber does not argue with such interpretations per se but rather suggests that they ought to be situated within a broader context, that is, within the overall intention of R's text.

Buber takes an opposite line of analysis: Accepting the fact that the book represents the words of two different prophets who are separated by some two hundred years of history, Buber shows that the second Isaiah uses carefully chosen guiding words to suggest that he considers his work a direct continuation of that of the first. He and the first Isaiah share a unity of purpose and deed. As such, they are parts of one, inclusive, continual effort to retain the dialogical relation to being. Consciously working from within the same ontology and as part of an ongoing stream of dialogical prophets, they see and experience naturally created and historically constructed realities in identical ways. This *seeing* supersedes their biographical separation. One might add that this reading of the biblical subtext is supported by the fact that the later prophet chooses to remain anonymous and blends into the personality of the first by assuming the name of Isaiah and by deleting any mention of his separate biography.

Buber begins his exegesis of the Book of Isaiah by reminding his readers of the principles that guide his interpretation: "Whenever an uncommon word appears in diverse biblical texts, it is imperative that one examine whether there is a special intention here to have the reader read the texts one alongside the other."[45] Reading two chapters from the Book of Isaiah that are evidently representative of the two separate Isaiahs, Buber asks whether these two historical figures represent different perspectives. In response to these questions, Buber singles out *limmud*, a rare derivation of the root למד (L\M\D, "to study"), as a *leitwort* constituting a key to understanding.

How does *limmud* become a guiding word, and how does it prove the unity of the Book of Isaiah? The word *limmud* appears six times in the Bible: four times in Isaiah and twice in Jeremiah. In Isaiah, it is a noun meaning "pupil" (or "disciple") and "a state of continuous study."[46] This form of the word appears once in a chapter attributed to the "first" Isaiah (8:16) and three times in chapters ascribed to the "second" (twice in 50:4 and once in 54:13). Buber points to this rare use of the word *limmud* as proof that the second Isaiah considered himself a disciple-descendant of the first.

According to Buber, in anticipation of the coming catastrophe, the first Isaiah declares that the time has come to "bind up the testimony, seal the teaching among my disciples [*limmudai*]" (8:16).[47] Practically speaking, this Isaiah has decided that from his time onward, *limmudim* (plural of *limmud*) will serve as living embodiments of the teaching that can no longer be transmitted as revealed instruction. Buber attributes to the first Isaiah the intention that this hidden form of transmission will persist until the *limmudim* are confronted by an unequivocal demand that the teaching be revealed. Metaphorically speaking, the teaching will be sealed in the "heart."[48] The second Isaiah is aware that he is a link in the line of hidden transmission initiated by the first. His carefully chosen words affirm that he, generations after the first Isaiah's time, considers himself a *limmud*. Hence his assertion that he has been given the "tongue" and the "ear" of *limmudim* (50:4), and hence his promise that in an age to come, the sons of those who have realized the magnitude of human suffering will be the *limmudim* of YHVH (54:13).[49]

Access to this testimony, which from the first Isaiah onwards becomes a teaching hidden from the public eye, will require special effort on the part of potential seekers.[50] The attitude befitting a seeker[51] who wishes to approach the "testimony" and "teaching" is spelled out in the verse that immediately follows Isaiah's declaration regarding the *limmudim* as a new form of transmitting the ancient teaching, וחיכיתי ליהוה המסתיר פניו מבית יעקב וקיויתי לו (*V'cheekeetee laYHVH hamasteer panav mebeit Ya'akov v'keeveetee loh*) (Isaiah 8:17).

This verse's translation into English is open to multiple versions, depending on the meaning ascribed to the root K\V\H (קוה) from which derives the word *vekeeveetee*. My own translation reads as follows: "And I will wait for YHVH, who hides his face from the house of Ya'akov, and I will incline towards him."[52] This translation opens the verse to the following interpretation: The *limmud* combines a state of anticipation, a form of alert inactivity (indicated by the phrase *heekeetee l'YHVH*, "I will wait for YHVH") and an inner inclination, an active form of longing (designated by *keeveetee loh,* usually translated as "I will hope in him" or

"I will look for him," although including the meaning I have emphasized, the use of the root K\V\H as also indicating "to incline toward").

Note that this verse (8:17) says that the *limmud* waits for YHVH,
who hides his face from the house of *Ya'akov* (Jacob), not from "the
house of *Israel*." I consider this a significant choice of words, for in the
next verse (8:18) we read that the "signs and portents" (אותות ומופתים)
are in *Israel* (and not in *Ya'akov*): ולמופתים בישׂראל מעם יהוה צבאות השׁכן בהר ציון
הנה אנכי והילדים אשר נתן לי יהוה לאתות (heeneh anochee v'hayiladeem asher natan
lee YHVH l'otot ul'mofteem b'Yisrael me-eem YHVH tsevaot hashochen b'har
tsion) (8:18). This verse translates as "Here am I and the children whom
YHVH has given me as signs and portents in Israel from YHVH of
hosts, who dwells on Mount Zion." The signs are embodied in the
children, who serve as living, visible metaphors for the part of Israel that
inclines toward the eternally present, YHVH. That is the meaning of
the reference to "the children" as "signs and portents *in Israel*." Israel
refers not only to the community of Israel, but also to the relation to
being that this community represents, to the inner transmutation indicated in the biblical distinction between Ya'akov and Israel. (The word
"Israel" may be read as *Yashar El*, Hebrew words that evoke multiple
associations, all related to *immediacy* and directness in the face of what is.
The name *Ya'akov*, in addition to connoting the word "heel," suggestive
of Ya'akov's grasping the heel of Esau, the name *Ya'akov* also implies
"one who will follow," suggesting *mediated* relation to what is—a contrast to the directness of Israel—perhaps symbolizing the reactive and
hence passive nature of thought characteristic of Ya'akov.)

Those whose relation to being is characterized by the expression
"the house of Ya'akov" are unaware of the possibility of experiencing a
more inclusive relation to being and therefore do not see the signs of an
alternative way of life, sent to them in the form of a child. This particular
exegesis of Isaiah 8:18 supports my understanding of Buber's brief mention of the significance of *limmud* as a guiding word: Those referred to
as *limmudim* are persons who are attentive to the element of being that
is granted symbolic form in the biblical distinction between "Ya'akov"
and "Israel." Their role is to bring to the surface of consciousness, and
to retain, the memory of this distinction, and to attempt to manifest in
their attitude to self and other the quality of presence indicated by the
word "Israel."

Verse 8:18 calls for additional interpretation. The allusion to the children given to Isaiah possesses multiple significance. From one perspective, it may be understood as referring to the *limmudim*—those who serve, together with Isaiah, as living signs of the relationship between the person and God. As such, the *limmudim* exemplify an openhearted naivete usually associated with children. An alternative viewpoint perceives the children as those designated in the preceding chapter of Isaiah: Verses 7:3, 7:14, and 8:3 mention a series of offspring—*She'ar-yashuv, Immanuel, and Maher-shalal-hash-baz*—whom Isaiah refers to as his own. These "children" are obviously allegorical figures whose significance merits separate interpretation and exegesis. In the context of the present discussion, it is important to note one feature common to all three: they embody the difference between the path of the "house of Ya'akov," characterized by ignorance and darkness, and that of "Israel," exemplified by active pursuit of the hidden teaching and testimony. Regarding the first child, *She'ar-yashuv* (literally, "the remnant will return"), Buber comments that Isaiah takes the boy with him to meet King Ahaz "as a visible word expressing the demanding mercy of his God."[53] In that meeting, the boy represents, in bodily form, the divine protest against the sacrifice of the firstborn, as well as a divine warning: "Now the decisive decision begins, who is of the remnant, who will return to me and whom shall I preserve."[54] It is the presence of the sign, and not solely the words of the prophet, that represents the greater reality that Ahaz is called to address.

Note the shift in presentation, for it illustrates the way guiding words open the reader to additional layers of meaning conveyed within one text. Initially, I drew attention to Buber's explicit use of the guiding word *limmud* as his way of validating the claim that the Book of Isaiah constitutes one indivisible literary unit. This exegesis was completed straightforwardly by pointing to this word's use by both Isaiahs.[55] Once that issue was determined, however, the guiding word revealed an opening to a far more significant observation concerning transmission of the teachings of Judaism through *limmudim*. Isaiah realized the futility of further admonishing people and kings to address the teaching in a manner befitting the "chosen people." Hence, he and his followers redirected their attention to ensuring that the seeds of prophecy were sown among the receptive few.[56] This layer of the biblical text was revealed through a concurrent reading of the biblical contexts that Buber alluded to and Buber's reference to these same verses in his own writings.

We thus encounter the full impact of one of Buber's most cherished convictions, a certainty that grew as he matured (historically and intellectually). In establishing the direct relation among the prophets of the Book of Isaiah, Buber shed light on what he refered to as a "great fact in the history of the Spirit";[57] he suggested that from Isaiah onwards, there have been circles of *limmudim* who embody the essence of Judaism. These disciples "seal" the secrets of *torah* and *te'udah* (testimony) in their existence, in their relation to life. We shall shortly read the full significance of these words, when contemplating the fact that the opening sentence of *The Prophetic Faith* includes these very words.

Before we do this, we should note that exegesis of the guiding word *limmud* would be incomplete without considering the two passages in Jeremiah that allude to this term. Jeremiah (the end of the seventh and beginning of the sixth century B.C.E) is evidently a link in the new chain of transmission initiated by Isaiah (the eighth century B.C.E). In Jeremiah 2:24, we read ישיבנה כל מבקשיה לא יעפו בחדשה ימצאונה פרה למד מדבר באות נפשו שאפה רוח תאנתה מי (*Pereh limmud meedbar b'avat nafsho sha'afah ruah ta'anatah me y'shevenah kol m'vaksheha loh yeafu b'chodshah yemtsaonah*). This verse is conventionally translated: "A wild ass used to the wilderness, in her heat sniffing the wind! Who can restrain her lust? None who seek her need weary themselves; in her month they will find her."[58] However, this verse is open to alternative translations based on interpretations inherent in the etymology of its text. The word *pereh* may represent fertility, as in Genesis 35:11 (*Anee El shadai preh urveh,* "I am God Almighty: be fruitful and multiply"); the word *limmud* may have the meaning it has in Isaiah. And the word *meedbar* may mean desert, symbolic of the period of wandering that followed the departure from Egypt and preceded the entry into the promised land.

These alternative translations are possible because the Hebrew Bible was punctuated and vocalized by interpreters, not by the original redactor. Accordingly, punctuation and vocalization constitute an act of interpretation. In seeking the original voices designated by the words of the text, one may go beyond the layer of meaning established by those who punctuated the present text (as long as such an alternative interpretation is corroborated by appropriate textual evidence). Letters strung into words (as visual text) may be infused with alternative meanings when the pronunciation of the words is changed (as audible utterance). By offering alternative vowel signs, I therefore offer an alternative interpretation that is bounded by the letters of the text.

Now, what do changes in vowel signs (and hence in phonetics) yield in terms of interpretation (and translation into English) of Jeremiah 2:24? Traditionally, Egypt and the desert may be interpreted as psychological states of mind that must be examined thoroughly before advancing to the state designated by entering the promised land of Canaan (Israel). Accordingly, the verse may be read as a blessing to the *limmud*: "Be fertile, *limmud* of the desert," that is, a *limmud* aware of the psychological state indicated by the term "desert" and determined to study it and know it thoroughly. Another reading yields "Be fertile, *limmud*, from speaking in sign[s]," if we read מדבר *midbar* (desert) as *medaber* (speaks) and באות, *b'avat* as *b'ot* (in sign[s]).

This interpretation of Jeremiah 2:24 is supported by the additional mention of *limmud* in Jeremiah 13:23, a well-known verse in which the prophet asks: היהפוך כושי עורו ונמר חברברותיו גם אתם תוכלו להיטיב למדי הרע ("*hayahafoch kooshee oro v'namer ch'varboorotav gam atem tochloo l'heyteev leemodei hare'ah*"). This verse is customarily rendered as follows: "Can the Ethiopian change his skin or the leopard his spots? Then also you can do good who are accustomed to do evil." Accordingly, a common interpretation perceives this verse as a declaration regarding the irreversibility of a state of existence accustomed to doing evil. Alternatively, however, it may be read as a message to the *limmud*: you can become good, *limmud*, if you study evil. Note that the Hebrew word *hare'ah* (infliction of badness) is preceded by *limmudei*, a derivative of the root L\M\D, enabling its translation as "the students of." The meaning of the verse would then change as follows: "remaining attentive to the situation termed badness, you will become good." The *limmud* can overcome evil by knowing it. This interpretation complements the earlier reference in 2:24 to the importance of studying the intermediate state between total servitude to material and psychological elements (symbolically referred to as Pharaoh and Egypt) and redemption (represented by the entry into Canaan and hence into the promised land of Israel).

In our reading of the two verses in the Book of Jeremiah that include the guiding word *limmud*, the prophet evidently emphasizes the need for practical, worldly efforts on the *limmud*'s part. The *limmud*'s existence is characterized by total immersion in the psychological reality

reflected in the political and religious chaos about him. He is differentiated from his surroundings by his determination to study the facts of
human existence that give rise to such misplacement of attention and
waste of faith and intention. He knows that the path to an unmediated
relation to reality is to be sought within, in the "heart." Jeremiah says
that the *torah* given to "the house of Israel" is "within them," written
"on their hearts" (31:33).[59] Considered in these terms, self-study of psychological reality is in fact, we may suggest, a study of the "seal" between the *limmud* and the *torah* embedded in his being.

Buber did not point out this connection between uses of the word
*limmud* in Jeremiah and Isaiah, perhaps because he read the verses in
Jeremiah differently. He might even have disagreed with the proposed
comparison, as he refers to the verses from Jeremiah as examples of the
"ordinary, commonplace" sense of a word accorded additional meaning
by Isaiah.[60] This difference in interpretation need not be considered
problematic, however, as it demonstrates the various ways in which the
Bible may be understood. To borrow a phrase developed by Steven
Kepnes, biblical hermeneutics is dialogical, "open and continually developing . . . not only between the reader and the text but also between the
reader and fellow interpreters."[61] Texts that intentionally apply biblical
hermeneutics—as Buber's does—are deliberately open ended, enabling
the reader to participate in an ongoing dialogue that originated in previous generations and will continue throughout his life and thereafter.

### The Hidden Circles of Prophets

Having addressed the role of *limmud* as a guiding word in Buber's
text, we now examine Buber's book on the prophetic tradition, *The
Prophetic Faith*. (The English translation misrepresents the original Hebrew title: תורת הנביאים, *Torat Hanive'eem*, should have been translated as
*The Prophetic Teaching*.)[62] From its opening line, this book calls us to
consider the hermeneutic principles that ought to guide a careful reading
of its text; as such, the first paragraph includes an indirect invitation to
consider a hidden message:

> The testimony of (*te'udato*) this book is to describe a *torah*, a teaching,
> that attained its final form in the works of writing prophets who wrote
> in the period between the last decades of the kingdom of Ephraim

and the return to Zion from the Babylonian exile; to describe both the course of its generation,[63] and its prehistoric development. The *torah* is the *torah* of the relation between the *Elohim* of Israel and Israel.[64]

The paragraph begins with the word *te'udato*, literally meaning "the testimony of . . . ," followed by the assertion that the testimony relates to a *torah*—a *torah*, not *the* Torah (the former means "teaching" and the latter means "Law," in addition, "the Pentateuch"). This choice of words cannot be mere coincidence. *Te'udah* appears in the Scriptures only three times; in two of these three instances, it is coupled with the word *torah* in two verses of the Book of Isaiah, chapter 8,[65] noted in the previous exegesis as those rare verses designated by the guiding word *limmud*! Isaiah 8:16 declares "Bind up the testimony (*te'udah*), seal the teaching (*torah*) among my disciples (*b'limmudai*)," while Isaiah 8:20 indicates that the place for "the house of Ya'akov" to seek understanding is in the teaching (*l'torah*) and the testimony (*v'lite'udah*).[66] According to Buber, these verses serve as indirect indications of the manner in which *te'udah* and *torah* are transmitted in the period following the first Isaiah.

Buber was surely aware that the inclusion of uncommon biblical words in the opening lines of a book about the Bible would be strikingly unusual. The anomaly is compounded when one considers that Buber, in a different essay, "The Unity of the Book of Isaiah,"[67] singled out the same two verses of Isaiah to demonstrate how guiding words serve as openings to hidden meanings in the biblical text. In his own terms, such words lead the reader to contemplate the possibility that beyond their conventional meanings, they may also serve as guiding words. In this case, the words guide our interpretation of passages in Buber's own text —*The Prophetic Faith*—that refer to these verses.

In his first reference to verse 8:16 in *The Prophetic Faith*, Buber attributes Isaiah's decision to create a new form of transmission (by establishing circles of *limmudim*) to Isaiah's unfruitful meeting with King Ahaz, during which Isaiah realizes that the "heart" of Ahaz "is hardened" and that his individual obstinacy is symbolic of a communal condition.[68] Isaiah assumes that the reasons for his failure to bring about a change of heart in Ahaz are identical to those that led to his failure to bring the people to *teshuva*, a (re)turn to YHVH. Buber concludes that in this encounter, one may detect the seeds of Isaiah's decision to "seal" the teaching in the "hearts" of "a circle of faithful" (*hug ne'emanim*).[69] This is Isaiah's testimony, his *te'udah*.[70]

To reorient transmission of the teaching towards a more private and intimate form of association, groups of *limmudim*, is, Isiaiah believes, the appropriate response to his observation that the people of his day (whose actual condition is that of the "house of Ya'akov") "no more wish to know God" and consequently, that "the reception of the revelation, which must be renewed in every generation, is interrupted."[71] Implicit in this attitude is the assumption that the social and political organization of the people of Israel should be subject to the primary goal of establishing the quality of relation to being that is designated by the word "Israel." The spiritual mission of "Israel" predates the establishment of a political Kingdom of Israel, and the latter mission ought to be determined by the former. Social and political forms of association and structures of authority should be commensurate with the overriding goal of transmitting the teaching that serves as the opening to revelation. Isaiah's renewal of the social structure of transmission thus conforms with the overall context within which Israel exists: when external social structures constrained by the limits of the prevailing ontology (i.e., association in a kingdom that includes a formal religious leadership) are detrimental to the primary purpose, they must undergo change. As social structures reflect ontological presuppositions, meaningful renewal of social structure is necessarily determined by personal ontological change.

It is important to emphasize that while Buber considered the decision to safeguard the teaching in the "hidden" line of *limmudim* to be Isaiah's innovative response to the dire social and psychological conditions he faced, Buber did not attribute to Isaiah a radical break with the past. Hidden circles of prophets had existed in the background of Judaism from time immemorial. In *Kingship of God*, Buber comments that from its earliest records of individual prophecy, the Bible indicates that the voice of the individual prophet represented a communal existence. All who spoke the words of the spirit, including the judges discussed in *Kingship of God*, "came . . . from the community of those persons open to the Spirit . . . from the community by which they [were] supported thereafter."[72] Buber describes the prophets as a movement of faith that was opposed to the tendency among the Israelite tribes to circumscribe faith within the confines of cult and ceremony. Communities of proph-

ets, such as those mentioned in *Amos* 2:11–12, were committed to retaining a direct, unmediated relationship with YHVH.[73]

Buber reminds us that Deborah,[74] Elijah[75] and Samuel[76] were associated with such groups. In 1 Samuel 10:5–6, Saul is informed by Samuel
that after he meets a group of prophets and joins them in their celebra-
tion of music and rhythm, he will experience an opening to the spirit of
YHVH; he will prophesy "and become a different person." Saul's new
state of being is described in terms of experiencing "a different heart"
(10:9). For Buber, this episode supports the proposition that the quality
of relation prevailing among members of the community of prophets
from whose midst Samuel emerged strengthens the individual member's
receptivity to the spirit and, consequently, to the word. The relation to
the spirit is established in the social space created among the members of
Samuel's group of prophets (the Between) and the word of prophecy
stems from the opening to the spirit.[77] Saul's spiritual powers seem to be
dependent on this social context, on those "men of valor whose hearts
*Elohim* touched" (1 Samuel 10:26). Buber writes: "Do not treat these
words [1 Samuel 10:26] lightly; they indicate that these are select and
chosen ones. . . . This group is not seen on the stage, but you sense its
presence behind the scenes."[78]

Saul's "heart turns" under the impact of the meeting with Samuel,
and his ability to prophesy manifests itself in the company of the group
of prophets. Ordinary people who see him prophesy "with the prophets" are surprised and ask: "Is Saul also among the prophets?" (1 Samuel
10:11). That Saul's refined relation to being is an effect of the meeting
with Samuel and subsequently with the group of prophets is apparent
from the description of Saul's downfall: Samuel turns his back on Saul
and thus brings about the loss of Saul's prophetic powers (1 Samuel
13:13–14, 19:9). Stripped of the quality of relation prevailing among the
members of this circle, Saul is deprived of his "new heart."[79]

Buber alludes to the communal background of the individual
prophet in an additional passage, one concerning the prophet Amos's
intimates in Samaria. He writes that Amos's promise that the "remnant"
of Israel will continue to exist in exile "is to be seen as *a form of will
[Amos] bequeaths to his intimates, those who share in the secret* [my italics—
D.A.]." Buber refers to Amos 8:11–12 without directly citing the text
or subjecting it to exegesis.[80] Let us see what he may have had in mind.
In Amos 7:10, Amatzia the priest complains to King Jeroboam that

Amos is conspiring against the king "in the midst of the House of Israel." In its simplest interpretation, Amos's prophecy (Amos 7:11) that the king will die and "Israel will be exiled from its land" implies that the "Israel" to be exiled is the political entity, the nation of Israel existing within the Kingdom of Israel. A further reading, sensitive to the inherent hermeneutics, may interpret Amos's prophesying in the midst of "the house of Israel" as referring to those who are privy to the relation designated by "Israel" (in contrast to "the house of Ya'akov"). Thus, Amos prophesies within the group of persons who can be properly referred to as "Israel," informing them that they will continue to fulfill the mission of "Israel" in exile, within the "house of Ya'akov," just as they do now, amid the misguided peoples of the political Kingdom of Israel.

This reading explains Buber's otherwise obscure comment that this prophecy is Amos's bequest (will) to his intimates in Samaria. A bequest conventionally constitutes something from which the inheritors may derive benefit. What is so positive about Amos's prophecy of (apparent) exile that merits consideration as a "will"? Reading the verses from Amos in terms associated with the essential background context—the hidden circles of prophets—we may suggest that the good news directed to this group is that, the political disaster notwithstanding, they will continue to exist in exile as a holy remnant. As a political, historical entity, the "Israel" addressed by Amos is the kingdom constructed at that particular time by the fundamental (and misguided) values of the men and women he criticizes. But present in Amos's audience are those privy to the additional meaning of "Israel," which represents the positive relation to existence. That part of Israel hears in Amos's words a different meaning, associated with the understanding that the twofold attitude to being that is granted symbolic form by the word "Israel" will be exiled with the historical entity termed "Israel" and will continue to exist in exile from the political world that it rejects. These apparently conflicting readings of the same biblical verse actually complement one another and exemplify the multilayered structure of biblical hermeneutics that enables the coexistence of diverse and, at times, ostensibly contradictory layers of meaning within one verse or passage.

Buber's discussion—opened through a careful reading of passages in his works and in the Hebrew Bible that are connected through the guiding-word principle—draws attention to the circles of prophets who operated outside the chronicles of recorded history. These groups were well established in the days of Isaiah, despite the biblical emphasis on the deeds of individual prophets. Buber even suggests that there may not be a substantial qualitative difference between the individual prophet whose word is recorded in the Bible and his supportive community whose presence is largely ignored in the text.[81] Community and individual alike serve the power that precedes the word; considered in this perspective, their actions are equal in merit. Buber portrays their collective presence as an opening to the spirit that, from time to time, "seizes" the persons receptive to its existence, "uniting them and driving them over the face of the land."[82] Buber's choice of words ("driving them over the face of the land") attributes to the community of prophets a human replication of the movement of the spirit over the face of the waters, as recorded in Genesis 1:2.

In sum, we see that Isaiah's innovation was not in establishing such circles of study but in granting them new meaning, purpose, and direction. His revolution was related to his replacing public presentation of teaching and testimony with private transmission of that tradition within the "hidden" circles of study that had existed in the shadows of history from the very beginnings of prophecy. As a result of Isaiah's deed, conditions are set for the continuation of the teaching in communal and individual settings, independent of external social and political turbulence.

From the days of Isaiah, the "heart" of Judaism gradually disappeared from the stage of history, "going underground," as it were, eventually to be exiled with the rest of the Israelites. This line of interpretation is commensurate with Buber's contention that Elohim is "the actuality in the existence of life. . . . It exists within all created beings but does not shine in all of them, but solely between them." The task of the person (in this case, the prophet) is to release that "light" by "unbolting" the "sublime stronghold of the individual." When this occurs, the person "breaks free to meet another person." Where this takes place, "the eternal rises in the Between, the seemingly empty space." That true place of realization "is community, and true community is that relationship in which the divine comes to its realization between man and man." Here is the succinct statement of faith: true community is present when and where human relationships reflect and enable the realization of "the divine." Accordingly, Judaism "is imbued with the will to create the true community on earth. Its longing for Elohim is the longing to prepare a place for him in the true community; its consciousness of Israel is the consciousness that out of it true community will emerge; its wait for the Messiah is the wait for true community."[83]

## The Suffering Servant, the Limmud, and the "Messianic Mystery"

Buber's belief in the existence of hidden circles of prophets came to our attention in an examination of the hermeneutic function of a biblical verse cited in the opening sentence of *The Prophetic Faith*. This observation, however, does not embody a complete reading of Buber's intentions. According to the hermeneutic principle of the guiding word, full comprehension may be achieved only by a comparative reading of all other passages in *The Prophetic Faith* that mention the guiding words we noted in the opening sentence.

Further reference to the relevant guiding verses may be found in the last chapter of *The Prophetic Faith*, entitled "The Mystery," which includes a three-page discussion of Isaiah 8:16 and 8:20.[84] The historical period discussed is that of the second Isaiah, characterized by Buber (following Isaiah) as a period of Elohim's "hiding his face," rendering himself inaccessible to ordinary vision (Isaiah 8:17).[85]

In this passage, Buber again explains his understanding of the critical role of *limmudim* in such a "dark" period. They are the hidden transmitters of "testimony," of "teaching." This is apparently the "real work" that Buber claims to be accomplished "in the shadow, in the quiver," alluding to Isaiah 49:2: "Official leadership fails more and more, leadership devolves more and more, upon the secret."[86] The *limmudim* sustain a quality of relation essential for ensuring uninterrupted continuity of humanity's relationship to the unity of creation of which humanity is but a part. Surrounded by ignorance, metaphorically referred to as "darkness," these efforts take place "in the shadow," unnoticed in ordinary perceptions of human progress and knowledge: "The way leads through the work that history does not write down and that history cannot write down."[87]

Buber's notion of a hidden history, not recorded in the ordinary chronicles of human events, will be considered in detail in chapter 4. For the moment, it is important to present Buber's description of the role of the *limmudim* in transition to a new age. Referring directly to the guiding verses from the Book of Isaiah now under consideration (8:16

and 8:20), Buber asserts that the word designates "those to whose heart [the testimony] was delivered."[88] This "testimony," he claims, will be revealed in a time of great distress. Then the seal will be removed "and those who can still see will see."[89] In this instance, the "seal" refers to the distance between the perceptions of *limmudim* and those of others regarding what is—in contrast to what seems to be—the source of life. This disparity of perspective is granted additional symbolic form by the biblical distinction between "the house of Israel" and "the house of Ya'akov." Implicit in Buber's reading is his assumption that the burden of the meeting with the *limmud* is on the seekers, on the house of Ya'a-kov; there is no purpose in revealing the testimony unless there are people willing, able, and eager to experience that which is revealed and thereafter transmitted.[90]

Buber's analysis of Isaiah 54:13 ("All your sons shall be taught by YHVH [*limmudei* YHVH] and great shall be the prosperity of your sons") places particular emphasis on Isaiah's promise that in the new epoch there will be no need for *limmudim*, because all of the "sons" will be *limmudim*: "All will be the *limmudai* (students) of Elohim: there will be no difference between teachers and students, and there will no longer be a thing to bind and to seal far away from the eyes of the people. There will be nothing but the public worldliness of Elohim, where all will learn from their king and teacher (Isaiah, 30:20) that which they are to learn."[91]

The words of Isaiah envision a time to come. What, however, is to transpire in the interim "dark" period, when the majority of humanity will be oblivious to the existence of teaching and testimony? The final appearance of the guiding verses in *The Prophetic Faith* addresses this question in a discussion of the role of the "suffering servant."[92] Buber's presentation of this image, which has exerted a profound influence on the development of messianic hope in the Western tradition, is demon-strably influenced by, and related to, his conception of the *limmudim*. His exegesis of the notion of "servant of YHVH" is based on an interpreta-tion of Isaiah 50:4–5:

> The Lord God has given me
> the tongue of *limmudim*
> that I may know how to sustain with a word
> him that is weary.

> Morning by morning he wakens,
> he wakens my ear to hear as *limmudim*.
> The Lord God has opened my ear,
> and I was not rebellious,
> I turned not backward.

Buber claims that the recipient of revelation experiences a moderate, ongoing relation with that which is revealed. The impact of the revelation is "not received as a penetration, but rather as a removal of a seal, as an 'opening.' "[93] In this interpretation, Buber attempts to approach the experience of the *limmud*. His exegesis, emphasizing the *limmud's* sense of an ongoing, openhearted relation to revelation, serves as a prelude to his presentation of the hidden servant, who is himself a *limmud*.

Buber indicates that the path of the servant comprises three stages. These stages are part of the servant's development irrespective of particular historical events. To understand the servant's existence, we may view Buber's depiction of Isaiah's specific path as symbolically representative of the universal path of the servant.

The first stage of the servant's path is the prophetic one, in which the prophet's work is experienced as futile, as reflected in Isaiah's meeting with King Ahaz. Isaiah does his best but has no impact on the "hardened" heart of the king. He knows that his attempts will encounter insurmountable resistance, yet he must go on. From the personal perspective, the prophet has to endure immense suffering during this stage without asking why. His acceptance is justified in his understanding that although he appears to be failing in his own time, his actions are not circumscribed by ordinary historical accounts of success. The prophet realizes that his true work includes an element of preparation for historical events that will unfold in an unknown future. Considering his deeds in the context of the mission of Israel, he knows that his presence in history ensures the continuation of a relation to being that serves all humanity, without distinction among religions or nations.

During the second stage, the suffering of the individual prophet is translated into "action." By enduring hardship and affliction, the prophet transforms the experience of suffering into a deed (*asiah*). Suffering is experienced as a necessary aspect of his mission among nations. Isaiah's description of such endurance, not mentioned in Buber's exegesis, begins with the opening of the servant's ear to hear "as *limmudim*"

(50:4), followed by a series of observations about the extent of his suffering. In 50:6–9, the *limmud* speaks of the physical, mental, and emotional abuse he suffers at the hands of the ignorant who surround him. He is beaten, spat upon, and shamed, yet he trusts in the light that is revealed when one turns to the source of being; the servant trusts YHVH. The light is within and is associated with the servant's trust in Elohim (50:10). As such, the prophet indirectly confirms that YHVH's promise of support, recorded in an earlier chapter, is fulfilled (Isaiah 42:1: "Behold my servant, whom I uphold, my chosen, in whom my soul delights; I have put my spirit upon him, he will bring forth justice to the nations").

As the servant experiences suffering, an element within him undergoes transmutation; he becomes quiet, still.[94] At this stage of the servant's development, his deeds are not recorded in ordinary historical chronicles. His silence is not noticed, not even as absence. Historical events develop, oblivious to the essential relation sustained by the silent, hidden servant. During this quiet stage, the servant (to whom Buber refers as a *limmud*) waits patiently, ready to respond to those who suddenly realize that their lives are wasted in a form of existence that is a mere disguise for what may properly be termed "life." Those who exist quietly, on the sidelines of history, are unaware of the exact historical timing of their emergence into the center of historical "action." However, they do realize that such a "coming out of the shadows" will occur when humankind experiences a form of suffering that engenders a powerful yearning for unity. When this moment transpires, writes Buber, the hidden will be revealed:

> Wait—thus addresses them Isaiah—until at a certain time, in a time of "distress and darkness" (Isaiah 8:22), the crowd will come . . . running toward you, you who wait patiently, who are now perceived as knowledgeable, and will entreat you, as beg those who know no dawn. . . . Then the hour will arrive: "To *torah*! To *te'udah*!" (Isaiah 8:20) Then you shall remove the seal and unravel the bind of the scroll that is in your hearts, then you shall respond: "The people who have walked in darkness have seen a great light." (Isaiah 9:1).[95]

The cry that Isaiah places in the mouths of a future generation—"To *torah*! To *Te'udah*!"—refers to the teaching that Isaiah had imparted in his times to the select few. The opening of the hearts of his spiritual

descendants will be dependent on their being approached by a generation that realizes that there is a quality of "knowledge" that is absent
from experience, yet is essential for realizing a true relation to being.
Until such a relation is established between the hidden few and the
bewildered crowd, the servant—the hidden *limmud*—should wait patiently, steadfast in his knowledge that he constitutes a beginning before
the beginning.[96] This passage also indicates that the relation to being that
is characteristic of the hidden servant is an active form of preparation
for the moment of communal insight that follows a period of intense
communal suffering.

The third stage consists of the successful culmination of the process
that unfolded in the preceding, preparatory stages. Humanity reaches an
extreme point of suffering that forces a turn inward, towards contemplation of the way of life that gave rise to the violence, destruction, and
insensitivity that goes by the name of "history." The prophet proclaims
"a new order of justice for the world."[97] This proclamation is an outcome of the opening of the seal protecting the "testimony" and "teaching" entrusted to the *limmudim*, an opening that occurs only when there
is an uncompromising demand for access to the heart of the teaching.

The hidden servant senses his relation to being as an "I" that is not
of a particular person but of the universal "Israel." He does not seek the
confirmation of others to justify his deeds. His relation to others is a
reflection of his relation to the eternal "I." This, notes Buber, is the
quality of relation that the servant of YHVH is determined to sustain.
The deeds of the suffering servant take place between the intention of
the Creator and the fulfillment of that intention. This intermediate position may be presented as three stages: Israel as it is intended to become
in the eyes of YHVH, the human servant in whom Israel appears in the
form of numerous lives, and the messiah in whom the true Israel is
realized as the true humanity. These three, writes Buber, "are one, three
manifestations of the one: the phenomenon as it arises in the thought of
YHVH, the phenomenon in the expanse of history, and the phenomenon in the breakthrough of eternity." Similarly, the deeds of the human
servant (presented as a human archetype) are oriented to the threefold
process of "redemption of the world": "the return of the person, the
return of Israel, and the return of the world."[98]

Buber considered the suffering servant to be a living symbol of, and
a textual metaphor for, a way of existence that persisted within Judaism

for many centuries after the prophets, including the centuries of exile following the destruction of the Second Temple. The servant of YHVH is a metaphor for the inclusive, openhearted relation to being that is characteristic of the hidden *limmud*. Buber describes this relation in the following terms:

> The "servant" is viewed as the embodiment of 'people's covenant,' (*brit-am*), as the very man, through whom the streams of the fulfilled covenant move from above downward, from below upward. [It is imperative that this human type] become the living symbol of the covenant.[99]

This passage implicitly assumes that the notion of "covenant" implies an active form of life that enables vital energies to flow according to the order of being. Persons whose way of life constitutes a participation in this flow become, by virtue of their deeds, "living symbol[s] of the covenant." Buber's understanding of the existence of these hidden "doers" apparently constitutes comprehension of the mystery and mission of Judaism. Hence, he refers to the presence of Israel in history as the "messianic mystery" of Judaism.

The paradoxical quality of the servant's hidden existence is accentuated when considered in the context of Buber's comment that this "servant," although addressed in the singular, is in fact a type of person rather than a specific historical individual. In Buber's words, the servant "is not a single person but a human type: those who from generation to generation keep returning."[100] This presentation is commensurate with the attitude exemplified in the relation of the second Isaiah to the first. The servant is referred to individually in the biblical text, yet the three stages of his development cannot be considered within the context of one life span. Hence a paradox: how can the apparently single path of one human being exceed one human life?

Buber contemplates this paradox when he asks whether the second Isaiah, as a servant of YHVH, knew how many life cycles and how many historical forms constitute the path of the servant. In this context, Buber considers alternative interpretations of the identity of the servant: as an ideal community of Israel, as a specific historical image (such as Moses, or Isaiah himself), as King Cyrus, or as an individual not yet born who will become a messiah (Jesus). Following exegesis of the biblical text,

Buber concludes that this image and its multiple possibilities incorporate both basic elements of "Israel": the rebellious, timorous, blind "house of Ya'akov" and the devoted, courageous, enlightened "house of Israel." Both are referred to by YHVH as "my servant." This, says Buber, is an intentional paradox. The paradox of the two servants, he continues, "should not be removed or uprooted. It is intended to be a paradox. We recognize in it the assumption necessary for that historical hour that ensures that Isaiah's messianic prophecy will turn into the second Isaiah's messianic mystery."[101]

## The Limmud *as an Opening to the "Inner History" of Israel*

Our special attention to the guiding words that begin *The Prophetic Faith* has uncovered the foundations of Buber's approach to the Jewish tradition and of his understanding of the role of Judaism in the transitional period between an age of concealment and a new epoch. Buber was profoundly aware of the possibility that a hidden mode of transmission, existing concurrently with revealed history, accompanied the work of the prophets throughout the ages, including the time in exile.[102] Buber concludes *The Prophetic Faith* with the assertion that a nucleus—a person or corporate entity—untouched by the changing fortunes of history and time exists within the portion of humanity properly termed "Israel." The members of this core group experience a voluntary form of suffering as part of their understanding of the distance between the path of existence appropriate to humankind and the forms of life that human communities create as "history." These hidden "doers" are the servants of YHVH.

The foregoing exposition of Buber's use of the guiding-word principle has illustrated Buber's application of biblical hermeneutical principles in his own studies of biblical interpretation. In "People Today and the Jewish Bible," we encountered the guiding word in the form of diverse repetitions of the same verb stem (P\T\CH) in a single text, focusing attention on an additional guiding word—*lev* (heart). In *The Prophetic Faith*, the guiding-word principle took the form of rare words that Buber considered to be guiding words proving the unity of the Book of Isaiah—*limmud, torah veteu'dah* (*torah* and testimony). These same guiding words then served as openings to layers of meaning inherent in Buber's own book. The use of guiding words in *The Prophetic*

*Faith* thus constitutes a more sophisticated application of the principle of repetition encountered in "People Today."

So far, our analysis has focused on the preliminary objective of corroborating Buber's use of the guiding-word principle as an interpretive apparatus guiding the reader of Buber's own works towards a hidden message. We have also begun to assemble a lexicon of Buberian guiding words that the alert reader may recognize as conveyers of multiple meaning. In the exegesis of *The Prophetic Faith*, we saw that certain words—"to open" and "heart"—were used in ways commensurate with our presentation of Buber's hermeneutic intentions in "People Today." Similarly, the word *limmud* and the cry "To *torah*! To *Te'udah*" are now part of the present text as words employed with particular care and attention.

However, some additional interactions have occurred between reader and text. As the indirect element in Buber's writing style was uncovered, the guiding words opened the text to a story that can be pieced together by noting the relations among the diverse passages that contain such guiding words or verses. For example, our analysis of Buber's writings referring to Isaiah 8:16 underscored the importance Buber attributed to hidden circles of seers and prophets mentioned in the biblical text. Furthermore, Buber's understanding of the task these circles fulfill in the shadows of the biblical text constitutes the background to his interpretation of Isaiah's decision to transform these circles into *limmudim*. Finally, the guiding words of the Book of Isaiah indicate the direct relationship that Buber discerned between the *limmud* of Isaiah and Isaiah's image of the "suffering servant."

According to Buber's reading, in their newfound self-conception as *limmudim*, the prophets create a human nucleus from which those whose task is to bring light to the nations emerge. This is the "inner history" of Judaism, a history that takes place "in the depths," oriented to the task of preparing all of humanity to fulfill their role as created beings who exist on earth.[103] This is the messianic mystery, the mystery of world redemption. The existence of persons privy to the "inner history" is the basis of Buber's enigmatic distinction between "apparent" and "hidden" history, a distinction inseparable from his proposition that the Bible includes reference to the existence of hidden "servants" of YHVH in the shadows of history.[104] We therefore move from the hidden hermeneutics to the hidden history.

# 4

# HIDDEN HISTORY: THE "TWO STREAMS" OF ADAM

As Buber's use of guiding words within his own texts becomes clearer and more self-evident, this and succeeding chapters will be more attentive to alternative conceptions of reality that Buber chose to communicate indirectly by use of these signifiers. The guiding-word principle will continue to be the interpretive key to this book, but there will be growing emphasis on the ideas Buber found difficult to present simply and directly. In a conversation he had with Aubrey Hodes toward the end of his days, Buber had the following words to say about history and the fathomability of its true sources: "The authentic forces that change and shape the world are deep and under the surface. So they move slowly. Real history is the history of the slow pace [of events]. The question is whether there will be enough people who see the deceit in the feverish tempo, withstand its temptation, and commit themselves to the truth of the slower tempo."[1]

The present chapter reveals Buber's convictions regarding the inadequacy of conventional notions of history. He was acutely aware of the difficulty his readers and listeners would have in hearing and accepting the distinction between "real" and "ordinary" history, between the "slow pace" and the "feverish tempo" of events. Nevertheless, this distinction is central to an understanding of Buber's intentions, and in this chapter we shall direct attention to the "real" history, to the "authentic" and "deep" forces that shape historical development. We shall address this aspect of Buber's work by discussing his division of history into the "apparent" (ordinary accounts of history) and the "hidden" (extraordinary accounts of what transpires in historical time) and his use of Jesus and of the Ba'al Shem as opposing examples of interventions in historical events of those privy to the complex ontology that Buber struggled to communicate in his writings.

Included in this analysis is a radical interpretation of the role of human life in creation, based on a reconstruction of Buber's uses of Genesis 1:26 and 1:27, the biblical verses that describe the creation of Adam. As I read side-by-side with these verses those passages within Buber's work that make direct or indirect reference to them, my attention was directed to an understanding of the purpose of human life and its function in creation that is grasped intuitively, in a manner that is wordless. Through this experience, I realized why some ideas are impossible to convey directly. For one thing, the reading suggested the existence within every human being of an element of self that is eternal and is part of an eternal order, yet I was accustomed to considering myself part of something temporal. For another, I was not used to contemplating a multidimensional symbolic world that assumes an order that precedes my apparently autonomous and independent movement. In addition, in my attempt to grant explicit linguistic form to a perspective that both R and Buber considered wiser to leave implicit, I felt that I was breaking a deeply ingrained taboo. Finally, contemplation of the guiding verses from Genesis help me understand why some ideas should indeed be encountered only through an extra effort required of the reader. Without the effort, there is no opening to self; without the opening to self, words are assimilated as authoritative statements that strengthen the inclination of self to depend on external authority when addressing fundamental questions of the purpose and responsibility of being human.

## GENESIS 1:26–27: THE NATURAL ADAM'S ROLE IN CREATION

In an essay written in 1918, before the publication of his magnum opus, *I and Thou*, Buber relates that an encounter with a book entitled *Tzva'at Ribesh* ("The Testament [Legacy] of Rabbi Israel Ba'al Shem") led him to realize the goal of his life's work:

> The Adam as created in the image of *Elohim* I grasped as deed, as becoming, as task. . . . The image out of my childhood, the memory of the *zaddik* and his community, rose upward and illuminated me: I

recognized the idea of the fully realized, whole person [*vollkommenen Menschen*][2] At the same time I became aware of the summons to proclaim it to the world.[3]

This passage points simultaneously to two ideas in the background of Buber's work: "The Adam as created in the image of Elohim"[4] and the idea of the "fully realized, whole person" whose life is oriented to the task of translating the first idea into actual, realized human life. (The term Elohim is differentiated from the other name of the Creator, YHVH, translated in standard editions of the Bible as "the Lord." Both terms are usually translated into everyday English as "God." For our purposes, Elohim is the force within which Adam is created and towards which Adam is instructed to turn when seeking self-perfection. The present section focuses on the first idea, with attention to its impact on Buber's philosophy. The second, derivative idea—the need to "proclaim [the first idea] to the world"—will be discussed in chapter 6.[5])

The existential implication of the reality indicated indirectly by the words "Adam as created in the image of *Elohim*" is revealed through study of the interpretation Buber grants to the biblical verse that these words echo, Genesis 1:26. That verse states that Elohim intended to "do" Adam "in our image, as our form" (or "in our image, after our likeness"). Yet in fact "Elohim created the Adam in His image, in the image of Elohim he created him" (Genesis 1:27). The difference between the two accounts raises an obvious question: why the disparity between the description of Elohim's intention "to do Adam in our image as our form" and the description of the act as creating "the Adam . . . in his image, in the image of Elohim"? What happened to the "form"?

Drawing on traditional materials from the Midrash, the Talmud, the Kabbalah and Hasidism, Buber interprets events in Eden in terms of Adam's turn away from his fundamental task of being a unity of opposites, in the image of Elohim.[6] According to these traditional interpretations, the disparity between the declared intention ("in our image, as our form") and the actual act ("in the image of Elohim") implies that Elohim intended the generic Adam and every particular Adam thereafter to complete the form by turning to the image of Elohim within which they were created.[7] To fulfill this task was a choice Adam was to accept and to undertake voluntarily.[8] Awareness of this potential and of its implied responsibility in relation to the order of creation implies cultivation of a quality of self-knowledge that is attentive to the original relation to Elohim inherent in the first and every Adam.[9] Hence the dramatic tenor of Buber's description of the moment of meeting with the magnitude of the mystery implied by verse 1:27: "The Adam as created in the image of Elohim I grasped as deed, as becoming, as task."

Buber attributes Adam's inability to fulfill his original purpose to a lesson learned from the Tree of Knowledge episode. This story points to Adam's having aligned his intention to self-perfect with the wrong faculty, that which emphasizes "knowledge of good and evil." Implicit in the story of the Tree of Knowledge is Adam's assumption that the turn toward the ability to know separation and difference is the capstone of "knowing." This leads to the first consequence of Adam's eating from the fruit of the tree: interpretation of his relation to Eve in terms of material separation of the two bodies (Genesis 3:7). On the level of material reality, the separation is a fact. Yet from a more refined perspective, the material separation is preceded by unity of the spirit. This development—consideration of self in terms of material existence—is in stark contrast to the original creation in the image of Elohim, of which it is written that "in the image of Elohim he created him, male and female he created them" (Genesis 1:27). The original unity of opposites (one Adam who is two, male and female) becomes, following the eating of the fruit of the Tree of Knowledge, a separation that does not know the way to the original unity (two separate beings, male and female, each able to experience the moment of "knowledge," yet forgetful of the perception that precedes their singularity as "knowing" subjects).

Buber summarizes his interpretation of this episode as follows: "The fall of the first human being consisted in his wanting to reach the likeness intended for him in his creation by other means than by perfecting 'the image'."[10] Adam's mistake was in misplacing his innate desire[11] to become whole—a passion in itself neutral—in the faculty that "knows good and evil," rather than seeking unity by turning to the faculty that knows "the image of Elohim" directly. The turn to Elohim should not be mediated by the faculty that distinguishes between the whole and its parts; to know Elohim is to be in a state of immediacy that needs no mediating, distinguishing thought. In Buber's reading, such a quality of relation is the necessary condition for subsequent knowledge of the choices a person must make on the way to fulfilling his or her purpose in life.[12]

Self-perfection of the soul in the image of Elohim is thus the primary, fundamental task of man:

> We perfect our souls "toward" *Elohim*. "Being like" *Elohim* is then not something which is unconnected with our earthly life; it is the goal of our life, provided that our life is really a perfecting of our soul "toward" *Elohim*. And this being so, we may well add that the perfection of a soul is called its being like *Elohim*, which yet does not mean any equality, but means that this soul has translated into reality that likeness to *Elohim* which was granted it. . . . "For in the image of *Elohim* made He man." It is on this that the imitation of *Elohim* is founded. We are destined to be like him, this means we are destined to bring to perfection out of ourselves, in actual life, the image in which we were created, and which we carry in us, that we may—no longer in this life—experience its consummation.[13]

Exposition of Buber's use of Genesis 1:27 as a guiding verse draws attention to Buber's understanding of the Scripture's presentation of the wrong cognitive turn that is the root of the psychological distance that human beings have created between their original ground of being and their imaginary ground of existence. The story of Genesis is thus an allegory for a potential not fulfilled: "we are destined to bring to perfection out of ourselves, in actual life, the image in which we were created, and which we carry in us." This is a radical proposition. Stated simply, it says that Elohim is within every human being. Such a statement, presented without its multiple accompanying perspectives, is clearly open to simplistic interpretations. The great potential for misunderstanding of such statements undoubtedly motivated Buber's very careful presentation. This interpretation of the meaning of the creation story recurs throughout Buber's mature works yet was never developed fully in one comprehensive study; apart from one essay,[14] it appears as an addendum to the study of some other primary question. Nevertheless, when juxtaposed, these diverse passages[15] yield the propositions presented here.

Buber returns to Judaism's role in transmitting the knowledge of man's potential for self-perfection in the image of Elohim by recounting a Hasidic story attributed to Rabbi Heschel of Apt. This *zaddik* interpreted a Mishnaic saying, "Know what is above you" (Avot 2:1), as follows:

Know that what is above, is of you. And what is above? Ezekiel tells us "and upon the form of the throne a form to be seen resembling a man upon it above" (*Ezekiel* 1:26). How can this be said of God? For it is written, "to whom will you compare me that I should resemble him?" (*Isaiah* 40:25). Yet it is true. The form to be seen resembling a man is of us. It is the form which we shape with the worship of our sincere hearts. With it, we make for our Creator without shape and likeness, for himself, blessed be he and blessed be his Name, a human form. When a man shows mercy and loving-kindness, he shapes God's right hand. And when a man fights the divine war and overcomes evil, he shapes God's left hand. He who is above upon the throne is of you.[16]

This tale confirms the basic belief that in the course of appropriate self-perfection, a person creates the "form" that he or she was assigned to complete at the moment of creation,[17] a form that "we shape with the worship of our sincere hearts," says the tale. The person who is aware of his or her "sincere heart" establishes appropriate relation to the reality signified by the word through a struggle with an illusion regarding the state of his or her knowledge. When the "reflection of the image" that one considers the source of knowledge is seen as indeed a mere reflection, this illusion "evaporates" and the heart is revealed as the opening to the way of Elohim.[18]

In contrast to conventional dichotomies between "mind" and "body," Buber's interpretation of these biblical stories reconciles the apparent separation between organ (body) and its inherent intelligence (mind). This reconciliation is suggested by extracting from the text its indirect references to a quality of perception that precedes the discursive construct. In this respect, Buber is attuned to the Kabbalistic understanding of God as a source of energy and of the human body as a receptor of that energy, a kind of "recycling system."[19] It seems that this perspective was inspired by the kind of Kabbalah developed in the sixteenth century by Rabbi Isaac Luria Ashkenazi (1534–72), later called the Ari ("the Lion"). Stated in extreme and incomplete brevity, one may summarize the Ari's teachings as follows: Elohim contracts within itself and thus creates a space that is not elohic. Only after the appearance of the non-elohic space does Elohim send rays of its light into the space of contraction and thus are worlds created. Consequently, in every world and in every moment, one encounters both contraction and light. Both forces are necessary for world creation: without the contraction, all will fall back into Elohim; without the rays of elohic light nothing will become. Everything, whether material or nonmaterial, whether objects or thoughts, expresses this basic confluence of forces.

In the Ari's teaching, the flow of creation moves in both directions, from above to below, and from below to above. This flow takes place within the human being, just as it takes place in other created forms. Adam is therefore an active tool or instrument in the one creative process. This point is significant, for it counters other forms of Kabbalah, which seem to suggest that Adam is a more passive vessel that accepts elohic light as it descends (in only one direction) in the tenfold ray of creation. The idea of contraction seems paradoxical, but in the words of Gershom Scholem, "it is alive; and even more precisely one may say: because it expresses life—it is full of paradoxes."[20] Moshe Idel adds that these apparently antithetical propositions (that Adam is a passive participant in the flow of creation and that he is active) in fact complement one another and can coexist in the anthropological context of the Kabbalah.[21] Both the human body and the system of spheres are parts of one recycling system based on principles of reciprocity. The human being is perceived as both a recipient and a source of energy, and the system of spheres both a prism and a recycling system.

Accordingly, Adam is considered a practical tool for perfection of the world. As worlds expand and create the human sphere of being, Adam is called to listen and to consciously and willingly accept the original movement and to participate in its manifestations. Energies flow up and down the ten worlds through which the ray of creation traverses. The responsibility of the human being is to willfully prepare itself to fulfill its role in this intricate system of spheres, vessels, and channels. This role implies perfecting the self in order to serve as a receptacle that channels life-energies.[22]

It seems that it is on the basis of this background understanding of the nature and purpose of the human form of life that Buber presents the development of humanity as a tale of two streams of consciousness that came into being as a result of the events in Eden. Prior to the episode of the Tree of Knowledge of Good and Evil, Adam was in direct relation with the source and purpose of his existence. This is "natural" Adam: in the original, "natural" state of Adam, there is one consciousness that is present to Elohim. Following the episode of the tree, Adam became "historical"; this is humanity's second "beginning."[23] This distinction implies that history is a specific form of consciousness, a particular form of shaping experience that relies on the wisdom associated with "knowing" of a certain, limited kind. This form of consciousness reduces the original relation to being to a specific pattern that is known to us as "history." The primary characteristic of historical consciousness is its use of cognition as a tool that enables the singling out of the clearest and most distinct elements that constitute a given phenomenon, and then dividing the elements into subjects and objects, and experiences into good and evil. This cognitive development constitutes a distancing from the relation to the original unity out of which the spheres of creation emanate and become apparently separate and self-contained.

Buber's distinction between two kinds of history, to be discussed shortly, is thus an expression of an elaborate and complex background. The historical people—Hebrews who evolve through history into Jews—are entrusted with the task of transmitting remembrance of the creative role of "Adam" in relation to the element of being that is referred to as "Elohim." This is their historical mission: to serve within history as a reminder of the ahistorical relation that precedes ordinary conceptions of birth and death, of origin and goal, of self and Elohim. When a majority of Hebrews forget the purpose of their communal existence, this remembrance is sustained in the deeds of those few who continue to transmit the memory of the original unity. These singular persons are the links of the hidden history of humanity, referred to in Buber's work through allusion to an additional verse that functions as a guiding verse—Isaiah 49:2.

## BIBLICAL LEADERSHIP: BETWEEN DIALOGUE AND HISTORY, BETWEEN GENESIS AND ISAIAH

Buber mentions Isaiah 49:2 in nearly all his discussions of a "history" of humanity that is not recorded in ordinary chronicles of historical development. In its biblical context, the verse reads as follows:

> (1) Listen to me, O coastlands
> and hearken, you peoples
> from afar.
> The YHVH called me from the womb,
> from the body of my mother he named my name.

(2) He made my mouth like a sharp sword,
in the shadow of his hand he hid me;
he made me a polished arrow,
in his quiver he hid me away.

(3) And he said to me: "You are my
Israel, in whom I will be
glorified."

(4) But I said, "I have labored in vain,
I have spent my strength for
nothing and vanity;
but surely my right is with YHVH
and my recompense with my
God (*Elohai*)."[24]

The prophet may appear to be uttering words of complaint ("I have labored in vain, I have spent my strength for nothing and vanity") but in fact realizes that his hidden existence constitutes a form of "doing" that participates in the development of humanity in a manner commensurate with the necessities of creation ("but surely my right is with YHVH and my recompense with *Elohai*"). The silence[25] of the servant in the "quiver" is an effect of the dominant ontology and his frustration is directed towards his fellow men, not towards him "[who] made [the prophet's] mouth like a sharp sword."

In Buber's works, Isaiah 49:2 is associated with the question of the messianic mystery, the mystery of those anonymous "servants of YHVH" whom we encountered in the previous chapter. Buber writes that these nameless "doers" exist in the shadows of history, fulfilling their mission without evident, tangible "historical" results. In Buber's interpretation of this verse, the deeds of those hidden in the quiver create a "hidden world history" (*Es gibt eine verborgene Weltgeschichte*).[26] Unnoticed in ordinary accounts of events, the quality of relation that they sustain is nevertheless eternally present. The relation among ontology, historical consciousness, and the invisibility of the covert "doers" is the background of Buber's comment that the hidden world history is not discerned by the historian whose work is part of "what we call the historical consciousness."[27] The constituent element of the hidden history, the hidden servant, reveals not a text about the absolute but rather a presence in the face of the absolute, not a thought about being, but rather a relation to being, not an attempt to reconstruct the past but rather a way to be present. As such, he is invisible to the science of history.

In the light of Buber's analysis of Genesis 1:26–27, it is clear that the mission of Judaism is to retain in the course of "historical Adam's" development the quality of relation to being that is indicated by the notion of "natural Adam." This is the "double mission" of the person and of humanity.[28] The later prophets are privy to this mission and attempt to fulfill it, while they are fully aware of the growing predominance of the "historical" element within the Israelite community.[29] In the Hebrew Bible, says Buber, the primary mission of prophets is their recurring demand that the leadership and the people remember the quality of relation that is immanent in the "natural" element of their being. This basic understanding is manifest in Buber's discussion of the five different types of biblical leadership: patriarch (*av*), leader (*manhig*), judge (*shofet*), king (*melech*), and prophet (*navi*). This classification follows the development of the biblical narrative and attempts to point to the inner significance of the changes in forms of rule that the narrative chronicles.

Buber emphasizes that Abraham, the first *av* (and also the first "Hebrew"), was sensitive to the distance that had been established between "natural" and "historical" Adam. Abraham's mission was to initiate a third beginning (after Eden and Babel), a third attempt to establish a social form of life that would be supportive of the original telos of Adam. His movement away from the land of his birth was symbolic of his rejection of contemporary notions of biography and existence in time. In Buber's retelling of the story, Abraham's image represents the experience of a fundamental change of heart, of a personal turn away from the ontology of his times toward a new form of relation. Buber's portrayal emphasizes the social factor. Abraham's personal change of heart is inseparable from his concern with the lot of humanity; Abraham founds a people as a "natural" extension of his own personal transformation.

How does personal experience translate into action that includes the fates of other persons and communities? What is it that distinguishes Abraham? For Buber, Abraham is first and foremost a "seer." A seer is one who experiences a suspension of the sense of separation between the person and the situation: "The man sees, and sees also that he is being seen." As a seer, "Abraham goes on to achieve the perfection of seeing." *Seeing* is the capacity that distinguishes prophets from other persons, a coexistence of *listening, seeing* and dialogue in one, powerful and empowering presence. In the words of Buber:

> If the gift of mediation between the above and the below, and between the below and the above, is the one great attribute of the prophet, then such seeing is the other. . . . "The prophet of our day was formerly called a seer," we read in the story of Samuel and Saul (1 Samuel 9:9). In its meaning, too, the "seer" is the older of the two concepts. Abraham *becomes* a prophet, but a seer is what he was from the very moment when God "let Himself be seen."[30]

Abraham was the first to be assigned the task of creating a people in a post-Babylonian world of separate peoples.[31] As such, his image influences Buber's interpretation of the task of founding a new form of communal life in a world of warring nations. "There no longer exists a homogeneous human community, but a multiplicity of peoples," writes Buber of the reality confronting Abraham, and continues:

> The new effort can begin only with this as a starting point. The aim can no longer be an undivided humanity, but only one that will overcome its division and achieve a unity beyond peoples, a joining of the peoples into a new human community, a people of many peoples. But how is this aim to be reached? In order that the multiplicity of people may become the one people of peoples, they must first be shown what a real people, a unity made up of the various many, is like. This cannot be shown by the world, but only by life itself—the life of a true people made up of many peoples. . . . A new people must arise, one that will come not only out of the natural begetting of generations but will be helped into being by the revelation, the promise, and the commandment from above. Its beginning must include its goal, so that it may fulfill its mission with regard to the ultimate goal of mankind. And this is what happens.[32]

Buber characterizes the patriarchs as a type of leadership whose deeds are determined by their ability to sustain a direct relation to Elohim. The nature of their actions excludes them from ordinary accounts of "historical" leadership, for as founders of a people they do not lead a historical nation. We shall see in due course that this image of creating conditions for the emergence of a people unlike other peoples inspired Buber's political agenda in relation to the raison d'etre of Zionism.

The founding of a nation is the task of the second type of biblical leadership, embodied in the image of Moses. This type of leader is the living center of community and of covenant,[33] who founds a nation that should consciously strive to live in ways "contrary to the laws of history." The nation he establishes is perceived as a historical entity, yet his intention is that the quality of relation particular to this nation be contrary to the one characteristic of the ontology that guides conventional historical development. In this nation, relation to the spirit ought to precede action in history; its leader, exemplified in the figure of Moses, attempts to do without structures of domination and power typical of the governance of other nations, substituting tangible symbols of power for the "imageless presence of the invisible, who permits himself to be seen."[34] The task of Israel as a nation is thus to set an example of how a historical community can create a social form of existence not bound by the laws of historical, divisive ontology.

Leaders of the third type, the judges, emerge as a response to the "total chaos" generated by the tension between the historical development of the people into a nation and the concurrent distancing of the people from their direct relation to Elohim. The judges emerge from the midst of the people as a particular form of response to political and historical crisis. Guided by their relation to Elohim, they fulfill a specific mission. On completion of the mission, they return to their original place among the people. Their presence in history is voluntary and temporary, lacking formal structures for succession of power. Buber comments that this voluntary form of leadership cannot be sustained over time: "the attempt to establish a society on pure voluntarism fails over and over again."[35]

Kingship, the fourth type of leadership, responds to the demand of a people who wish to be ruled like all historical nations, giving rise to even greater confusion than prevailed during the period of the judges. On the one hand, the king is the *mashuah*, "the anointed one" (the word *mashiah*, "messiah," derived from the same root, has come to connote selection of singular persons for the fulfillment of Elohim's rule through the judicious use of earthly office), yet on the other hand kingship entails hereditary succession, with no guarantees that the successors will be worthy of the original anointment. From this point on, the question concerning the messiah becomes inextricably bound up with that of human leadership: "The history of the great religions, and in general all great history, is bound up with the problem: How do human beings stand the test of what is here called anointing [*meshiha*]?"[36] In hereditary kingship, unlike among the judges, the voluntary nature of leadership is absent, as is the option for eventual return to ordinary membership in the community; kings do not relinquish their formal position of authority on completion of their particular mission.

Prophets, the fifth type of leadership, arise from within the historical conditions created by the failure of kingship. The prophet opposes not only the people in office but also the ontology that accords these forms of rule and domination such centrality and importance in "historical consciousness." Hence Buber's telling emphasis: the prophet "*is appointed to oppose the king, and even more, history.*"[37] Note that the prophet is explicitly in opposition to "history," implying opposition to the dominant ontology ("historical consciousness"), as well as to those who swear by the norms of the historical hour (kings and the common people). "It goes without saying," writes Buber, "that not only the rulers but also the people treat the prophet as their enemy in the way in which, as a matter of history, it falls to the lot of such men to be treated."[38]

The typology of leadership in the Bible is presented as a chronological development of ideal types of leadership that arise within Judaism as responses to changing historical situations. One may extrapolate from Buber's typology a schematic representation of the development of the ahistorical spiritual form termed "Israel" into a historical entity: From a quality of unmediated presence, "Israel" becomes associated with one of the begetters of the people, the *av* Ya'akov-Israel. From a single historical patriarch, "Israel" becomes a people through the transition of leadership from patriarch to leader (and founder) Moses. From a people, "Israel" becomes a nation, a form of identity that assumes the practices and anticipations of existing nations, a situation that gives rise to the transition of leadership from a "leader" to judges. In the transition from nation to kingship, "Israel" becomes progressively more and more identified as a historical territorial entity that in due course divides into two separate kingdoms; from an established kingdom, "Israel" becomes an exile of dispersed communities, first deported by Babylonian troops in 722 B.C.E., then by the Romans in the second century. These remnants of the historical, political kingdoms of "Israel" continued to exist in exile as "Jews" (descendants of the exiled kingdom of Judea) until the twentieth century and the return of the people to the land in the form of a Zionist nation-state. Each stage of distancing of "Israel" from its spiritual origin includes the previous layer of meaning from which the new meaning emerges. The layers of meaning do not indicate a process of replacing old with new, but rather transmit all that preceded in a new form. Comprehension of the original formless relation implied by "Israel" requires insight into the nature of the formations within which "Israel" developed into a historical entity.

Buber summarizes the lesson of the Bible with the conclusion that the five forms of biblical leadership represent diverse manifestations of the same essential relation to being. From the patriarch Abraham to the prophet Jeremiah, the biblical leaders "are the foreshadowings of the dialogical person, of the person who commits his whole being to Elohim's dialogue with the world, and who stands firm throughout this dialogue."[39] We thus see that in the five types of leadership Buber discerns a common characteristic that "foreshadows" a sixth type not presented explicitly: the dialogical leader. In the background of Buber's text is the assumption (or vision) that in an age yet to come, the dialogical leader will emerge as one adequate to the needs of a new epoch of humanity. This background understanding of Buber's multiple uses of the notion of dialogue is crucial to note, for it is the rationale underlying his writings about the philosophy of dialogue and dialogical communities, writings that do not explicitly mention Buber's biblical interpretation and the symbolic world he includes in the innocuous term "dialogue" and "dialogical leadership."

The gradual incompatibility of dialogical leadership with "historical" leadership implies that the last category of biblical leaders, the prophets, have to awaken the attentive sensitivity to creation and to natural forms of life necessary for "the gradual overcoming of history."[40] This is accomplished by the prophets' intentional disappearance from historical consciousness and their concomitant fulfillment of their responsibilities as hidden leaders, as *limmudim*. Hence Buber's assertion that "the arrows God leaves in his quiver in all their shining strength are in no way inferior to those he shoots."[41]

A paradoxical element is apparent in this exposition: the very people who transmit the teaching and testimony, the people of Israel, repeatedly misunderstand the practical implications of the words they retain and transmit. They are like a faithful messenger who is unaware of the message he bears. Intent on fulfilling the external function (to transmit a memory of the mission), they overlook the internal telos (to fulfill the mission). The deeds of the people of Israel, often performed in the name of an interpretation of the teaching (*torah*), "harden their hearts" and cause them to act contrary to their telos. Nevertheless, the testimony (*te'udah*) remains and is transmitted throughout the generations in the form of a "longing of human beings to adhere to the truth."[42] A select few continue to do what is to be done. In Buber's account, their deeds will be revealed when under the impact of unblinking insight, humanity will despair of conflict and domination as the way to relate to one another and to being. Directly encountering the horrifying way of life that has emerged as historical "reality," ordinary consciousness will be shocked into self-recognition. Only then will the hour of "true history" transpire through movement towards "torah and testimony."[43] Buber thought that in his lifetime he had witnessed the emergence of conditions that would shock Adam into such self-recognition. In 1950, in the immediate aftermath of the Holocaust and the introduction of nuclear weapons, Buber wrote of "the greatest crisis ever experienced by the human being."[44] His belief in the possibility of twentieth-century Adam overcoming apparently insurmountable historical conditions was rooted in the perspective developed in his biblical studies.

In sum, we read that in Buber's account, biblical leadership changes in a manner precisely commensurate with the growing disparity between *a dialogical leadership*, sensitive to the essential unity of being, and *a historical leadership* which leads according to the divisive perspective characteristic of historical consciousness. This tension was noted in the preceding chapter's discussion of events leading to Isaiah's decision to seal the torah and testimony in the hearts of the *limmudim*. The story of the meeting of (the dialogical prophet) Isaiah with (the historical leader) King Ahaz is a metaphor for the inability of an inclusive dialogical relation to being to speak to a "hardened heart" of historical consciousness.

At this point, we may return to the guiding verses from the Book of Isaiah that drew our attention to the significance of Buber's typology of leadership in the Bible. Before explicating the five ideal types of leadership in the Bible, Buber writes as follows:

> This existence in the shadow, in the quiver, is the final word of the
> leaders in the biblical world; this enclosure in failure, in obscurity,
> even when one stands in the blaze of public life, in the presence of

the whole national life. The truth is hidden in obscurity and yet does its work; though indeed in a way far different from that which is known and lauded as effective world history.[45]

This passage indirectly alludes to Isaiah 49:2 ("existence in the shadow, in the quiver"). The significance that Buber attributed to his interpretation of this verse has been either overlooked or misunderstood by his critics. Buber was aware of this situation. Towards the end of his days, in a detailed reply to a fine collection of interpretive essays devoted to his work, Buber refers to this verse in unequivocal terms: "In my writings I have ever again pointed to what it means when a man steps forth arbitrarily out of the hiddenness of the 'quiver' in which God has sunk him as a 'polished arrow' (Isaiah 49:2), and accords to himself and his actions the redeeming function."[46]

Critics who *have* noted Buber's unusual use of this verse have not always been attentive to its hermeneutic function in Buber's work. One outstanding example of such misunderstanding is Harold Bloom's critique of Buber's interpretation of the verse. Evidently unaware of the application of the *leitwort* principle in Buber's writings, Bloom comments that Buber's "beautiful allusion to Second Isaiah (49:2) subverts the meaning of that lament, whose point is that the true prophet ought *not* to be concealed in the shadow and in the quiver." Like most commentators, Bloom too is unaware of Buber's use of guiding verses in his writings, and therefore cannot read Buber's references to Isaiah 49:2 in the comprehensive manner available to those aware of such hidden hermeneutics.[47]

In contrast to Bloom's reading of Buber's essay on biblical leadership, which characterizes the essay as "anti-historical," "astonishing," more like a "gnostic or Cabalistic point of view than like a biblical one," a "beautiful allusion" and a reflection of "Buber's personal darkening of the prophetic faith," our reading is not detached from the overall context of Buber's works and intentions—his meditation on the nature of the messianic mystery and the mission of Israel.[48] Hence, this rather obscure reference to the words of Isaiah is now meaningful, at least in terms of the discourse Buber creates.

We are now prepared to encounter the additional mention of the guiding verse in the same essay. Concluding his study of biblical leadership, Buber writes that the Bible chronicles a process in which "official leadership fails more and more, leadership devolves more and more upon the secret." He continues with the following proposition: "The way leads through the work that history does not write down, and that history cannot write down, work that is not ascribed to him who did it, but which possibly at some time in a distant generation will emerge as having been done, without the name of the doer—the secret working of the secret leadership."[49]

Buber concludes this enigmatic passage with the comment that the anonymous leaders are those relegated to the shadows of history, where they do "the real work." From the biblical point of view, writes Buber, this "real" work is "the late-recorded, the unrecorded, the anonymous work. The real work is done in the shadow, in the quiver." Buber lets the biblical reference linger without additional explanation. These references to the work done "in the shadow, in the quiver," cannot be understood if not considered in the context of the other passages in his writings that include explicit or implicit reference to Isaiah 49:1–3.[50]

## HISTORY: APPARENT AND HIDDEN

Our examination of Buberian passages that include direct or indirect reference to Isaiah 49:2–3 has drawn our attention to Buber's assumption that concurrent with ordinary, "apparent" history, there is an additional, hidden "history" of the human type referred to in his biblical studies as the suffering servant of YHVH.[51] This is the background for understanding Buber's overall perception of history, including that of "the secret working of the secret leadership."[52] We move now from a reconstruction of Buber's assumptions regarding the significance of "Israel" as an element of humanity to a discussion of the categories that he developed in the context of his writings about history and humanity in general.

In this section, the background assumption is that the growing mass of humanity (and not only the people of "Israel") accumulates countless memories of successes and failures. These are the narratives of apparent patterns of "historical" order and progress. Together with these memories, humanity develops ways of existence in response to historical events. As this ontology and its characteristic forms of life (power and domination) become increasingly dominant, fewer and fewer people retain the essential relation to being that is not merely an automatic reaction to historical events but rather a response to the call of the eternal source and end of life. Hence the distinction between the two kinds of "history": one chronicles the forms of life and memory created by those who are blissfully ignorant of the source of their being (historical Adam); the other, those created by the select few who are aware of the distance between what they appear to be and what they can and should be (natural Adam). In the language of scholarly discourse, Buber presents this tension as that between "apparent" and "hidden" history.[53]

Apparent history is recorded on the surface of consciousness and is written on the pages of the exoteric layer of the biblical text. It is registered as descriptions and accounts of deeds retained and transmitted as memories, organized in manners commensurate with the linear, cause-and-effect mode of thinking that characterizes "historical consciousness."[54] The ontology that underpins this form of consciousness focuses attention on the external, exoteric details that create the facade of events. Hidden history is the record of an inclusive consciousness and is registered in the esoteric dimension of the biblical text. The perspective guiding this kind of "history" does not fit easily into the patterns of thought characteristic of apparent history; hence the need for a special kind of writing to transmit the insight that constitutes the hidden history. This distinction is the basis for Buber's (otherwise enigmatic) comment that "what we are accustomed to call history is, from the biblical standpoint, only the facade of reality."[55]

Apparent history judges actions or deeds in terms of the "success" of the hour, a success that manifests itself as an accumulation of power and the maintenance thereof.[56] Apparent historical "successes" are based on the outcomes of struggles and manipulations that occur on the battlefields of physical force and psychological cunning, harnessed in the quest for political power.[57] In contrast, hidden history is oriented towards "the other law, the law of the covenant, a true covenant between the peoples, so as to overcome that other first law, and rule the world alone."[58] The true worth of the human presence in hidden history is thus considered in terms of the ability of this human type to sustain a radical alternative to the divisive perspective characteristic of ordinary historical consciousness.[59]

Historical consciousness creates a sensation of progressive order that is, in fact, only an external, superficial description of events constructed by a particular form of consciousness. The biblical text and Buber as its interpreter and emulator challenge the reader to read through the facade, to see what is concealed by immoderate faith in the part of consciousness that provides the external description of reality. Buber is extremely sensitive—perhaps uniquely so—to the realization that the word is not the object described and that the biblical word is an afterimage of the original event, the experience of being that precedes the word. As such, the words of the Torah are garments of reality.[60] Like garments, they endow the body with presence; they serve a function. Once this function is completed, the garments are removed and the naked reality remains present without the mediation of external form.

Buber evidently experimented with different forms for presenting the perceived tension between the two ways of being in the world. Hence his additional distinction between history "seen from above" (apparent) and history "seen from below" (hidden). This distinction is more focused than apparent in contrast to hidden history in its attempt to subvert from within notions about the progress of history, and thus is characterized by an absence of biblical nomenclature and by allusions to the more common notions accompanying discussions about the nature of "history."

"Seen from above,"[61] historical events are judged in terms of the external, objective, transcendental criteria that one claims to know. This perspective assumes that history is a sequence of developments that register the success or failure of human endeavors in terms of standards attributed to an external, "higher" source of events. According to this perspective, knowledge of God (or of reason or of the dialectic implicit in the law that orders history) is accepted as a source of authority. Apparent history thus becomes the history of struggles over control of such authority; persons or social groups associated with authority do not willingly relinquish the positions of power that come with their social status, nor are they particularly interested in reexamining their assumptions about the nature of being. The "view from above" draws on a religious perspective (institutionalized dogmas about God), yet holds sway over much of secular "scientific" thinking (institutionalized dogmas about reason).[62] At bottom, both "religious" and "scientific" accounts *of this kind*[63] assume that the individual subject has little to no influence on the events experienced; a power external to the subject determines the outcomes regardless of what the subject may assume.

"Seen from below,"[64] historical events are considered the outcome of the relation between human agents and the eternal order of being. That is, what happens *between* the agent and being is what matters (and not the imagined desires or dictates of a transcendental force, law, or god). Buber calls this perspective the "Cinderella" of human recollection because of the lack of attention accorded to this point of view.[65] The history thus established "is the action which takes place between Elohim and the one who is in dialogical relation with him." This observation implies that ordinary accounts of progress, with their inordinate emphasis on the deeds of those in positions of power, are inadequate: "both those with and those without power take place in the dialogue of history." In terms of the guiding verse, this idea is articulated as follows: "Equal in merit to the arrows released from the quiver are those sharp and chosen ones that are hidden in the shadow of his quiver. These exercise power, and these suffer from power."[66] Keeping in mind Buber's transitions between areas of discourse, these presentations can be integrated as follows: The "view from below" considers history to be an event that develops in the dialogue between Adam and Elohim. "Adam" signifies the element of being that is unique to the human species, while "Elohim" signifies the opening of Adam to the multiple energies of being, to the "down-flowing of the abundance."[67]

Central to Buber's distinction between the two kinds of history is his assertion that one's formal station in life is of no necessary consequence for an insightful understanding of the chronicles of humanity. An individual's having accumulated power does not indicate that his life is of exceptional value. The view "from below" maintains that there is no necessary or causal connection between the position a person holds and his deep, genuine effect on the development of humanity. One may detect in this proposition a critique of theologies or philosophies that consider power, honor, or wealth signs of "God's" or "reason's" approval of the deeds of one who is blessed with such earthly fortune.[68]

Buber's distinction between two kinds of history, manifestations of two different kinds of relation to (or "uses of") consciousness (i.e., two different ontologies), guides his understanding of the development of humanity. Profound, effective revolutions are reflections of ontological turning points and are manifested in deeds of singular individuals whose personal "turnings" towards being challenge conventional ontology and create new forms of relation to being. This understanding underlies

Buber's discussion of the "powerful revelations that stand at the beginnings of great communities, at the turning points of human time."[69] The leaders of such historical moments are not primarily political leaders but rather the great, unique founders, those who establish ways of life within which human beings can more fully know themselves. In our experience, such founders emerged in the first millennium before Christ, in the period Karl Jaspers and others have named the Axial Age. The notion of the Axial Age alludes to the intriguing fact that during this period, each of the major contemporary civilizations of humanity—Greece (the age of the philosophers), Israel (the period of the later prophets), China (Confucius and Lao-Tzu), India (the Mahabharata), Persia (Zoroaster)—underwent profound ontological revolution that changed its conception of how to relate to self and being. Hence Jaspers' comment that at that time, "man as we know him, came into being."[70] Against this background we can comprehend Buber's proposition that regardless of social, cultural, and historical boundaries, at the source of all great cultures one finds persons who have experienced an "original encounter, an event at the source when a response was made to a You."[71] This "event at the source" refers to one's opening to the multidimensional dialogue with both the absolute and fellow humans. One who has experienced it is Buber's "dialogical person," "the person who commits his whole being to Elohim's dialogue with the world, and who stands firm throughout this dialogue. . . . [W]hatever the way, man enters into the dialogue again and again; imperfect entry, but yet one which is not refused, an entry which is determined to persevere in the dialogical world."[72]

This person has undergone an experience that enables him to shape society, the human cosmos, in the image of the greater cosmos he has come to know by virtue of his meeting with the absolute. The unique person at the source of a great society or civilization therefore establishes a paradigmatic conception of human perfection at the moment of founding. His encounter inspires future generations and gives purpose and direction to their efforts to renew their societies: "Reinforced by the energy of subsequent generations that points in the same direction, this [original encounter] creates a distinctive conception of the cosmos in the spirit; only thus does a human cosmos become possible again and again."[73] Such an encounter can occur in any cultural environment. In this respect, the image of the dialogical person may apply universally to

all communities. In terms of the present analysis, these points of regeneration (or—in the absence of appropriate persons and conditions—of de-
generation) are moments of an opening of the mind to the inclusive
consciousness sustained in the hidden history. Translating this insight
into sociological and cultural analysis, S. N. Eisenstadt (who was Buber's
student at the Hebrew University) summarized Buber's specific sociological or social philosophical concern in the following terms: "[To de-
fine] the nature and conditions of social and cultural creativity, the
conditions of those of stagnation or of the demise of societies and cultures. He sought to identify the situations where creativity really can
occur, and he believed that these situations exist to some extent in all
cultures but that their fullest development occurs only rarely."[74]

Sensitivity to a refined quality of relation unnoted in the annals
of historical consciousness thus constitutes one means of understanding
Buber's distinction between the two kinds of history. In Buber's works,
we indeed encounter a persistent preoccupation with the conditions that
would enable individuals, within small communities or under conditions
present in larger societies, to experience the opening to a more inclusive
relation to being. Such rare moments of meeting between hidden and
apparent history are thus the significant turning points in the annals of
cultures or societies. They are points of ontological revolutions.

However, "significant" does not necessarily signify "good." "Ontological revolution" does not necessarily imply a turn toward the good,
nor does it necessarily imply "positive." In Buber's analysis, there are
cases of premature "intervention" in apparent history of those privy to
the hidden history. We now proceed to examine the distinction between
accurate and inaccurate timings of "exit from the quiver," represented
in Buber's works in his analysis of the fate of "Israel" as it transpired in
the deeds of Jesus and of the Ba'al Shem.

## JESUS, THE BA'AL SHEM, AND SPINOZA

In Buber's narrative, Jesus is an example of a hidden servant who
emerged prematurely and without adequate preparation into historical
consciousness. Premature "emergence from the quiver" such as Jesus'
causes unintended effects that may be detrimental to the desired meeting
between apparent and hidden history, a meeting that occurs when the

mind is ready to accept the shock of self-recognition. Jesus' actions led to results opposite from his intentions. This figure thus serves as a negative example that illuminates the problematic facing individuals who realize the revolutionary nature of the task they have encountered. A reading of Buber's Jesus helps us understand the kind of dialectic that Buber thought takes place *within hidden history* between, on the one hand, those content to remain hidden and to operate in ways not easily discernible to the historical eye and, on the other, those who use their hidden knowledge to influence historical events in ways that—for Buber— inevitably lead to distortion of the teaching and testimony that they seek to revive.

Buber notes that to fully understand the actions of Jesus, one must understand that he came from the ranks of those "whom the nameless prophet spoke of . . . when he said that God had made him a polished shaft, and then had hidden him in the quiver." Jesus was the first who "stepped out of the seclusion of the servants of God, which is their real 'Messianic secret.' "[75] Like the other "servants" or "arrows of YHVH dwelling at one time or other 'in the darkness of the quiver,' " writes Buber, "Jesus too does not know without doubt whether he is destined to be taken out, to be shot. . . . [H]e does not even know without doubt whether he must not offer himself for that purpose if it should take place legitimately."[76]

Since Jesus was a true servant of YHVH, the nature of his deeds is comprehensible to those who are members of this tradition. Accordingly, Buber writes that "we Jews knew him (Jesus) from within, in the impulses and stirrings of his Jewish being, in a way that remains inaccessible to the peoples submissive to him."[77] With these comments in mind, we can fully appreciate Buber's candor when he states:

> I firmly believe that the Jewish community, in the course of its renaissance, will recognize Jesus; and not merely as a great figure in its religious history, but also in the organic connection of a Messianic development extending over millennia, whose final goal is the Redemption of Israel and of the world. But I believe equally firmly that we will never recognize Jesus as the Messiah Come, for this would contradict the deepest meaning of our Messianic Passion.[78]

Buber does not question the sincerity of Jesus' motives, nor does he doubt that as a person, Jesus was privy to the experience of the "double history" of Adam. However, Jesus could not know for certain whether he should stay hidden in the quiver or whether he was destined "to be shot to the target."[79] Buber explicates the nature of the dilemma facing Jesus by contrasting Jesus' actions to those of the hero of Buber's pseudo-novel *Gog Umagog*, the "Holy Yehudi" of Pshyscha, who confronts an existential dilemma: his teacher and master, the "Seer" of Lublin, demands that the Yehudi use his knowledge of the esoteric practices of the Kabbalah to influence the course of historical events (in this case, to help Napoleon bring about the calamity—symbolized by the notion of *Gog Umagog*—that would herald the end of the historical epoch and the consequent ushering in of the messianic era). The Yehudi refuses his mentor's demands, leading him to painful confrontations with the teacher he respects and eventually bringing about his early death. Responding to a critique of *Gog Umagog*, Buber explained the considerations that guided his characterization of the Yehudi, indicating that the Yehudi did not emerge from the hiddenness of the quiver. Furthermore, Buber added: "It is our duty to see this fact: both this hand, which first sharpens the arrow and then hides it in the darkness of the quiver, and the arrow remained faithful."[80]

The Yehudi remained faithful to the hiddenness that is essential to the servant of YHVH's "doing." Buber writes that in contrast to the Yehudi, Jesus *did* emerge from the darkness of the quiver. Buber attributes Jesus' actions to the urging of his disciples: Jesus turns to "those termed 'his students,'" to whom he was sent, and he asks them who they think he is . . . and if he is answered as he is answered, then occurs, as if from his heart, what occurs—the hurrying of the end—and it happens in a pure heart and in innocence."[81] To "hurry the end" is a Jewish idiom that refers to human attempts to intervene in historical events in a manner that would bring closer the advent of the messianic era. It is often used in negative connotations, implying imprudent and ultimately harmful actions undertaken in the name of "God's will." Jesus attempted such intervention upon the urging of his disciples; his actions stemmed from "a pure heart" and "innocence." His good intentions notwithstanding, the results of his acquiescence to immediate demands were detrimental to the kind of revolution—personal and communal—that he had intended for his disciples and for humanity.

Buber's explanation of Jesus' decision to make his mark on history appears somewhat difficult to accept. However, a thorough examination of the issue would not be relevant to the present discussion. It suffices to note that in Buber's understanding, Jesus was a servant of YHVH who revealed himself and his wisdom to a generation not prepared to fathom the depths of understanding he was eager to share. Jesus' inaccurate intervention in history led to an effect that was the diametric opposite of his intention: incomplete interpretations of his historical presence gave rise to a religion that institutionalized and perpetuated the separation between Adam and Elohim that Jesus, as a servant of YHVH, sought to bridge. This is the background of Buber's critique of Paul and of Christianity. Buber writes that Jesus could not anticipate the interpretation that Saul of Tarsus, Paul, would ascribe to his teaching, an interpretation that diverts attention from presence in the face of being to belief in the Son of God;[82] neither could Jesus anticipate the Church that would be established on the basis of Paul's misunderstanding.[83]

It appears that the words Buber puts in the mouth of the Yehudi reflect Buber's critique of Jesus' actions: "All calculations concerning the end of time are false and all attempts to bring nearer the coming of the Messiah must fail . . . Truly there is a mystery here. But he who would perform it will surely fail; only he who does not attempt it dare hope to have a share in it. Redemption is at the door. It depends only upon our return, our *teshuva*."[84] *Teshuva*, a Hebrew word that connotes the (re)-turn to Elohim, is a personal experience that cannot be mediated by the actions of others, nor can it occur in a single, decisive, irreversible moment. It represents an attitude to being that is renewed at every moment of a person's life. The religious form of life that rose from interpretations of Jesus' proclaiming the coming of the Kingdom of YHVH articulated and perpetuated a dualistic relation to being that is far from the original teaching. Consequently, Buber considers the development of Christianity to be proof that Jesus acted in an inaccurate and irresponsible manner. Accordingly, whatever the reasons for Jesus' actions, Buber considers him the first in a series of *premature* attempts to enter the world of historical consciousness with the intention of bringing about a change of heart.[85] That is why, Buber writes, Jesus was the first of those "tremendous and weak saints"[86] who attempted to do good in ways incommensurate with the demands of the historical hour.

Jesus was transformed into a historical image (the biography "Jesus of Nazareth, son of Mary and Joseph") of a hidden reality (the hidden servant of YHVH, the preserver of the messianic mystery). The historical image replaced the dialogical relation that characterized the hidden servant's way. Those who followed the religion based on the apparent teachings of Jesus interpreted his deeds as a call to turn to Elohim through turning to the image of his son, Jesus the *mashuah*, the anointed, the Christ.[87]

In an ironic twist, Jesus' premature emergence from the quiver gave rise to a belief system that propagated the very duality that he—as a human being, not as the image transmitted in apparent history—sought to overcome. By becoming a mediating presence in Christian eschatology, the image of Jesus became a symbol for a belief system that—as a construct of thought—developed into a barrier to the development of the direct, dialogical relation to being that the Hebrew tradition sought to retain.[88] As Catholic Christianity came to differ so markedly from Judaism on an issue essential to Catholicism's self-conception, belief in the importance of having Jews accept Jesus as the human Messiah became one of the central dogmas of Catholicism. Consequently, Catholicism's quarrel with Judaism became pivotal to its belief system and to its institutional history.

In contrast to Jesus, the Ba'al Shem (1700–1760), founder of the Jewish movement of religious revival called Hasidism, serves in Buber's narrative as an exemplary figure who attempted to create a historical form of social life that would ensure the continued transmission of teaching and testimony without creating a new religion. Buber explicitly situates the deeds of the Ba'al Shem in the context of the mission of the hidden servants of YHVH. In Buber's story, the Ba'al Shem is a hidden servant who decides to renew Judaism from within.

What were the particular conditions facing the Ba'al Shem, and how did he initiate responses that were more commensurate with the needs of humanity than those of Jesus? We have seen that the basic assumption of the Hebrew tradition is that humanity's most dangerous tendency is to forget the unity of being and to consider partial aspects of human existence as independent of the rest of life. The Ba'al Shem, living in the age of the great secular reaction to centuries of religious impositions, was aware that the emergence of Western rationalism included rejection of the validity of propositions that could not be proved by scientific thought, including those that were attuned to the essential unity of being. The modern subject was becoming detached from a quality of "knowing" that is not located in its reasoning faculties. In this particular historical context, a new form of challenge to the life of the spirit emerged: the inclination of thought to attribute to human existence an autonomy that is separate from the rest of creation. This was perceived by many sensitive thinkers as constituting a fundamental threat to the free life of the spirit. In response to the challenges posed by this development within the historical form of consciousness, the Ba'al Shem sought to create a form of social life that would balance the emergence of a subjectifying ontology. This is why, Buber writes, "what is of greatest importance in Hasidism is . . . the powerful tendency, preserved in personal as well as in communal existence, to overcome the fundamental separation between the sacred and the profane."[89] The inclusive tendency of Hasidism balances the divisive tendency of modern subjectification. In Buber's presentation of this historical event, the Jewish thinker Baruch Spinoza was a major force. Defending reason in the face of ignorance perpetuated by religious institutions, Spinoza was a major turning point in the release of the mind from superstitions. Yet his interpreters focused on the apparent autonomy of reason that his teachings emphasize, without heeding his understanding of the unity of consciousness. Consequently, Spinoza represents (in the context of this discussion) the turn to reason as a rejection of the wisdom transmitted in Scripture.

From one perspective, the founding of Hasidism was the Ba'al Shem's active response to the development of the modern subject, symbolized by the philosophy of Spinoza. But in Buber's narrative, the deeds of the Ba'al Shem were aimed at checking an additional development, one that was particular to Judaism: after centuries of suffering and persecution under Christian rule, including the traumas of the Catholic Inquisition and the expulsion in 1492 from Spain and Portugal, many Jews felt that their suffering could be justified only in terms of their being the last generations before the coming of the messianic age. The time was ripe for redemption, for the coming of the Messiah. The yearning for personal and communal redemption became for many a desire to follow a human savior, a human messiah. Against the background of these hopes appeared the person known retrospectively in Jewish history as *the* "false Messiah" of Judaism—Sabbatai Zevi. Appearing as if from nowhere, Sabbatai ignited messianic fervor in Jewish communities throughout Europe and the bordering Mediterranean (particularly regions close to the Middle East). When his messianic "doings" ended in the conversion of Sabbatai and many of his followers to Islam, the resulting crisis of trust within Judaism was of unprecedented magnitude. The effects of the Sabbatean movement thus were not merely disillusionment with a particular person but also the possibility that Jews would relinquish faith in the messianic idea that Sabbatai had so effectively claimed to represent.

It is worthwhile to quote Buber's remarks about this event at relative length, as they are comprehensible in the context of our analysis of Buber's use of implication and indirect reference to biblical guiding verses. In Buber's terms, Sabbatai was a particularly degenerate form of the misguided servant of YHVH, the last in a series of such persons, "stepping out of the hiddenness of the servant of YHVH."

> [Sabbatai] sank into the deepest problematic, slid over from an honest self-assurance into a pretended one, and ended in apostasy. And it was not a small band that clung to him. . . . Rather Jewry itself adhered to him and accepted his statements as legitimate proclamations, statements which they once would have found intolerable and would have taken as evidence against any divine summons. . . . The catastrophe prepared the end not merely of this one event, but of the whole form of the event: the meeting of a man who had taken the fateful step from the hiddenness of the servants of YHVH to messianic self-consciousness, with a group who took it upon themselves to begin the kingdom of YHVH.[90]

Presented simply, the dashing of messianic hopes on the rocks of Sabbatai's conversion to Islam made a farce out of messianic belief; the latent, mysterious yearning for a new epoch was channeled into the Sabbatean attempt to "hasten the end" and to "begin the kingdom of God."[91] In contrast to the openhearted yearning evoked by the messianic mystery, Sabbatai directed the emotional energies of this state of being to expectations of the one, single "Messiah" who claimed to be a guide to a newfound relation to being. Like the Church and the image of Christ that it advanced, Sabbatai substituted himself for Elohim.

The Ba'al Shem thus encountered a dual challenge to the hidden history: in his times, the possibility of experiencing the unified consciousness *and* the possibility of fathoming the messianic mystery were simultaneously threatened by changes that had crystallized within historical consciousness through the deeds of two Jews, Spinoza and Sabbatai Zevi. Spinoza offered a philosophy that assumed inordinate trust in reason as the existential, thought–laden foundation of the individuated modern subject, while Sabbatai eliminated a rare and refined yearning (similar to the platonic eros) for relation to eternity. In Spinozan philosophy, there are grounds for a misunderstanding that would legitimize conceptions of the self as a being separate from creation (an objectifying subject separate from other objectifying subjects), while Sabbateanism represents the most extreme form of the Jewish notion of a single, human messianic redeemer, a human break in time after whom history will end and humanity will experience redemption. In Spinoza, there is unprecedented understanding of the power of reason, an understanding that inadvertently strengthens the basis of modern philosophy's consideration of the thinking subject as the foundation of being; in Sabbatai, there is unprecedented harnessing, in the service of a misleading personality, the false Messiah Sabbatai Zevi, of the energy contained in generations of messianic yearning.

Buber's choice of Spinoza as one whose philosophy posed a threat to the teaching and testimony of Judaism is surprising. Indeed, considering Buber's total and deeply felt rejection of institutional religion, one would expect him to embrace Spinoza's teachings wholeheartedly. Examination of Buber's critique of Spinoza reveals that it is directed not at the philosophy per se but rather at one of its unintended consequences. While approving of Spinoza's rejection of religious conceptions of Elohim as a kind of elevated personality, Buber criticizes Spinoza's dismissal of the possibility of relating to Elohim in the immediacy of life. In other words, Buber faults Spinoza for coupling (justified) rejection of idolatrous interpretations of the nature of Elohim with (unjustified) rejection of the hidden, real teaching of the Torah.

Turning away from the teaching, Spinoza looked inward toward reason. In Buber's interpretation, Spinoza's philosophy unwittingly led to the glorification of a form of reason that considers the inner movement of thought as the sole source of understanding. Buber considers Spinoza's philosophy a milestone on the modern path to "monologism," to the "monologizing hubris" of modern philosophy.[92] Buber's critique of Spinoza is therefore in the context of the effect Spinoza had of accelerating "the tendency of the Western spirit toward monological life."[93] For Buber, Spinoza represents a state of forgetfulness of the *desire to address* that is the force giving rise to language and to its carriers— thoughts and words: "Spinoza undertook to take from Elohim his being open to address."[94] We note in passing that Buber's critique of Spinoza conforms with his understanding of the Hebrew Bible as an address that precedes the written word and hence engenders it. This is in contrast to Spinoza's critique of the authority of Scripture, which is based on the assumption that most believers suspend individual reason and subject their understanding to the authority of established religious leaders. Spinoza's philosophy, stemming from a rejection of both blind acceptance of religious dogmas and base interpretations of Scripture, is a corrective to the kind of ignorance that seeks justification in the words of religious authorities. In contrast to Buber, Spinoza does not assume that one will come closer to truth through a refined reading of the biblical text; for him, rejection of the deeply ingrained authoritative status of Scripture is essential for attaining an experience of freedom through the exercise of reason.[95]

It is clear that Spinoza cannot be accused of being inattentive to the depths of consciousness and the unfulfilled potential of human reason. His works challenge a philosophy of mind that assumes fixed limits to the infinite possibilities of understanding that are present to consciousness. He wished his readers to judge reality according to the light of reason, not of dogma. One may even read him as an attempt to save the secret of Judaism (the relation to Elohim as the opening to eternal being) from the ignorance of rabbinical authority. These are intentions and criticisms that Buber shared. However, Buber's writings about Spinoza and other philosophers, like Buber's critique of Jesus, often focus on the way those philosophers were misinterpreted rather than on their original intentions. Buber's critique therefore relates to the impact of Spinoza's work on the relation of successive generations to the hidden aspects of the teaching. That is why Buber presents Spinoza as one who did not see the hidden wisdom transmitted within the institutionalized form of religion he so perceptively considered ossified and misleading. In the course of rejecting the authority of rabbinic Judaism, Spinoza unfortunately also rejected the secrets transmitted by this cultural tradition. Hence, while acting "out of a primal Jewish instinct" in his opposition to the "dualism of life that had become current in his life" (a perspective that Buber approves), Spinoza, in rejecting the biblical Elohim, "swung beyond this legitimate object" and misunderstood Judaism. By rejecting the hidden Elohim, Spinoza inadvertently closed the "opening" to becoming "natural Adam." As with his critique of Jesus, Buber detects in the deeds of Spinoza a good intention gone astray.

In Buber's narrative, the Ba'al Shem was aware that a turn toward reason as a kind of inner foundation of being was gaining force in human consciousness. Hence Buber's (otherwise obscure) comment that while the Ba'al Shem may not have heard of Spinoza personally, he certainly realized that Western consciousness was rapidly developing into a struc-ture of thought that was self-enclosed, self-adulating, and closed to the finer quality of consciousness that is concealed by the movement of thought. In Buber's narrative, the Ba'al Shem *listened* and "heard" with the refined ear characteristic of those hidden in the shadows. The Ba'al Shem's response, too, bore the mark of such refined understanding.

> The Ba'al Shem Tov probably knew nothing of Spinoza; nevertheless he has given the reply to him. In the truth of history one can reply without having heard; he does not mean what he says as a reply, but it is one. And that the reply of the Ba'al Shem did not come to the attention of the spirits who received the speech of Spinoza, also does not diminish its significance; in the truth of history even what remains unknown can be valid.[96]

The Ba'al Shem sought to correct the emerging modern misunder-standing of the nature of reason by establishing a way of life that would be based on the assumption that Elohim and Adam are inseparable and that Adam can renew the relation to Elohim in every action and encoun-ter. Hence Buber's assertion that in Hasidism the division between "life in Elohim" and "life in the world"—two apparently different dimen-sions of relation—is recognized as "the primal evil of all 'religion' " and "is overcome in the concrete meeting between Elohim and Adam."[97]

As mentioned, the other threat to the teaching and testimony sus-tained and transmitted in the hidden history came from within Judaism, in the form of Sabbatai Zevi, a Jew who claimed to be the Messiah. Buber interprets the actions of the Ba'al Shem as a response to the de-spair and crisis of trust that came as a reaction to Sabbatai. The Ba'al Shem realized that Sabbatai's deed had to be countered by acts of a no less persuasive nature. Judaism needed concrete proof that Jewish messianism is not belief in an event happening once at the end of time and in a single human figure created as the center of the event.[98] Hence

Buber's comment that the Ba'al Shem filled the void created by the failure of rabbinic leadership to prepare the people to combat the false messianism of Sabbateanism.[99] The Ba'al Shem's presence "establishes the new type of leader. The appearance of the Ba'al Shem Tov is the founding act of Hasidism."[100]

However, aware of the experience of Jesus and of Sabbatai, the Ba'al Shem had to lay foundations for a new form of transmission that would ensure that the teaching and testimony were transmitted precisely and that this new form of transmission would not degenerate into a new kind of worship of himself or of any other figure associated with creative Jewish revival. The founding of the Hasidic community was his way of renewing Judaism from within. When discussing Buber's theory of community in chapter 6, we shall see that the Hasidic community thus becomes for Buber a paradigm of true community, one that aims at overcoming the limits of modern forms of social organization.

## THE BA'AL SHEM, ISAIAH, AND BUBER'S INTENTIONS

It may be useful to compare Buber's presentation of the Ba'al Shem with his depiction of Isaiah. Both images figure in Buber's narrative as positive examples of intervening in history in ways that do not threaten the original purpose of transmitting the teaching. It would seem that Buber's assessment of the deeds of the Ba'al Shem contrasts sharply with his earlier depiction of Isaiah's critical decision to remove "teaching" and "testimony" from revealed history. The Ba'al Shem decided to *revive* the apparent, manifest communal form of transmitting the tradition, whereas Isaiah chose to *remove* the community of faithful from the stage of history. The apparent contradiction between these two decisions is indeed apparent; each of these "hidden servants" acted in accordance with what he considered crucial to the continuation and transmission of the stream of consciousness referred to as the "hidden history" *within the ontological underpinnings and historical constraints unique to his times*.

Under the historical conditions of Isaiah's time—the existence of a political Kingdom of Israel—the response took the form of initiating a hidden line of *limmud* that would create a response adequate to the conditions of an inevitable exile. Considering this analysis, one might claim that exile begins with the transfer of teaching and testimony from public to private forms of transmission, not with the political exile of the kingdom.

In contrast, the historical conditions confronting the Ba'al Shem— exiled communities threatened by a loss of faith and the enticing alternative of modern subjectivity—necessitated the return to a public, visible form of transmission. Like the relation established between the second and the first Isaiah—historically indirect, yet ontologically a direct continuity of intention and deed—their work and self-conception are experienced as links in an ongoing chain of transmission. My reference to Isaiah's *limmud* in this discussion is not incidental; it is based on Buber's indirect reference, evident in his careful choice of words, to the Ba'al Shem as a member of the ongoing line of *limmudim* initiated by Isaiah. Buber refers to the Hasidic *zaddikim* as those who know the "teaching" that "has been written in the heart of men, so that they perceive Elohim directly"[101] as "true embodiments of a torah," as "the teaching."[102] Through the symbolic existence of such persons "is said what there is to be said."[103] They manifest the teaching and testimony of the *limmud*, and those who can discern will see the reality that they serve and symbolize. From our examination of Buber's use of the guiding words of Isaiah 8:16, we know that what Buber is saying is that these persons continue the chain of transmission that is continually present in the chronicles of "Israel."

Having presented the apparent merits of the Ba'al Shem, we may ponder Buber's presentation in the context of his critique of Jesus. The comparison is problematic for readers like myself who wonder why Buber attributed to the Ba'al Shem a certainty that what he was doing was substantially different from what Jesus did. Stated differently, Buber's analysis leaves us with a troubling question: Why did Buber attribute accurate "doing" to the Ba'al Shem but refer to Jesus as one who "left the quiver" prematurely? It seems that the response is in the effects of the person's actions, not in the intention or action itself. If that is the case, then Buber leaves us with no real criteria for judging in our own lives and times the deeds of others; the judgment seems to be situated in our understanding of historical effect, not in hidden (and hence invisible) intention.

I think that Buber would have responded by justifying the juxtaposition of Jesus and the Ba'al Shem in terms of the background story that he elicited from his reading of the layers of meaning implicit in the

Hebrew Bible. Buber judged the two in terms of his interpretation of what Isaiah intended when Isaiah initiated the hidden line of transmission of Judaism's "teaching" and "testimony." Buber assumed that both Jesus and the Ba'al Shem shared a common goal: to ensure that the accelerated development of a historical consciousness would not result in a total and irrevocable forgetfulness of the essential relation to being that is available to the "natural" element of Adam. Buber read texts with these concerns in mind. The reaction of his listeners or interpreters is dependent on their sensitivity to this background understanding. It is clear that Buber thought that a sensitive interpreter can "hear" and decipher the meaning of a dialogical moment recorded in a text by reading between the lines of the text according to his experience and understanding of the nature of dialogue. Such an interpreter justifies his interpretation by eliciting from the ancient text those clues that substantiate his reconstruction of the original moment and then interprets his consequent retelling of the story thus reformed.

Since Buber's insight and consequent convictions developed over time, and since he was allusive and indirect in his presentation of the truths he held most dear to his heart, most of his critics were not privy to his implicit intentions. This led to inevitable "mismeetings" between Buber and scholars or theologians who read his writings about particular concerns without being privy to the intricate web of meaning that emerges only from study of all of his works. Consider, for example, the following exchange with a number of eminent American scholars that took place in 1957, as recorded by Maurice Friedman:

> Buber dealt with the interpretation of a number of verses, particularly from the New Testament. At one point he remarked that the passage in Matthew that came directly after "Since the days of John the Baptist men have tried to take the Kingdom of Heaven by violence" did not seem to him genuine. When asked for his reason, Buber said, "it is merely my own subjective feeling." After several continued to press him, he finally stated, "I do not hear the voice of Jesus in it." At this James Muilenburg became very red in the face and pounded the table, saying "That's pure subjectivity!" "But I told you," said Buber mildly.[104]

It seems that Buber was not forthright when he agreed that his reading of the passage from the Gospel of Matthew was on the basis of "pure subjectivity." This "subjectivity" was grounded in his perception of the ontological and the historical effects of the New Testament. Ontologically, the New Testament strengthened assumptions about "fallen man's" sinful, dual nature, symbolized by the presentation of apparent conflict between flesh and spirit and redeemable only through recognition of the messianic presence of Jesus (this is a form of "history from above"). Historically, the emphasis on the "fallen" and sinful nature of man gave rise to a theology that institutionalized the mediating function of Jesus and of the Church, thus creating a form of worship diametrically opposite to that characteristic of the hidden servants ("history from below") from whose midst Jesus emerged.

In other words, Buber's basic critique was not of Jesus but rather of the canonical text about Jesus (the New Testament) and the institution (the Church and Church dogma) that, in the name of Christ, mediates between the person and the Creator. Jesus' mistake is thus manifest in the effects of his mission. His followers created a new form of transmission that separated itself from the source, from the Hebrew *miqra'*. By becoming the new source of textual authority, the New Testament deprived its faithful readers of the opportunity to discover the unmediated relation to being that is the core of the teaching transmitted in the Hebrew Bible. Buber's quarrel is with the institutionalized religion that directed subsequent generations to a source of wisdom that was (in his opinion) an incomplete and indirect rendering of the dialogical situations experienced by (the hidden, Jewish servant) Jesus both in relation to Elohim and in relation to women and men. The new texts (parts of the Gospels, like the passage from Matthew mentioned above, but primarily the Epistles of Paul) clearly replaced the Hebrew Scripture with a new testament and thus deprived generations of Christians of a direct meeting with the "secret" granted textual form by the Hebrew Bible. (The Gospel of Thomas, discovered in the twentieth century, presents a portrait of Jesus that is surprisingly similar to the image projected by Buber and thus renews questions raised by Buber and others about the distance between Jesus the person and Jesus as institutionalized by the Church).

Buber turns to the Ba'al Shem as a neat contrast to Jesus because the former renewed the Hebrew tradition *from within*. Unlike Jesus, the Ba'al Shem did not enable the inadvertent creation of a new canon that would be subject to misguided interpretations. At bottom, this is the rationale guiding Buber's critique of Spinoza too. Buber thus applauds the Ba'al Shem for having engendered a new social structure that did not lead to disavowal of the mission it sought to preserve, *mesirah* (transmission) and *kabbalah* (reception) of the original. We thus see that Buber justifies his comparison between Jesus and the Ba'al Shem, on the one hand, and between Spinoza and the Ba'al Shem, on the other, in terms of the effects of their deeds on historical developments. On the basis of the deeds of Jesus, there sprang a tradition that (in Buber's eyes) institutionalized the very kind of mediation that Jesus thought destructive to the life of the spirit. On the basis of the teachings of Spinoza, there developed a way of secular life that rejected in toto all that is preserved by religion. In contrast, Buber depicts the Ba'al Shem as one who was exceptionally attentive to creating a social structure that would prevent both an institutionalization of charisma and an exclusive belief in the autonomy of the individual subject.

## LIVING IN BETWEEN THE TWO STREAMS

Having presented the rationale guiding Buber's contrasts among the Ba'al Shem and Jesus and Spinoza (with the majestic figure of Isaiah in the background of Buber's comparison), I am still dissatisfied with Buber's analysis. At the end of the twentieth century, less than two hundred fifty years after the death of the Ba'al Shem, many Hasidic communities are organized around the charismatic presence of their leading *zaddik*. In some cases, charisma is institutionalized and the mantle of leadership passes from father to son (or to another next of kin). The fact that Buber criticized this development ("most of the powers of the Hasidic community itself have been given over to decay or destruction")[105] does not solve our question: whether Buber's criticism of Jesus—based on the historical results of Jesus' teachings—should not apply to the historical development of Hasidism. After all, both attempts to challenge orthodoxy ended up with the same result—the creation of new forms of institutionalized religion predicated on a belief in the extraordinary powers of a central charismatic figure. Spinoza still has much to teach us in this respect.

Perhaps the puzzlement raised by Buber's juxtapositions may be best addressed from the perspective of the task that Buber gradually realized to be his personal destiny. It was sometimes suggested to him that he present the essential teachings of Judaism as a universal, "unfettered teaching of mankind." Such a course would have implied a total rejection of the cultural tradition of his ancestors. Aware of the historical effects of previous attempts to revitalize the teachings of Judaism by proclaiming them to be universal—whether by granting the religion a universal dimension (Jesus) or by rejecting the religious text and offering in its stead a universal rationality (Spinoza)—Buber chose a middle ground between the various alternatives that he had detected in the "hidden, true, history of humankind." This middle ground is encapsulated in a statement that Buber wrote in 1957, toward the end of his life:

> It has often been suggested to me that I should liberate this teaching from its "confessional limitations," as people like to put it, and proclaim it as an unfettered teaching of mankind. Taking such a "universal" path would have been for me pure arbitrariness. In order to speak to the world what I have heard, I am not bound to step into the street. I may remain standing in the door of my ancestral house: here too the word that [the teaching] utters does not go astray.[106]

This metaphor is striking. Buber hovers between his home and the world. Facing the street, his back is turned to the home. He does not step into the street, nor does he invite those outside to come in. He speaks "what [he has] heard" (a choice of words that connotes the "hearing" of the prelinguistic "voice") yet does not attempt to cause his listeners to make a choice between "home" and "street," between their established dogmas and their carefree movement on life's paths. Those inside do not hear him (for he turns outward), and those on the street do not attempt to enter (for by standing on the shadowy threshold that demarcates the house and the street, he is a bodily presence blocking the entrance of those who might be attracted to the source of the words they hear as they pass). His presence is effective as a word that is heard, not as a person who is seen. His presence subverts all institutionalized forms of the teaching, for he disregards entirely the need to choose between alternative institutions. Those inside the "ancestral home" may remain inside, and those who walk the streets may also continue to proceed along their respective ways.

All that Buber suggests is transformation of attitude: remain human, continue in your individual path, but be open to the possibility of radically transforming your relation to self, to other, and to the cosmos. That is all that is required:

> The Hasidic word says that the worlds can fulfill their destiny of becoming one through man's (Adam's) life becoming one. But how can this be understood? . . . Israel's confession of the oneness of Elohim says, indeed, not merely that outside of him there is no Elohim, but also that he alone is unity. *Here the interpreter must come in. . . .* Adam cannot approach the divine by reaching beyond the human; he can approach him through becoming human. To become human is what he, this individual man, has been created for.[107]

To "become human" is what Buber's work is about—to become aware of the nature of life, and of the responsibility to creation that is part and parcel of such awareness. Such a commitment is not predestined to be the sole responsibility of a particular cultural tradition. However, Buber was firm in his conviction that one who seeks to fathom the implications of this deceptively simple precept should begin with him- or herself, within the particular culture that shapes his or her worldview. That is why Buber refused to rid himself of the fetters of his particular background.

What may seem to one as "fetters" may become for another an opening to refined understanding. The exact effects of one's life-circumstances cannot be predetermined by intervention of external authority. The experience of wonder in the face of individual existence cannot be planned by another. The most one can do is indicate alternative possibilities and let the other decide whether what the other experiences as a full sensation of life is "fettered" or not. To do so, one must be attentive to the language of the other, to ensure initial communication. Those "in the street" do not share Buber's biblical or Hasidic discourse. Consequently, Buber must speak to them in their own language. In this context, we shall examine Buber's philosophy of dialogue, a region of language that uses concepts and forms of argumentation familiar to any educated Western reader. However, we shall also attend to the inseparable connection between this form of writing and Buber's biblical works, by drawing attention to Buber's use of biblical guiding words in his philosophical discourse.

To this area of Buber's work we now turn, to philosophy.

# 5

# DIALOGICAL PHILOSOPHY:
# BETWEEN THE WORDS OF TEXTS
# AND THE CONTENT OF THOUGHT

After bearing witness to two world wars, the Holocaust, the atomic bomb, terror, and violence-based totalitarian regimes, Buber seemed to believe that there was no more distance to cover in man's disengagement from himself and from his essence. In 1951, he wrote that the most fundamental ground of human existence was at stake: "It seems that all original relations are about to break asunder, and all original being about to fall apart." In his eyes, the magnitude of the crisis of humanity left little room between two alternative futures: either a renewed relation to being or the annihilation of the human form of life. The existential question that he perceived and articulated was thus clear and sharp: "In what way shall we become what we are from the very nature of our being?"[1]

Buber's mature philosophy reflects his responses to this question. In a manner that may initially seem paradoxical, Buber's philosophy of dialogue is oriented towards activation of a quality of attention that is present to the voice of silence that precedes thought and speech (and therefore precedes the existence of "I" as thought). Buber considered his primary task—as a human being, as a member of the cultural tradition that had taken upon itself to transmit the remembrance of the original relation, *and* as a philosopher—to direct attention to "the heart" as a place of reception, as an organ of understanding.[2]

Previous chapters have established Buber's proposition that appropriate reading of Scripture enables listening. As we have seen in our reading of his use of biblical hermeneutics, Buber sought to awaken a quality of listening that would enable renewed attention to the voice that is in the background of creation and of Scripture. This chapter goes further and claims that for Buber, the experience of listening was ultimately more important than the interpretation of Scripture.[3] The Bible exists in the service of the listening; if the latter is experienced, the former becomes an auxiliary artifact that has completed its purpose, an example of Stanley Fish's "self-consuming artifact."[4] In pursuing this goal, Buber appears to have aligned himself intentionally with the prophets whose works he had studied so carefully and whose writings repeatedly allude to the necessity of finding the way to a renewed relation to being as the ultimate message of the Hebrew tradition.[5] This is the mission that Buber undertook to "proclaim."[6]

Buber's writings about the Hebrew Bible and the mission of Judaism and his philosophical discourse therefore complement one another rather than presenting apparently distinct modes of discourse. In contrast to conventional dichotomies, it seems that Buber's primary concern was, rather than to argue about the relative merits of theology or philosophy, to direct attention to the insight that is prior to one or the other system of thought.[7]

This chapter therefore aims at uncovering the basic insight perceived as the common root of Buber's disparate forms of writing (biblical interpretation, philosophical commentaries and essays, Hasidic legends, and social criticism): his turning to the silent place of attention that precedes language, thought, and speech. That this apparently paradoxical proposition is discovered through real philosophizing, yet not open to systematic articulation, is the basis for Buber's comment, in the late 1950s, about his method of philosophizing: "I *must* philosophize; there is no other way to my goal, but my goal itself cannot be grasped philosophically."[8] His philosophy is a search, not a clearly structured statement; an urge, not a final edifice of thought. His work is motivated by the most fundamental eros of an inquiring soul, to comprehend the life that he embodies. His philosophical writings grapple with the noblest of philosophical questions: What am I? How do I know what (or who) I am? Why am I here? Where have I come from? Where do I turn from the place that I am?[9]

To comprehend Buber's responses to these and similarly perplexing questions, we turn to Buber's insight regarding the origins of thought in a thoughtless movement of attention. We shall approach this issue indirectly, by eliciting the philosophy implicit in many of Buber's Hasidic legends. Following the exegesis of legends that indirectly address philosophical concerns, we shall turn to explicitly philosophical writings in which Buber attempts to grant discursive form to the understanding implicit in his legends and other "nonphilosophical" writings.

## SILENT PRESENCE AS THE ORIGIN OF CONTEMPLATION

We begin by examining the story for which the Hebrew collection of Buber's Hasidic tales, *Or HaGanooz* (Light of the Hidden), is named: Rabbi Elazar said:

> "Light that the Holy One, blessed be he, created on the first day—Adam sees through it from one end of the world to the other. Because the Holy One, blessed be he, looked at the generation of the flood and at the generation of the division and saw that their deeds were wicked, he stopped the light and hid it from them. For whom did he hide it? For the *zaddikim* (the just) who are yet to come."
>
> Hasidim asked, "Where did he hide it?"
> They answered, "In the Torah."
> They asked, "If so, won't the *zaddikim* find some of the hidden light when they are studying Torah?"
> They answered, "They will find and find."
> They asked, "If so, what will the *zaddikim* do when they find some of the light hidden in the Torah?"
> They answered, "They will reveal it in their way of life."[10]

Buber's choice of "Light of the Hidden" as the title for his Hebrew collection implies that these legends, and perhaps all his writing, were an indirect form of "revealing" in *his* way of life (primarily, as a writer) whatever he had found in his many years of study and contemplation.

The perspective guiding Buber's use of legend in the service of indirect communication of his ideas is present in the following allegory—one of the pearls in his collection of Hasidic tales. In this story, Buber uses biblical interpretation, inserted into a Hasidic legend, to alert his reader to his basic assumptions about the tradition of writing within which he himself writes:

Rabbi Levi Yitzhak said: "It is written in Isaiah: 'For Torah shall come forth from me.' What Torah is discussed in the text? Surely, we believe with perfect faith that the Torah received by Moses on Mount Sinai will not be replaced and that the Creator, blessed be he, will give us no other Torah. The Torah cannot be changed, and we are forbidden to touch its letters. But, in fact, not only the black letters but also the white gaps between them are letters of the Torah. However, we cannot read the white gaps. In the future, the Holy Name will reveal the white hiddenness of the Torah."[11]

We read in this tale an allusion to a hidden reality indicated by the white gaps between the black letters. Its absence is only apparent, an effect of the reader's focus on the foreground of the text at the expense of noting its inseparable background. We can see and read the black letters and ordinarily do not pay attention to the gaps between them. To render the white gaps relevant to our understanding, we first have to see them as signs, as letters (the Hebrew word for letter, *ot*, also means "sign") necessitating a release of the attention that is ordinarily focused on the black, dominant script. This release, in turn, requires us to recognize the sensation of attention that is entrapped by a continual focus on the dominant black script and to know how to release this attention. Perceiving the black letters differently, in a manner that would bring the white gaps to the fore as "letters," implies seeing the page through revised sight and experiencing the reading of the Torah in a new way. This interpretation of the legend, which emphasizes a new way of seeing and experiencing reality, is one way of considering Buber's use of legends as conveyor of philosophical insight.[12]

Buber's rendering of Rabbi Levi Yitzhak's description of the rationale underlying relation to the Torah as a text with esoteric dimensions provides us with a convenient analogy to Buber's presentation of the nature of thought. Based on philosophical justifications that can be traced to the work of Descartes, the modern subject identifies itself as the movement and content of its thought as-if they were "real" entities. It senses itself as an "I" whose sensation of being is identified with the sensations evoked by its thinking. That sensation of being (i.e., the one the "I" experiences when "I" identifies with the content of its thought) grants to the "I" a sense of apparent singularity and thus feeds the impulse to abstract and objectify reality continuously. In Buber's dialogical

philosophy, this misplaced sensation of self and its relation to its surroundings is called the I–It relation to being.

The process that sustains "I" as a self-made thought-world is analogous to the one that focuses on the black letters of the Torah in the
Hasidic tale. Just as meanings inferred from the black letters are accorded
dominance, "I" considers as "real" only those thoughts that move
within its mind in reaction to one another and to the associations evoked
by the stimuli of ordinary sensory perception. The silence between the
thoughts and the stillness that is the background of their movement are
absent from I's experience; this absence is the "white hiddenness" of
thought. Present as an absence, it is not heard. Listening to the still
silence between thoughts is analogous to seeing the white gaps as letters
of the Torah.

Another Hasidic tale illustrates Buber's use of simple Hasidic homi-
lies to present understanding that would otherwise necessitate dense
philosophical justification:

> Rabbi Yitzhak's two sons went to see [Rabbi Benjamin after the death
> of their father]. "Children," [Rabbi Benjamin] said to them, "I wish
> you would tell me how we are to interpret the words in the Scrip-
> tures: 'And all the people saw the voice . . .' (*Exodus* 20:18). Rabbi
> Ya'akov David, the elder son, gave a most perspicuous interpretation,
> but Rabbi Menahem Mendel, the younger, was silent as usual. "And
> what have you to say?" asked Rabbi Benjamin.
>
> "I say," answered Menahem Mendel, "that we must take it to
> mean that they saw and realized that one must take the voice into
> oneself and make it one's own."[13]

The same Menahem Mendel figures in several legends as one whose
silence enabled him and those who entered into dialogue with him to
experience the extraordinary silence that precedes thought and creation:
"Once Rabbi Menahem Mendel spent an entire night in the company
of his Hasidim. No one spoke, but all were filled with great reverence
and experienced great elation. Finally the rabbi said: 'Happy is the Jew
who knows that "one" (*echad*) means "one"!' "[14] To know that "one"
means "one" indicates an immediacy of understanding that is difficult
to justify in simple philosophical discourse as description of verifiable
fact. It implies knowledge of the indivisible oneness of unity that the

Hebrew tradition transmits through the generations (the Hebrew word for "unity," *achdut,* derives from the word "one," *echad*).

For additional examples of paradoxical propositions difficult to express in the discursive, linear form of philosophical presentation, yet amenable to Hasidic legend, we may consider the following interpretations of esoteric meanings associated with biblical verses:

> Rabbi Menahem Mendel once commented on the verse in the Scriptures: "For God hath heard the voice of the lad" (*Genesis* 21:17). He explained it in this way: "Nothing in the preceding verses indicates that Ishmael cried out. No, *it was a soundless cry* and God heard it."
>
> On another occasion he discussed the Scriptural verse that describes Pharaoh's daughter in these words: "And she opened it, *and saw . . . a boy that wept*" (*Exodus* 2:6). "What we should expect to be told," said he, "is that she *heard* the child Moses weeping. But the child was weeping inside himself. That is why we subsequently find these words: "and (she) said: This is one of the Hebrews' children." It was the Jewish kind of weeping. [When asked what constitutes a true Jew, he responded:] "Three things are fitting for us: *upright kneeling, silent screaming, motionless dance.*"[15]

These stories contain a mixture of metaphors unacceptable in systematic scholarly writing or in the kind of philosophical discourse that considers logical, systematic thought structures a sine qua non of exposition. Yet these metaphors are necessary for the communication of paradoxical propositions (to hear silence, to see a voice, to scream silently, to dance motionlessly) in a literary form amenable to such perspectives. Contemplation of paradox is as integral to philosophizing as are statements that constitute a paradox's apparent resolution. In the Hasidic legend, Buber found a form congenial to the arousing of such philosophical experience.

The role of Hasidic legend as indirect support for Buber's alternative philosophical perspective—that which grounds the "I" in a prelinguistic, prethought foundation of unmediated relation to being—is given explicit form in the following final illustration:

> The Maggid of Mezeritch said: "Nothing in the world can change from one reality into another, unless it first turns into nothing, that is, into the reality of the between-stage. In that stage it is nothingness and no one can grasp it, for it has reached the rung of nothingness,

just as before creation. And then a new creature is created, from the egg to the chick. The moment when the egg is no more and the chick is not yet, is nothingness. And philosophy terms this 'the primal state which no one can grasp' because it is a force which precedes creation; it is called chaos. It is the same with the sprouting seed. It does not begin to sprout until the seed disintegrates in the earth and the quality of seed-dom is destroyed in order that it may attain to nothingness which is the rung before creation. And this rung is called wisdom, that is to say, a thought that is not yet part of revelation. Then this thought gives rise to creation, as is written: 'In wisdom hast Thou made them all.' "[16]

In this tale, we read of the in-betweenness that cannot be described yet constitutes a key to understanding the origin of everything in a still nothingness. This story indirectly illustrates Buber's propositions about the quality of the perception that precedes thought. In this tale, wisdom is presented as an embryonic thought, an understanding that has not been granted communicative form, a thought "that is not yet part of revelation." We also read in this tale an allusion to early Greek philosophy, perhaps to Anaxagoras' definition of the primal state as chaos that persisted prior to the intervention of *nous*.

The philosophical meaning that Buber wishes to transmit through this particular Hasidic legend echoes the philosophy of Heraclitus. As pointed out by Paul Mendes-Flohr, there is an affinity between Buber's call to hear the eternal voice and Heraclitus' call to listen to the eternal Logos.[17] This proposition is substantiated by a reading of fragments 1 and 50, in which Heraclitus is credited with the saying: "Not after listening to me but after listening to the account (*logos*), one does wisely in agreeing that all things are [in fact] one [thing]."[18]

Buber's affinity to pre-Platonic philosophy (and hence to pre*system-atic* philosophy) may be augmented by an additional feature common to Heraclitus and Buber, explicitly referred to by Buber himself. Heraclitus writes that "one thing, the only wise thing, is unwilling and willing to be called by the name of Zeus."[19] Reading this along the lines indicated by Buber, we may interpret it as a suggestion that naming comes after perception. Hence Heraclitus' reference to Zeus's discomfort with being named. Like Buber, Heraclitus' Zeus is not sure what will happen to the mind that names: Will it become enamored of this capacity and consequently forget the reality that the name represents? Will the reality "Zeus" remain a living presence in the experience of the namer? According to Diogenes Laertius, Heraclitus feared that thinking would turn from a blessing into a source of misfortune: "thinking is an instance of the sacred disease and . . . sight is deceptive."[20] In Buber's analysis, such Heraclitean questioning is absent in mainstream modern philosophy; objectification has replaced the meeting, and today—in particular in the postmodern (and post-Buber) "present"—one encounters thought and words, not the reality that precedes them.

The unconventional nature of this analysis is evident from a brief examination of Leo Strauss's critique of Buber's way of philosophizing. In contrast to the relation to being indicated by Buber's dialogical philosophy, Strauss prefers (what he calls) the reductionist attitude of traditional philosophy and its modest acceptance of the limits of human relation. In Strauss's reading, Greek philosophy assumes that the eternal elements of existence "cannot be experienced by man, by the whole man, but only be inferred or thought by him."[21] Strauss thus assumes that contemplation is an activity of thought and that discussions of experiences that apparently precede thought are—ultimately—constructs of thought. Such discussions are thoughts about a prethought relation to eternal elements of being. Like Descartes, Strauss ends up assuming that we cannot relate to truth without the mediation of thought, an activity that he identifies with contemplation.

This preference for Greek philosophy is present in the background of Strauss's critique of Buber's philosophy of dialogue:

> The phenomenon which is now called the I–Thou–We relation was known to the classics by the name of friendship. When speaking to a friend I address him in the second person. But philosophic or scientific analysis is not speaking to a friend, i.e., to this individual here and now, but speaking to anyone concerned with such analysis. . . . When speaking about someone with whom I have a close relation I call him my friend. I do not call him my Thou. . . . By speaking of "the Thou" instead of "the friend," I am trying to preserve in objective speech what cannot be preserved in objective speech; I am trying to objectify something that is incapable of being objectified. I am trying to preserve in "speaking about" what can be actual only in "speaking to." Hence I do injustice to the phenomena; I am untrue to the phenomena; I miss the concrete. While attempting to lay a foundation for

genuine human communication, I preserve an incapacity for genuine human communication.[22]

In short, Strauss considers Buber's philosophy of dialogue (I–You) to be a poor substitute for classical Aristotelian philosophy, because the former is, ultimately, an objectification that replaces "concrete" relationships. This reading is extremely ironical when we consider the conclusions of the present analysis, which suggests that Buber's philosophical work is a multilayered attack on the tendency of the mind to objectify and then relate to the abstract thought as if[23] it were a real entity, a position that Strauss attributes to Buber's philosophy. Strauss's critique stems from his considering unauthentic the "addressing" element of the I-You relation.

In his own text, Strauss's reference to Buber seems to be detached from the surrounding context, for after the paragraphs cited above, he turns to Plato's *Laws*, never to return to Buber and this motif. However, this turn to the *Laws* is a return to the Athenian Stranger, whom Strauss praises as one who (realistically?) tries to demonstrate the existence of the final salvation and security.[24] The Athenian Stranger is thus a contrast to Buber's "I–Thou–We." Strauss's turn to the Stranger reflects his preference for sincere attempts to demonstrate the existence of ultimate being over discourse regarding its experience. This is in diametrical opposition to Buber's perspective, articulated succinctly in the wry comment "To the man who is no longer able to meet yet is able as ever to think, the only possible religious question is whether man can ascertain the existence of the Gods."[25] I believe that this quote would reflect Buber's response to Strauss's critique.

Let us conclude the discussion of Buber's use of Hasidic lore to indirectly convey philosophical understanding by reading a short legend that communicates the silent, yet eloquent, experience of presence, the experience that precedes learned discourse: "Rabbi Leib, son of Sarah, the hidden *zaddik* who wandered over the earth, following the course of rivers, in order to redeem the souls of the living and the dead, said this: 'I did not go to the Maggid in order to hear Torah from him, but to see how he unlaces his felt shoes and laces them up again.' "[26] The meeting between the "hidden *zaddik*" and the great teacher, the Maggid, is based on direct relation: the anecdote seeks to emphasize deeds, not words. In these deeds, we discern not only the Maggid's act of tying shoelaces but also the relation between the one who ties and the *zaddik* who silently observes. The dialogical moment occurs in the meeting of the two, in a relation that transcends separation.

## THE ORIGIN OF THOUGHT, SPEECH, AND TEXT IN A PRELINGUISTIC RELATION TO BEING

Our examination of selected Hasidic legends has demonstrated Buber's conviction that a form of philosophizing that considers thinking the ground of being is *fundamentally* flawed because it lacks the concrete relation to reality that is prior to the activity of thought.[27] This belief does not negate the observation that for all practical purposes, we do create self, culture, and society as extensions of our thoughts. The problem with this (modern) ontology is not that it is a wrong representation of reality but simply that it is incomplete. Just as the black letters of the Hasidic tale dominate perception and blind one to their white background, so do our mental structures exist within us as if they were the background of our being. However, in Buber's philosophical writings, we read that contrary to prevailing conceptions of self as an entity grounded in its thought-world ("I think, therefore I am"), mental structures are the "black script" of self; they are inseparable from their "white background." Were we attentive to their background and to the experiential origins of the arising of thought, we would not deplete so much energy in retaining these structures intact after they have fulfilled their limited (and absolutely necessary) communicative function.

We may extract Buber's final insight regarding the origins of the spoken word from a reading of one of his later essays, "The Word That Is Spoken," first published in 1960. Part of Buber's philosophical expositions, this essay can be read as an attempt to grant discursive form to insights communicated indirectly in Buber's Hasidic and biblical writings. In this essay, we read that the origin of language is in a first, primal form of relation, where the movement of attention is wordless. (The Hebrew word for "attention," *tsoomet lev*, literally means "that which is placed into the heart.") Initially, before striving towards language, the movement of attention "wander[s] without meeting a word."[28] The body, perceived to be an organ endowed with the potential to be aware and attentive, activates its linguistic potential only *after* the event that merits articulation. Thought and words are preceded by the body's awareness of, and relation to, the situation; the silent movement of attention becomes word when it crosses an invisible boundary beyond which are thought, words, and speech. This invisible boundary is called "language" (*safah*).

The intriguing nature of language in its Hebrew meaning (as *safah*) is worthy of particular attention. In Hebrew, the word *safah* means "language" as a generic term; a particular language, such as French or English, is called *lashon* (tongue). In ordinary language, *safah* may also denote an invisible boundary. For example, the seashore, the transition from sea to land, is called *sfat-yam* in Hebrew, representing the invisible place that is neither water nor sand. Similarly, the area where a tabletop encounters the open space surrounding it is called *sfat-shulhan*. The word *safah*, then, points to the demarcation of an edge of one form of substance and the beginning of another. Considering language in these terms, we see that in its elemental condition, language exists essentially as an indication of an invisible transition, a boundary that delineates a change of form so striking that it is rarely perceived as a transition; noting the separate substances, one rarely contemplates the nature of the invisible place that is neither one nor the other.

Returning to Buber's propositions concerning the origin of language, language marks the transition from *perception* of reality to *communication* of perception. That, perhaps, is the background for the Hebrew tongue's reference to the lip as *safah* and to both lips, which serve as the body's gate to speech, as *sfatayim*. Keep the *sfatayim* closed and the tongue (*lashon*) remains inactive; open the lips and the tongue is released. Like the transition from water to sand, the transition from perception to communication occurs in the movement from one side of *safah* to the other.

Buber writes that "striving toward language," toward communication of unmediated (i.e., unmediated by thought) perception, is an expression of a person's desire to "come into being," to relate to another. This gives rise to a movement away from the original attention and creates a "second stage"[29] *of relation to reality*. We may note in passing an implicit assumption: a person is a being who desires to share insight, to become him- or herself in relation to like-minded beings. It appears that for Buber, this desire is basic to human nature, creating the transitional stage from wordless relation to the emergence of language in the third stage of the schema implied in his presentation.

Buber writes that the "third stage" is the entry to "the true level of language." Here, language arises to fulfill the desire awakened in the second, intermediary stage. Thought turns to memory, words are chosen, and the conditions for communicating understanding are set. Language is still "soundless" (as it arises "within" the person) but "already recognizably spoken" in the sense that the nameless other, for whom language is formed, is so far an invisible presence, a catalyst that awakens the desire to be understood.[30] Returning to the seashore metaphor, the substance of relation changes from wordless attention to verbal, spoken communication. The transition is invisible, but it takes place nonetheless.

Together, the second and third stages of the emergence of language (not as invisible boundary but as *lashon*, "tongue") prepare the words that will enable communication with an other. Attention to this process reveals that language is a temporary distancing from relation that arises in the service of relation.[31] In fact, language exist not in itself but rather, so to speak, in a permanent state of temporariness, fluid and changing. Hence the inherent ambiguity of words and the need for constant attention to the exact use of a given word and its meaning in a particular, specific context. (In this respect, Buber's description of language anticipates and accommodates the sensitivities of Wittgenstein and his followers.) Language designates the ontological distance between the words communicated and the sight that gave rise to the communication. It indicates the understanding *seen* in the original relation, an understanding that is wordless and unmediated by the vehicle of language, thought.

The existential origin and function of the spoken word, of speech, thus lie in the original wordless relation. Thought, language, and words are used to relate the understanding of that which was *seen*; speech is the expression of that process. Speech thus used is a unique characteristic of human beings, setting them apart from other created beings.

Our presentation of the origins of language (as both *safah* and *lashon*) depicts a separation of consciousness into two distinct streams. These two streams originate in the two separated movements of attention that are on either side of the boundary for which language serves as an indicator. On one side of the boundary is the wordless fluid attention that observes and receives without comment; on the other side is the intricate structure of thoughts, held together by focused, entrapped attention. On the prelinguistic side of the boundary created by language is "natural Adam," who is part of the timeless order created out of the primal unity;[32] on the other side, where language emerges as a form of communication, is "historical Adam," a "coming-to-be"[33] that creates the world of time and of differentiated "order."[34] Both sides of Adam exist in every individual. This, in Buber's words, is "the double nature of Adam." This analysis helps us to fathom Buber's assertion that "the mystery of the coming-to-be of language and that of the coming-to-be of Adam are one."[35]

In sum, we read that on one side of the "boundary" of *safah* is a prelinguistic form of relation and on the other are modes of description, articulation, and spoken communication. The origins of *safah* in formless insight precede its form as thought; thought arises on the far side of *safah*, serving as an image of the original understanding, as a mode of communicating a prelinguistic relation to being. As explained below, Buber regards the crisis of humanity in the twentieth century as a reflection of the human subject's forgetting of the existential origin of thought, which results in misunderstanding of the origin and foundation of being.

## DIALOGICAL PHILOSOPHY AS A CRITIQUE OF "I THINK, THEREFORE I AM"

Many philosophers have argued that any philosophy worthy of attention must propose reformed conduct that leads to a new condition of self and that includes as its principal benefit the capacity to see and know the world more truly *as it is*. Stated differently, any meaningful philosophy seeks to effect self-transformation that enables the world to be experienced in a new, more intelligent way than that experienced ordinarily and unreflectively.[36] The root impulse of such a philosophy is an unresolved contradiction in the spirit of a single human being, whose particular experience is relevant to all human beings because it stems from the chaos of human existence, not only of his individual life. Robert Cushman addressed this dimension of philosophy succinctly: "As called forth by a destructive distortion in human life and experience, philosophy offers itself as a therapy. But it begins with diagnosis, and only thereafter supplies its distinctive method of release and transformation."[37]

Buber's writings adhere to these understandings of the purpose and function of philosophy. However, his philosophy is unusual because its diagnostic dimension includes a fundamental challenge to the practices of what is usually referred to in modern culture as philosophical activity, that is, the articulation of a coherent structure of well-ordered thoughts that support or expand a fundamental ethical premise or proposition. Accordingly, Buber's method of philosophizing may be considered "anarchical" (compared with common practice) because it challenges the assumption that well-structured thinking is an authoritative source of understanding. This proposition may be clarified by a more focused discussion of Buber's critique of Descartes, providing an example of Buber's use of Western philosophical discourse to undermine the most fundamental ontological and epistemic premises of that tradition of thought. Similar to his critique of Jesus and of Spinoza, Buber's critique of Descartes is actually a critique of the influence Descartes had; Buber's primary concern is with the way Descartes was used to justify using reason in the service of the self-adulating modern subject. We now turn to the analysis that gives rise to this understanding of the incomplete nature of Cartesian notions of self.[38]

In Buber's reading, *ego cogito* means to Descartes not simply "I have consciousness" but "It is I who have consciousness." Understood as such, *ego cogito* therefore ends up identifying the foundation of one's existence with an "I" that is the abstract and abstracting subject of consciousness.[39] Buber refers to this as a triple abstraction. It seems that what he means is as follows: First, I say that the only sure proof of my existence is my certainty regarding the fact that I think. Then I say to myself (I think . . . ) that if I think—and I am certain that thinking is real—then I am. Finally, I conclude that since I know that I am only through the experience of my thinking, "I" (as self) am first of all a thinking being. Turning to Descartes's writings (one of Buber's weaknesses as a philosopher is lack of reference to the sources he critiques), we read that "thought is an attribute that belongs to me; it alone is inseparable from my nature." Descartes concludes that he is "only a thinking being, that is to say, a mind, an understanding, or a reasoning being . . ."[40] Therefore, his certainty, articulated in the form of the first principle of his philosophy, is "I think, therefore I am (or exist)."[41]

Now, Buber must have known that Descartes was deeply concerned with the question of the source of thinking, of that experience that granted him certainty. That is why Descartes ended up assuming that there was an idea of God in the background of his thinking.[42] However, Descartes's recurring attempts to relate his philosophy to the idea of God are absent from Buber's writings about Descartes's influence. It seems that the reason for this apparent oversight is to be found in Buber's intention. He sought to address Descartes's influence, the way Descartes was (perhaps incompletely) understood, and not to directly analyze Descartes's texts as self-contained bodies of knowledge. As with Buber's discussion of Spinoza's influence on Western philosophy, Buber's writings on Descartes attempt to deal with the conventional misinterpretations Buber encountered when examining the justifications that ground contemporary ontology. It is the partial readings of past meditations that have been the source of increasingly erroneous and misguided interpretations of serious thinkers.[43] It is this ignorance, in its present form, that Buber addresses. Hence his critique of Descartes addresses base interpretations of that great philosopher, without alluding to the fact that Descartes could not philosophize without the idea of God as a necessary first cause for the existence of thought.

Considering this interpretation of Descartes in the context of Buber's propositions regarding the origins of thought in insight, we may articulate Buber's critique in the following terms: Enamored of the power of its own thought, the thinking subject ("I") traps the original attention in the structures of thought that were intended initially as a temporary representation of reality, a representation that arose in the service of interpersonal communication. The intricate complex of structures of thought, of trapped attention, becomes a self-reflecting thinking subject—"I." This subject, considering itself solely in terms of the thoughts it has about itself, is oblivious to the origins of its self-referential thoughts in the primal relation of attention to what is.

The ability of thought to abstract and objectify is a source of the modern subject's strengths and weaknesses alike. On the one hand, the subject's apparently boundless objectification potential is beneficial to human life because it creates progressively elaborate ways of interpersonal communication concerning the reality abstracted in thought. Used in this manner, thought supports the aforementioned innate desire to communicate perception and to become active and creative in relation to reality. On the other hand, the ability to objectify weakens human beings when the evident effects of the objectifying power of thought (for example, the ability to develop technological innovations or to influence the psychological condition of other persons) cause the thinking subject to identify with the sensation of thought as though thought it-self—and its sensation—were the source of existence. This is the funda-mental error of modern anthropology, ontology, and epistemology: instead of addressing thought as a tool to be used when necessary and put aside otherwise, the modern subject has identified with thought as if it were existence itself. Accordingly, to be empty of thought is associated with not being; if "I" does not think, "I" does not exist. Proceeding in this direction, much of modern philosophy has overlooked the simple fact that thought is merely a mode of communication, to be activated in service of insight. Moreover, as thought is not reality, it cannot be a proof of one's existence, unless one adheres to a philosophy that claims that nothing is real and hence one form of self-illusion is as good as another. This perspective is clearly unacceptable to a thinker such as Buber.

This interpretation of Buber's latent intentions may assist readers in their attempt to make sense of the following remarks of Buber:

> The world, as objective and self-contained connection of all being, natural and spiritual, would not exist for us if our thinking, which develops in our philosophizing, did not melt together the sensations that come to us from the world. It would not exist for us if our think-ing did not merge these sensations of the world with one another and with all that man has ever experienced and has ever comprehended as experiencable. . . . Only through the fact that philosophy radically abandoned the relation with the concrete did that amazing construc-tion of an objective thought-continuum become possible, with a static system of concepts and a dynamic one of problems. Every person who can "think" may enter this continuum through the simple use of this ability, through a thinking comprehension of thought. . . . A content of being is objectively communicable and translatable only through philosophy, consequently only through the objectifying elaboration of the situation.[44]

The above passage indicates that the problem of the modern subject is not the development of the objectifying capacity of thought per se, but rather the forgetting of the original relation to being that preceded the objectifying movement. The original relation is genuine; the abstraction is not. Hence, philosophy fulfills its function as long as the thinking subject remembers the original relation and insight. In the words of Buber: "Systems of thought are manifestations of genuine thought-relations to being made possible through abstraction. . . . [However,] thinking overruns and overwhelms all the faculties and provinces of the person. In a great act of philosophizing even the finger-tips think—but they no longer touch."[45]

"I" exists as a mechanical system of responses, largely predetermined by the particular formation of self as one particular configuration of thought-clusters or another. It is unaware of the mechanical, reactive nature of thought or of the barrier erected by thought between self and the world:

> Each and every one of us is encrusted in an armor. . . . All orders of science promise us: "Be still, all that takes place occurs according to the proper way, is necessary, but is not directed at you. . . ." Every one of us is encased in an armor that we almost do not feel because of habit. There are only fleeting moments that penetrate the armor and urge the soul to accept.[46]

The "armor" metaphor refers to clusters of thought that organize events in ways that correspond to predetermined patterns held together within these clusters. The "I" loses sight of the immediacy and singularity of relation to the event, a relation that in itself is not part of any single pattern. Modern philosophy reflects this development; philosophizing in its modern sense means making the world conceptually comprehensible, an object of thought. However, in the process of contemplation, a tragic misunderstanding occurs. The contemplating subject, "which appeared to be joined to being in order to perform for it the service of contemplation, declares that it itself produced and produces being."[47] As a result, the self-enclosed subject meets the world from within its self-encasement, an ontological "armor" comprising an intricate web of tightly held thought structures.

Enamored of the sensation accompanying the thought "I think, therefore I am," modern philosophy has developed an anthropology that considers "human nature" in terms of a self-reflective subject that constitutes the objectifying structure of thought.[48] It follows that the culture of modernity is an ongoing edification predicated on this misunderstanding. This mechanical way of relating to being is what Buber seems to refer to when writing that "the sequential and distorted system that forces all that takes place to become part of it, is the gigantic project of humanity. Even language has come to serve it."[49] Considered in light of his critique, the goal of a renewed philosophy adequate to the needs of the modern subject should have been to lead the subject to see the misguided self-conception that conditions his relation to self and to being. However, that development did not transpire. Hence Buber's alternative perspective.

In Buber's eyes, having established itself as the source of its own being, the modern subject continues to develop according to its inner logic:

> The next step already takes us to the stage in development familiar to us, the stage that understands itself as the final one and plays with its finality: the human spirit, which adjudges to itself mastery over its work, annihilates conceptually absoluteness and the absolute. . . .[50] The spirit as an independent essence cannot exist anymore; from now exists only what is called "spirit," and it is the product of human individuals, who hold onto and secrete spirit like mucus and urine, and are destined to "release" it—with all its weighty actuality—in the hour of their dying (if it has not devoured them prior to that).[51]

In a life thus formed, only death releases thought. Following the logic of Buber's presentation of the origins of language, this comment implies that in a "self" grounded in thought, only death enables the release of entrapped attention. The energy that should have been released intentionally, through the meeting of Adam with *Elohim*, is released mechanically with the moment of death. Buber articulates this premise through a mixture of religious and anatomical metaphors: "Only at this stage does the release-in-thought of *Elohim* take place, because only now philosophy cuts off its own hands, the hands that enabled her to catch and hold onto him."[52] The "hands" in the above passage refer to the subjects' (mis)understanding that the "spirit" exists only as a product of thought; in fact, the "spirit" is entrapped in thought. When thought dies, the "spirit" is released.

The claim regarding the heart of Buber's philosophizing—the paradoxical distancing of self from the foundation of its being through the misplaced identification of self as thought (or as the images associated with and sustained by thought)—is buttressed by Buber's description of a meeting between two persons who have forgotten the ground of "life as it is." The following passage illustrates the comic, yet tragic, state of interpersonal relationships in a culture that adores and therefore sustains and nurtures a self who lives and acts "according to the image" (the distinction between "life as it is" and "life according to the image" is emphasized in the original Hebrew version of the 1953 essay from which the passage is taken; unfortunately, the translator into English did not sufficiently emphasize the distinction). Buber describes such a meeting as follows:

> Let us imagine two persons, Reuven and Shimeon [who live accord-ing to their images]. They are sitting one alongside the other and are speaking with one another. Let us count the number of faces who are acting in this play. First, here is Reuven as he wishes to be seen in the eyes of Shimeon, and Shimeon as he wishes to be seen in the eyes of Reuven. Next, Reuven as he really seems in the eyes of Shimeon—that is, the image of Reuven in the eyes of Shimeon, which is usually not the image preferred by Reuven—and vice versa. Add to these Reuven as he seems to himself and Shimeon as he seems to himself, and finally Reuven with all his sense organs and Shimeon with all of his sense organs. Two live beings [who meet through] six imaginary images, a ghostly audience that very often intervenes and interferes in the conversation![53]

This passage illustrates the proposition that the modern subject not only is forgetful of the ground of its existence but is even unable to effect a consistent projection of the image it has adopted as the "real I."

Having established the indirect link between Buber's critique of the Cartesian "I think, therefore I am" and his other forms of writing—the Hasidic legend and the biblical guiding verse—we return to our point of departure, his critique of contemporary philosophical discourse. It appears that for Buber, Descartes's "I think, therefore I am" represents the modern version of the original error of judgment that characterized Adam. In the modern subject's turn toward thought as the ground and end of its own being, Buber discerns a contemporary twist on Adam's misguided attempt to turn to knowledge of good and evil in a context that is incommensurate with the uses and intended functions of that form of knowing. It is the modern form of the ignorance of "historical

Adam" that in this age constitutes the obstruction between sincere desire to know being and the actual ability to experience this quality of knowledge.

## DIALOGUE

We can now summarize Buber's notion of dialogue with appropriate sensitivity to its unique and paradoxical nature. The dialogue of the person who is open to an I–You relation is not necessarily spoken, although it includes speech. It may transpire as silence, as a release of the spell of thought. In the words of Buber: "The lifting of the spell has happened to him—no matter from where—without his doing. But this is what he does now: he releases in himself a reserve over which only he has power. Unreservedly communication streams from him, and the silence bears it to his neighbor."[54]

Dialogue may exist in three distinct forms: "genuine," "technical," and "monologue disguised as dialogue." It is *genuine* when each of the participants "has in mind the other or others in their present and particular being and turns to them with the intention of establishing a living mutual relation between himself and them." Dialogue is *technical* when "prompted solely by the need of objective understanding," that is, by the need to understand the object that is present as the focal point of the meeting. *Monologue*, a distortion of dialogue, is the characteristic of most speech. When conversations occur, we tend to refer to them as "dialogue" merely because two or more persons are conversing. Yet to consider any exchange of words or one's inner chatter as "dialogue" is wrongheaded; in Buber's parlance, this is "monologue disguised as dialogue."[55]

Considered on a communal scale, the most dangerous manifestations of "monologue disguised as dialogue" are those that further the ideology (or dogma) of a party (or sect) or of the state (or a centralized religious institution).[56] These perversions of dialogue are particularly troubling because they serve as justifications for violence and abuse of power in the name of "higher" purposes. Their power stems from manipulations by those who are aware of the fact that people take their thoughts all too seriously, as if their entire being is to be dedicated to the perpetuation of the contents of thought. The meeting between organized power (be it of the state or of religious institutions) and the gullible individual is possible because it is embedded in a form of life that attributes more importance to thoughts than to the facts that give rise to the inner reaction we experience as thoughts—more importance to thoughts than to what actually is. Because "monologue disguised as dialogue" is so commonplace, most people cannot imagine (or envision) an existence that is in true dialogue, quietly attentive to facts, utilizing thoughts and words only when needed to communicate to others the facts observed and the deeds to be done.

In contrast to the prevailing, reactive order of self, the fundamental fact of a dialogical person is presence: presence to what is, presence to the other without negating presence of self, presence to the inner voice(s) without excluding the voice(s) that are addressed from without. The key to a dialogical presence is awareness. Accordingly, "the limits of the possibility of dialogue are the limits of awareness."[57] The more unencumbered the awareness, the less entrapped it is in the service of holding thought-clusters together and the greater is the person's ability to face the concreteness of the immediate situation. In a nutshell, in a dialogical presence there is attention to all voices, an attention that is in dialogue because it is capable of listening, of inclusion. It does not privilege the voice of self over the voice of other selves. (But this comment by no means implies suspension of judgment regarding what is seen and heard! On the contrary, such presence enables more accurate responses to what the situation entails.) The dialogical person experiences reality (including relationships) from a place that silently listens. Attention flows from him or her and creates in the sphere of the interpersonal that quality referred to in Buber's philosophy as the Between.

## DIALOGUE AND THE "HEART" OF BIBLICAL DISCOURSE

Let us turn now to a brief consideration of the way guiding words familiar to us from our study of Buber's biblical writings constitute links that connect his disparate writings. The implicit connection between Buber's biblical and philosophical discourse hinges on attention to the crucial role of guiding words. In the following reading of one of Buber's philosophical essays, the key word that connects philosophical and biblical insight is *lev* (heart). Having encountered the use that Buber makes of "heart" in his opening of the prophetic writings, we know that this word conveys multiple associations, meanings that reveal themselves in direct relation to the reader's conscious efforts.

In 1953 Buber wrote (in Hebrew) an essay titled "The Elements of the Interhuman" (יסודותיו של הבין אנושי), an exposition of his philosophy of dialogue. In the four-page concluding section of that essay, called "The Conversation (or 'Dialogue') in its Actuality" (השיחה כהווייתה)[58] Buber uses the word *lev* thirteen times, in diverse forms. The heart of this section consists of the following lines:

> I must attend to the fact that what is in my *lev* at this moment—but which as yet is not granted the form of language (as *lashon*, "tongue")—I shall raise to the inner word and after that to the spoken word. Utterance is nature and human activity as one, safeguarded and created as one, and must forever renew the unity of the two wherever [such renewal] is dialogical and appears in the enlivened place of the great faithfulness.[59]

In this passage, Buber concisely encapsulates the understanding of language we encountered in his essay "The Word That Is Spoken."[60] When manifested in spoken form, true dialogue utilizes speech to convey the insight that precedes language. First, there is the silent knowing of the heart. When an opportunity for dialogue with another appears, the silent knowing "rises" to words, moving into the area of *safah* (language). Then, after finding the precise words to be uttered, the tongue (*lashon*) releases them. The knowing of the heart is both eternal (in the sense that one does not invent something new through language but rather renders what is present in linguistic form) and creative (in the sense that the speaker must be creative in the choice of words that bridge the distance between the eternal and the temporal).

The "heart" is thus a metaphor for direct address to the immediate situation, without premeditated thought or utterance: "In a dialogue as it truly is," writes Buber, "the turning toward the other conversant occurs in all truthfulness; that is, it is an address of the heart." Each participant in such a conversation "must be ready in his heart always to say that which is in his heart." Of course, the ability to speak what is in one's heart demands attention to this part of one's being. If one does not speak from the heart, one may consider conversation an opportunity to aggrandize one's own self-importance. In such situations, dialogue does not come into being. In the words of Buber:

> If instead of turning to the word that I must utter, I intend to draw attention to the importance of my "I," I have damaged beyond repair my intention to say what I was to have uttered. The word enters the conversation in a faulty way and hence the conversation itself is faulty, because conversation is essentially an ontological sphere, which builds and expands on the reliability of the present, of what actually is. [Every eruption of appearance that comes instead of truth may disrupt dialogue.][61]

This intricate web of intention and meaning is lost in the English translation by Ronald Gregor Smith. *Lev*, which serves as a key word for this essay, and leads to the passage cited above, is translated only once as "heart." In other instances, it is translated in various ways that are inattentive to Buber's hermeneutics, creating misleading alternatives. Smith employs the expressions "a turning of the being" (instead of "an address of the heart"); "he must be willing on each occasion to say what is really in his mind" (rather than "he must be ready in his heart always to say that which is in his heart"); "I must not keep it back, keep it in myself" (rather than "I must not repress it in my heart"); "we wanted to discuss together how the catastrophe, which we all believed was imminent, could be avoided" (rather than "we intended to discuss in common how to prevent the approaching catastrophe prophesied by the heart"). *Da'at halev* (the knowledge of the heart) is translated as "becoming aware." These examples are not mere quibbles; they demonstrate that the English translation, while retaining some sense of the original meaning, deprives the reader of the hermeneutic relation to the heart as the place that is open to direct reception of "signs."[62]

The diagnosis in the background of Buber's articulation of his therapeutic philosophy of dialogue dovetails perfectly with his understanding of the nature of the rationale underpinning the hidden hermeneutics of the Hebrew Bible. Stated simply, Buber's claim is this: Modern philosophy grants an epistemological and ontological rationale for a form of life (Wittgenstein's term, not Buber's) that does not allow the individual to sense being unless it is mediated by thought and the self-images that thought sustains. Thus, thought has become the primary ground and sensation of existence, and other sensations are discarded as irrational or irrelevant unless they are granted place in the order constructed by thought. Accordingly, in terms of the "hidden history" initiated by the Hebrew prophets, the "thought" that prevents "relation to being" in Buber's philosophical discourse is analogous to the "seal" covering the "heart" of his biblical discourse. Both represent barriers to a quality of refined relation to being that must be released through conscious intention and effort.

## WRITING ABOUT PHILOSOPHY (AND ABOUT ELOHIM) IN SCHOLARLY PROSE

We now turn to Buber's critique of other philosophers, focusing on the cognitive barrier that Buber claims conventional philosophizing has created between the person and the self and between the person and the reality presented in symbolic form in the word "Elohim." This final section thus refers discussion of Buber's philosophy back to his direct writings on the subject, with particular attention to his use of the word "Elohim." In this latter form of discourse, Buber develops an apparently surprising conclusion: the need to remove the word "God" from philosophical works. Paradoxical as this suggestion may seem, it is shown to be commensurate with the insight and goals of all Buber's writings, whether dealing with philosophy or other subjects.

Considering the path the discussion has followed until now, including examination of Buber's writings on biblical interpretation, one might very well ask why we do not state straightforwardly that the silent voice of the prelinguistic relation to being is the voice of "Elohim." A cursory review of Buber's prolific writings may indeed tempt one to signify the silent voice with the word "Elohim," usually translated as "God."[63] But that reply is inadequate. The reader need only examine his or her reaction to this possibility to realize how conditioned we are in our relation to mention of "God." This word, perhaps more than any other, has lost its original power as the expression of a reality that it claims to represent.[64] Buber *does* mention the word "God" frequently in his philosophical works, but the most frequent context concerns the problematics of its use, particularly in philosophical and political discourse.

Consequently, to understand why the word "God" is meaningless as an indication of the original voice, one may examine Buber's critique of its use in the writings of other philosophers.[65] In this sphere of discourse, Buber uses the word "God" to negate its (mis)use in the works of others. Underlying this enterprise is the assumption that most of modern philosophy is an ongoing construction of conceptual structures within which ideas gain meaning. *Implicit* in Buber's critique of many philosophers' use of "God" is their unexamined assumption that meaning is created as part of the subject's experience of thinking.[66] Meaning is indeed created in the course of thinking, but is thinking the ground of being? Is meaning solely a matter of thoughts? Is there no experience of being, meaningful and significant, that is not grounded in thinking? Does language indeed originate in thought?

Citing numerous (mis)uses of the word "God"—as "a moral condition within us" (Kant), as "love in love with itself" (Hegel) and as "the center of all ideas, the idea of truth" (Herman Cohen)—Buber repeatedly concludes that for many modern philosophers, the word lacks grounding in experience of the unmediated reality that it seeks to communicate.[67] Hence, when such philosophers use the word, they replace the original reality with "the image of images, the idea."[68] Note Buber's careful choice of words. The "image of images" is a term that indirectly refers to the biblical command not to worship man-made idols and images.[69] By alluding to the language of the Book of Deuteronomy, Buber is indirectly suggesting that the Mosaic insistence on the danger of man-made images refers not only to material artifacts but also to the images and idols constructed in thought and in imagination.

The original biblical text is indeed open to such interpretation. In Deuteronomy 4:12, we read that the words that were spoken were sounds without form or image: "there was only a voice." To experience through images is to deprive the voice of its unmediated presence. Hence Moses' long discourse on images (Deuteronomy 4:1–40) which he delivered *before* he enumerated the Ten Commandments (Deuteronomy 5:6–21). Moses' tone is one of resignation to the fact that warnings[70] notwithstanding, the ability to hear the voice will be impaired because of misuse of thought and imagination in the service of goals foreign to their original telos ("you will serve gods of wood and stone, the work of men's hands, that neither see, nor hear, nor eat, nor smell"). Moses adds that the words he is transmitting will be present to those later generations to whom he addresses the following: "seek YHVH your Elohim, and . . . you will find him, if you search after him with all your heart and all your soul. When you are in tribulation, and all these things come upon you in the latter days, you will return to YHVH your Elohim and obey his voice" (Deuteronomy 4:29–30).

From this perspective, Buber's discourse on thought and words seems to echo that of Moses. Whether this is intentional or not, Buber clearly granted the biblical prohibition on worship of images a meaning relevant to what he considered to be the primary problem of the historical hour: worship of "the image of images, the idea." As such, impressive as its subjective articulation may seem, the use of "God" in most of modern philosophy does not exist outside of the world of ideas, that is, outside of the "inner monologue" between clusters of the thinking subject's multiple structures of thought.[71]

The obstructive presence of thought is the basis for Buber's well-known notion of "the eclipse of God." The eclipse of Elohim is like the eclipse of the sun; it takes place between objects, between poles of relation. Just as the solar eclipse occurs not in the sun or in the eye but rather as a result of the moon's intervention between the two, so too is the eclipse of Elohim from Adam a result of a barrier that comes between them—thought. Philosophy's fatal mistake, writes Buber, is its insistence on seeking and revealing the power that may unravel the mystery of the eclipse "from within the domain of earthly thought."[72]

At this point, Buber's discussion attains a surprising climax. He writes that even if a person rids himself of all ideology and apparent structures of thought, the veil of darkness may still exist in the form of the word Elohim. It is this word that stands between the person and what the word represents. In the words of Buber: "It is incumbent upon the human being to get rid also of the name Elohim, for it by necessity creates a relation based on an assumption of nearness."[73] The problem with the assumption of nearness is that it leads the subject to disregard the separation implied in "nearness." What is near may also be distant; in any event, it is separate.

Buber's philosophy of dialogue is thus grounded in the firm belief we encountered in a previous discussion, that Elohim and Adam are metaphors for a complex relation of mutual reciprocity, wherein Adam is a possibility that is adorned with a body and Elohim a place of renewal of being, a potential for renewal of self and world that becomes actuality when Adam overcomes the man-made barriers between self and Elohim. Hence Buber's concluding comment in the essay "The Eclipse of the Light of Elohim": "Although each epoch is a continuation of that which preceded it, each continuity may be either confirmation or rejection." In language strikingly similar to that used in his mention of the hidden history, Buber continues: "Something is occurring in the depths, which as yet should not be called by name. . . . It is possible that even tomorrow the thing will happen. . . . The light of Elohim has been eclipsed, but not turned off. It is possible that even tomorrow the barrier will be removed."[74] Expressed in terms that are not limited to biblical nomenclature, the barrier referred to is that of thought, the intermediary construct that prevents unmediated relation to being.

Through examination of Buber's quarrel with philosophy's use of "God," we encounter a more fundamental problem: the intrinsic subjectivity of *any* structure of thought that develops *within* a subject's "inner monologue." From this perspective, the use of "God" is but one instance of the way all ideas emerge as centers of clusters of interrelated thoughts that are inherently not present to what is. Thoughts cannot be present because thinking is of the past, is the past. Thinking (like texts) is a process that reorganizes preexisting thoughts into new clusters of association. Words and thoughts are drawn from the memory, which is a remembrance of what was. Hence the proposition regarding the nonpresent nature of thought that arises as a reaction or corrective to other thoughts. We continually change the organization of our thoughts because we continually confront events that call on us to interpret and grant meaning to them. Change the thought-cluster and you have changed meaning. Change meaning and "reality" is experienced in a different way. But all this takes place within thought, not as a direct experience of the event but rather after the event, as its "after-arising image." We attribute to such thought-cluster changes the sensation of "life." Some consider them a change of "self." Indeed, *if* sensation of self, of "I," is determined by the thoughts one retains about oneself and one's beliefs, *then* change of content may indeed be experienced by the subject as change of self.

Construction of a philosophical statement about the quality of the dialogical moment is elusive, as it attempts to communicate an invisible, yet very real, substance—a quality of in-betweenness that is recognized when it transpires yet cannot be recreated in thought or written word because of the inherently limited capacity of words to describe their origin. This difficulty is similar to the one Buber appears to have experienced in his characterization of the invisible nature of the reality indicated by the word *safah*. Accordingly, the use of indirect reference to transmit the sense of the original dialogical encounter in written form may have been Buber's response to the difficulty of justifying his perspective in clear philosophic parlance. This may be the ultimate explanation for Buber's resorting to allusion and indirect reference—for example, through the situations and comments included in his Hasidic legends—to present his philosophical insight.

The difficulties Buber encountered in granting his understanding coherent expression in strictly philosophical parlance are absent when he turns to reconstructing dialogical moments through the retelling of Hasidic tales. The dense and convoluted prose characteristic of his writings about the "philosophy of the interhuman"[75] stands in stark contrast to the simple and direct statements he presents in the form of Hasidic legends, particularly after having granted these legends their final Hebrew form in 1946.[76] In the Hasidic legends (including the classic *Gog Umagog*, considered by Gershom Scholem to be "the most personal of Buber's works about Hasidism"),[77] Buber seems to have found respite from the rigorous demands of academic discourse and systematic philosophy, forms of writing not easily amenable to the need to communicate the immediacy and simplicity of the dialogical moment.[78]

Indeed, Buber's philosophical writings are largely inaccessible to the average reader and not much more intelligible to expert philosophers. Why is this so when, after all, Buber uses such a light and airy style when recounting Hasidic tales and other stories? Some may blame the nature of scholarly discourse that requires attention to the works of others and thus obfuscates one's own statement. Others may suggest that Buber feared his findings would brand him a "mystic" and therefore unworthy of serious consideration in scholarly circles. There is an additional possibility that should not be ruled out: Buber's later writings, from the 1940s on, when he was over sixty years of age, reflect tension between increasing clarity and sincere perplexity regarding the implications of his insight. His philosophical and anthropological writings, twisting and turning about the question of language and the nature of interpersonal relationships, at times reflect refusal to accept the full consequences of his deepening perception of the origins of thought in a prelinguistic relation to being.[79] This latent ambiguity about the implications of Buber's insight is characteristic of the human condition that he addressed and sought to overcome.

What about relationships? Since the process of thought described above is considered characteristic of contemporary notions of self and self-knowledge, the possibility of mutual understanding is immediately understood to be no easy matter. The self, constituted by its thoughts, is an elusive entity, not always transparent to the thinker and certainly invisible to the other. When two or more subjects meet, they bring to the encounter the same mechanism: thought-clusters that may be at times fixed and rigid, at other times flexible and fluid. These thought-clusters support different images in different contexts, as is apparent in our earlier example of the meeting between Reuven, Shimeon, and their six images. To weaken the self-structure—to open oneself to the reality of self and of other in concrete situations—becomes the challenge of existence and hence of philosophy. Observation of the limits of thought raises fundamental and immediate questions of how we exist: How can we be present to ourselves and to an other, who faces us with precisely the same mechanism of thought, a mechanism that is intrinsically a reproduction of the past through rearrangement of thought-clusters? We all think and we all speak. What would it mean to think and speak from a place that is not thought, as suggested by the worldview that emerges from a close reading of Buber's dialogical philosophy? For such an experience to transpire, we need communal conditions conducive to the life of dialogue.

We therefore turn to Buber's theory of community.

## 6

# DIALOGICAL COMMUNITY: THE THIRD WAY BETWEEN INDIVIDUALISM AND COLLECTIVISM

B uber's attitude toward politics stemmed from his understanding of the need to radically transform the nature of the interpersonal. He was one of the first social thinkers in modern times to develop a critique of modernity based on the realization that our spiritual lack is no less acute than our economic lack. Like his teacher Simmel, he thought that growth in the quality of relationship is as important as material welfare and economic growth.[1] That is why he repeatedly returned to refining his early concept of *das Zwischenmenschliche* ("the Between," also imply-ing in this context "the interhuman") to convey a new understanding of the nature of the space created by human beings as a direct effect of the quality of their presence in relation to what is.[2] In Buber's words:

> On the far side of the subjective, on this side of the objective, on the narrow ridge, where *I* and *Thou* meet, there is the realm of "be-tween." This reality, whose disclosure has begun in our time, shows the way, leading beyond individualism and collectivism, for the life of future generations. Here the genuine third alternative is indicated, the knowledge of which will help to bring about the genuine person again and to establish genuine community.[3]

From the personal perspective, the Between is an effect of the opening of the person to dialogue, in its Buberian meaning: a lifting of the "spell of thought" and an enabling of the meeting of Adam and Elohim. From an institutional and structural perspective, the growth of the Between necessitates release of centralized state control over the development of community and society. Hence Buber's vision of a global, dialogical "community of communities" that would render obsolete the modern nation-state, its institutions, and its characteristic forms of relationship (power and domination). The ultimate pinnacle of Buber's social vision is thus a commonwealth of communities bound together by a common trust, a shared relation to the "eternal (and innate) You."[4]

While most studies of Buber's political and social thought focus on his political essays as communicators of his political and social philosophy,[5] the present chapter will continue to illustrate the importance of Buber's *non*political works as indirect communicators of his insight, this time in relation to community and its founding. This reading of Buber's intentions continues to emphasize his use of legends, myths, and symbols as vehicles for presenting society with a new paradigm for personal conduct and communal life. The legends, myths, and traditional symbols that Buber includes in his writings constitute the background for his writings that directly address social and political issues. Considered in this light, Buber may be best described as a political thinker whose primary vocation is the creation of social and political symbols and images.[6] This places Buber well within the tradition of Western political philosophy, where one finds many thinkers who, to borrow Eric Voegelin's terminology, reinterpret their societies' symbols in an attempt to redirect society's self-definition and consequently its self-illumination.[7]

Buber's political theory reflects his insight regarding the origin of language and of community: *when* in the course of addressing one another people are attentive to the pre-linguistic original relation to being (a presence that for Buber is the primal source of address), the interpersonal is *then* permeated by an I–You mode of existence. This constitutes a movement to relation and establishes in the interpersonal space the quality that Buber calls the Between.[8] The Between, then, belongs to the I–You relation.[9] It must be emphasized that (contrary to the critique voiced by Emmanuel Levinas)[10] the Between is not dependent on reciprocity or mutuality (although it creates conditions congenial to such relationships); it comes into being as an effect of presence, and presence is first of all a characteristic of a single person. That is why Buber attempts to foster the emergence of dialogical "living centers" of his ideal community by presenting his readers with images of such ideal persons that become historical metaphors for the reality he envisions.

The quality of social relationships is thus a direct effect of the quality of presence that materializes in a given situation. This quality cannot be institutionalized. People cannot be legislated into "relation," the word Buber uses to describe the Between ("relation" is the English translation of the German word *Beziehung*, and of the Hebrew word *zeeka*). However, social structures and cultural norms are the background conditions that either encourage the creation of the Between, or, conversely, impede the development of such a sphere of relation. In Buber's social theory, people who are attentive to the invisible, yet real, quality of the interhuman sphere of the Between are those whose presence he terms "dialogical." The significance of the Between in attainment of a fuller, inclusive relation to being may be clarified by addressing Buber's notion of the interpersonal as a substance serving as a conduit for interaction between separate spheres of being. The metaphor that comes to mind is that of electricity: to transfer electrical energy between one object and another, a conductor is required, a special substance that can transmit that energy.

The shared relation—whether between individuals or between communities—stems from actual attitudes that need to be continually renewed by live persons who are attentive to the need to sustain relation, to foster the growth of the Between. This conception of community is, of course, a way of envisioning an alternative to conventional assumptions about the social and political spheres, with their emphasis on preexisting structures of authority as the primary determinants of the nature of relationships. Hence, the importance of "God"[11] in Buber's thought notwithstanding, it is living persons who are responsible for the creation of such "true" community (*die wahre Gemeinde*).[12] The emphasis on the responsibility of individuals to create the quality of their social space (and hence to create conditions for fulfillment of individual potential) thus goes against two strongly ingrained beliefs: (1) that there is an external force (God, the Law of History, Spirit) that is the ultimate "mover" of earthly events, and (2) that social and political regeneration must begin by replacing one form of social and political association with an alternative structure of authority. Buber's theory of community emphasizes conscious individual effort as the sine qua non of social and political revolution. He assumes that the turn to self is at once a turn to the eternal element of being and to other persons. The sensitivity that comes with such a "turn" is ultimately what sustains the Between. This contrasts with inordinate trust in political structures as the necessary context for creating a social sphere worthy of a full and rich human life.

## COMMUNITY AND THE BETWEEN

Buber's interest in interhuman relationships and in their correlation with politics grants his social theory permanence and direction. The emphasis on the generation of an appropriate attitude to relationships, concomitant with the transformation of one's limited, unreflective attitude to being, is the opening, universal theme of *I and Thou*. Basic modern ontological convictions notwithstanding, "the world is twofold for man in accordance with his twofold attitude."[13] Buber considered change of attitude to the nature of being to be the hidden, but nonetheless decisive, factor determining one's perception of reality. Change in perception of reality, in turn, leads to change in conduct.[14] Transformation of an attitude to being from one that assumes division, separation, and conflict as "natural" to one that questions fragmentation as "unnatural" is the ontological shift that is Buber's version of Plato's minimal "least change" necessary for the establishment of a true community.[15]

Buber's turn to relation (as inclusion), stemming in part from his critique of the Cartesian *ego cogito* (as separation), does not imply that the transformation of one's relation to being is a single, self-shattering moment. The I–You attitude to relation is not a permanent state of being and cannot be sustained over an extended period of time. It is a moment—albeit a moment of full attention to what is—and like every other moment, it includes equal opportunity for continually renewed attention or, conversely, for a return to less attentive and more "thoughtful" forms of addressing reality. Accordingly, Buber suggests that the "I" of the I–You relation to being cannot retain a permanent state of unity; it is subject to recurring fragmentation into the separate I's of the I–It attitude to being.

We should focus on this proposition, for it presents the logic that underlies the notion of the Between. Buber calls the movement generated by the I–You attitude "entering into relation" (*In-Beziehungtreten*).[16] Entering into relation is presupposed by primal distancing; following Buber's logic, it is possible to enter into relation only with what is at a distance and therefore has become an independent opposite.[17] In his mature works, Buber applies this insight to social reality and seeks the greater reality of existence in the context of the interhuman, "in the great phenomena of [man's] connection with an otherness which is constituted as otherness by the event of 'distancing.' "[18] Persons are thus subject to continual alternations between states of being, between inner unity and fragmentation. In a balanced society, there will always be enough persons who at a given time will be attentive to sustained relation; these very same persons may, on other occasions, benefit from the attention of others to this need. Accordingly, Buber's conception of community and of society does not divide society into those who participate in social growth and those who do not; each and every person experiences alternations between an I–You and an I–It relation to being, and what matters for communal welfare is the sum effect of the many attitudes in a given time.

This proposition is the basis for an additional distinction Buber draws between two basic orientations contending within each person for mastery over his or her essential attitude to being: the "ego-oriented I" and the "person-oriented I." For the ego-oriented I, self-knowledge is knowing of a limited, partial aspect of one's existence and considering it to be the whole; for the person-oriented I, self-knowledge is knowing self as being.[19] The person-oriented I is one who can shift from an erroneous perception of him- or herself as the center of being to recognition of relation as this center. We may note in passing that the language Buber uses here is free of religious or biblical overtones; Buber uses common discourse in discussing the self as a psychological construct and attempts to reform this perspective from within its region of language.[20]

Buber emphasizes that the ego/person duality represents two poles of one's intrinsic humanity, *not* two kinds of human beings. No human being, says Buber, is pure person, and none is pure ego: "Each lives in a twofold I. But some men are so person-oriented that one may call them persons, while others are so ego-oriented that one may call them egos."[21] Consequently, the primary reality of the I–You dialogue lies in neither of the subjects of the relation, I and You, but in the relation itself, in that which is indicated by the hyphen. It thus becomes crucial for Buber to present a vision of community that would, above all, emphasize the quality of interpersonal relationships desired by all members.

It follows that Buber's distinction between an ego-orientation and a person-orientation harbors implications beyond individual existence. Buber establishes a clear connection between the prevailing ontology and the culture and modes of association stemming from it:

> [The] more a human being, the more humanity, is dominated by the ego, the more does the I fall prey to inactuality. In such ages the person in the human being and in humanity comes to lead a subterranean, hidden, as it were invalid existence—until it is summoned.[22]

The oblique mention of "a subterranean, hidden, as it were invalid existence" refers to the hidden history of "natural Adam." When the insight guiding Buber's distinction between apparent and hidden aspects of being is applied to modern realities, Buber's analysis leads him to conclude that uniquely *human* enterprises (such as civilization, culture, history, and individual biographies) are created between the poles determining personal and collective identity, between the ego-orientation and the person-orientation. Buber seems to suggest that in modern times, the person-orientation has only a marginal existence and that, consequently, the sphere of relationship into which contemporary humans are born and within which they act is dominated by the ego-orientation, which posits separation as the determining characteristic of the human condition.

The domination of the ego-orientation in modern societies is most blatantly manifest in the primary form of social organization created by modern human beings—the nation-state. The nation-state may be a collectivity of sorts, but it is not a community in the Buberian sense; the "typical individual" of contemporary times relates to the state as if it were the highest authority within his reach and to the nation as if it were his "expanded ego."[23] Consequently, for Buber, the central challenge facing today's societies and their social theorists and activists is to clear the (ontological) way for the emergence of a community characterized by the predominance of the person-orientation. A redress of the modern imbalance between the ego-orientation and the person-orientation, occurring as a result of transformations in an individual's relations to being, would give rise to a form of social organization that would reflect this new balance between the competing orientations. Such action would be in line with Buber's belief that the human world is meant to become a single body through the deeds of human beings themselves.

Note the anarchical elements implied by such a theory. From the personal perspective, Buber's teachings imply reliance on self as the place of renewal (and not on external authority). From the perspective of the existing world order, Buber's ideas imply that the nation-state has completed its historical role and that the demands of the current historical hour call for a transformed organization of social life, from nation-states to a global "community of communities." The two perspectives—a newfound relation to self and a rejection of the existing world order—create the need for a radically transformed notion and experience of community. That is why Buber's social theory is primarily concerned with the idea and practice of community. In addition to expanding on this point in the present chapter, we shall return to Buber's vision of community in chapter 7, when we contemplate his criticism of Zionism's demand to establish a Jewish nation-state "like all of the nations."

## THE DIALOGICAL BUILDERS OF COMMUNITY

In a key passage of *I and Thou*, Buber asserts that at the center of community is a living person he calls the builder. A genuine community does not exist if people merely "have feelings for each other." There are two further requirements:

> *All of them have to stand in a living, reciprocal relationship to a single living center*, and they have to stand in a living reciprocal relationship to one another. The second event has its source in the first but is not immediately given with it. A living reciprocal relationship includes feelings but is not derived from them. A community is built upon a living reciprocal relationship, *but the builder is the living, active center [aber der Baumeister ist die lebendige wirkende Mitte]*.[24]

Buber emphasizes that the relationship at the heart of true community is not grounded in mere feelings, sentiments, or sentimentality.[25] For Buber, neither a sense of shared devotion to God nor a romantic sense of shared "feeling" or "love" can replace the human, living center of community. Feelings, intense as they may be, are by nature transient and ephemeral. Buber would thus have serious reservations about a theory of community in which the community is to be constituted and maintained primarily by "mutual affection."[26] The members of a true community may indeed share feelings of mutual affection, yet Buber argues that a community "includes feelings but is not derived from them."[27]

It is evident from the passage quoted above that the members of a true community aspire to share a common relation to a divine center, the "eternal You"; however, it is equally obvious that such a relation can emerge only from social frameworks that allow for this shared attitude. The attitude is developed in the context of lived relationships, not in solitary contemplation or worship.

The concept of a *"living,* active center" required for founding or renewing true community has been overlooked in studies of Buber's social and political thought. In an article that speaks of Buber's concept of the center and social renewal, Paul Mendes-Flohr claims that "a *Gemeinde,* Buber held, is founded when a host of men encounter and realize a common revelation, a thou which addresses them collectively." Mendes-Flohr thus concludes that, for Buber, true community is founded "by a 'situational' revelation."[28] This interpretation is not supported by our analysis. A community may be formed in a moment of revelation, yet the decisive element in creating that moment is the appropriate communal context established by virtue of the efforts of the ones at its center.[29] Buber thus comments that "the meaning of revelation is that it is to be prepared,"[30] prepared by living persons, not by transcendent deities. Mendes-Flohr's analysis, in contrast, would lead us to conclude that the origin of true community is essentially an act of grace rather than the product of human efforts. Overlooking Buber's emphasis on the necessity to prepare the social context conducive to revelation, Mendes-Flohr concludes that a Buberian community faces "inherent discontinuity."[31] This comment would be a complete rendering of Buber's position only if revelation were envisaged as a fortuitous event, independent of action by those privy to the experience. Buber, however, argues that revelation is granted to a community that has developed an attitude to being that enables revelation to occur. Personal and communal renewal precede the opening to the greater reality of what is. In this sense, the hidden community of "servants" is inherently *continuous,* although in ways not readily apparent; they are the "movers" of "real history" that we referred to in chapter 4.

Mendes-Flohr concludes that the transition from ordinary community to true community is attained by a kind of metasociological, inexplicable revelation. Yet Buber does not confuse the problem of founding or renewing a community with that of ensuring the continuity of the true community over time.[32] These issues are interrelated yet not identical. Mendes–Flohr is correct in pointing to the question of continuity as a central problem in Buber's theory of community. However, this problem arises after the community is established, not in the period of its founding. Buber, as the division of themes in *I and Thou* indicates, draws clear distinctions between the community's founding or renewal and its ongoing life. The members of a true community do indeed aspire to share a common relation to a divine center; however, the advent of such a relation is dependent on the prior creation of social frameworks that create this shared attitude.

The problems of founding a community and ensuring its continuity do converge in Buber's work when considered in the context of his notion of social renewal. For a community to retain its "true" nature, it must be constantly renewed. Here, too, the decisive element is the transformed person; only the continual influx of persons capable of being "living, active centers" can guarantee that the community will retain its "true" character. From this perspective, we may appreciate the centrality of the notion of social renewal for Buber's social and political theory. The ongoing revolution that guarantees social renewal is a continuing transmission of the teaching, which enables individuals to perceive their "natural" selves and experience the "turning." The precise social form that such a community creates is dependent on the contingencies of the historical and political hour.

In the Hebrew Bible, we read that such communities exist in the shadows of the biblical text, appearing in history through the deeds of individual prophets who demand that kings and people change their relation to being. This form of a single prophet's intervention in ordinary events is apparent to historical consciousness and is thus recorded and transmitted. In our reading of Buber's depiction of the Hasidic community, the "true" community exists as a social phenomenon, serving as testimony to the desired change by manifesting the necessary exemplary quality of relation in everyday social situations. Both singular leaders (prophets and *zaddikim*) and singular members (the community of prophets and the Hasidim) are equally responsible for creating conditions that sustain genuine community. From this perspective, the distinction between leader and led, usually associated with the language of power, authority, and domination, is useful only as a description of social structure, not as a description of the essential quality of such a community. Such a community is judged by the essence of the interpersonal sphere that transpires between its members, regardless of their functions within the social order.

The living center is concerned with social renewal and consequently constitutes a historical, revolutionary force. But it is even more concerned with transmission of the truth regarding man's spiritual estrangement and ways to overcome this condition. That is why culture and society represent two aspects of the same responsibility. Society has to develop a framework for transmitting the spiritual teaching that the culture transmits between generations; culture cannot attain *social* significance, cannot enter the social sphere, if it does not undergo transmission and acceptance. Culture is thus not merely the artifact or idea of a particular generation; a culture develops diverse forms to transmit a teaching. As such, it has *two faces*, creation (*yetsira*) and transmission (*mesira*), granting it a paradoxical quality: although culture is revolutionary in its creative dimension, its dependence on established patterns of transmission also accord it a conservative dimension.[33] Creative revolutionary activity serves transmission of the conservative force, while revolutionary social renewal is auxiliary to the primary goal of conserving and transmitting the unchanging teaching about the true nature of being in relation to creation.[34]

The tension between the revolutionary and conservative aspects of culture is allayed by the actual moment of transmission. A living tradition is marked by repeated encounters between a generation that has reached full development and one that is still developing: "What matters is that time and again an older generation, staking its entire existence on this act, comes to a younger with the desire to teach, waken and shape it; then the holy spark leaps across the gap."[25]

The persons involved, both those who teach and those who learn, become the transmitting agents. What remains fixed is the presence of a certain quality of relationship that enables the transmission to take place. This is the Between. To attain that quality, social structures and communal settings may undergo radical transformations. The process of transmission influences not only the form of the relationship that enables the transmission, but also the form of the teaching: "For tradition does not consist in letting contents and forms pass on, finished and inflexible, from generation to generation. . . . [A] generation can only receive the teachings in the sense that it renews them."[36]

In sum, Buber distinguishes between the problem of renewing a community and and that of guaranteeing its continuity. In both cases, the solution requires persons who have turned to the "twofold nature of being" and who show their fellow human beings the way to that turning. In this respect, S. N. Eisenstadt's emphasis on social and cultural renewal as the focus of Buber's sociology is a more accurate interpretation than those tendered by Mendes-Flohr and others. Buber's social theory indeed reflects what Eisenstadt has referred to as a lifelong concern with "intersubjectivity and cultural creativity,"[37] identifying the "transformative, creative potential" that may be present in ostensibly routine situations as well as in periods of great social and cultural upheaval. Based on Buber's writings and on personal acquaintance, Eisenstadt writes that Buber did not focus his search on one particular problem, "but rather . . . the crucial issues [were] the continuous quest for such creativity and the readiness to retain an openness toward the variety of ways, methods, and content of the solutions." However, whereas Eisenstadt suggests that Buber's search was oriented to "the transcendental, to absolute *values*," this book assumes that it was directed at discerning conditions that would support the phenomenon of ontological opening to the experience of direct relation to the absolute. In other words, in contrast to Eisenstadt's emphasis on values, I consider Buber's primary concern to have been to undermine the unreflective trust in clearly articulated ethical sentences that in modern culture and society often replace unmediated trust in being and inclusive relation to what (or who) is.[38]

In the largest sense, Buber's social and political theory aims at rendering the modern state, its institutions, and characteristic forms of relationship (power and domination) obsolete,[39] supplanting the modern system of nation-states with a global "dialogical civilization."[40] This goal is to be attained in three stages. The first is by creating "true" communities as the basis for a new mode of society. This is the first stage in a global process leading to the second stage, creation of a global "community of communities,"[41] a commonwealth of communities bound together by a common trust, a shared relation to the "eternal" You.[42] The goal of the new (global) social system is the third stage of the development that Buber envisions, the creation of social conditions conducive to acceptance of the dialogical moment.[43] These three stages of development may also be considered as three levels of social life—individual, communal, and global. These three stages of development (and levels of social existence) are interrelated in a reciprocal manner, for the coalescence of individual persons whose relation to being includes direct experience of the dialogical moment is the beginning and end of "true" community and of the new global order.

Contemplation of this schema reveals that the originating element, the singular, human effort that enables this ongoing process to begin in a manner ensuring continuity, is crucial to the vision. Thus, interpretations of the source of renewed community in a shared revelation or shared relationship to a transcendent archetype common to all appears to apply to the second and third stages of Buber's political and social vision. However, on the *first* level, the basic unit and point of departure for the other levels of the envisioned social system, the decisive focus is the transformation of society. The builder, the dialogical person, is at the center of that process.

Why have many interpreters of Buber's work overlooked the idea of the builder when discussing the passage from *I and Thou* that deals explicitly with the founding of true community?[44] One possibility is that the idea of the builder of community is considered an anomalous indiscretion that detracts from what are perceived as more important aspects of Buber's theory of community. This line of reasoning would justify omission on the grounds that mention of the idea of the builder would create unnecessary confusion among students of Buber's thought. Another possibility is fear that the concept would be misunderstood and consequently associated with unattractive, antidemocratic and nonliberal conceptions of community.[45] This concern may reflect the nature of our times: the twentieth century has taught many people to be wary of ideas that evoke initial associations of strong leaders whose personal charisma may blind their followers to the ramifications of their deeds.

Buber did not advocate some form of benevolent authoritarianism, as several commentators fear an inattentive reader may erroneously assume. Buber, whose personal biography includes a childhood in late nineteenth-century Eastern Europe and adulthood in pre- and post-First World War Germany, was well aware of the dangers of misguided leadership. Buber refers to Mussolini and Hitler as the most dangerous examples of leadership with the guidance of a true way.[46] Such commanding leaders base their rule on their ability to manipulate to the utmost the political power inherent in the centralized structure of the modern state. Totalitarian states whose leaders' rule is based solely on their control of political power are the extreme instances of the exploitation of organs of control made available to the leader of the modern state. A totalitarian leader takes over the organs of state by utilizing what Buber calls "negative charisma" and, in the name of grace, strips real freedom and judgment from the ruled.[47] Such a leader is totally immersed in the political ends of attaining and retaining power. In terms of the themes we have discussed, such a leader (regardless of his fallacious self-conception) is thoroughly identified with his egotistic self and is devoid of relation to his innate You or to the eternal You. He is the ultimate subject, himself an armor of self-perpetuating clusters of thoughts and self-adulating fantasies that cannot be open to the "hidden light."

Considered in the context of the categories of *I and Thou*, Buber says that such leaders fall outside the scale of the I–You and I–It relation. He refers to leaders like Hitler as the "demonic You," persons who, like Napoleon, know only their association with their cause and experience no real relation to any You. Relation to a cause implies relating to dogmas as if they were real, as if they were transcendent "realities." Such leaders recognize no one as being, so that everything around them becomes an object and subservient to their cause. The demonic You for whom no one can become a You, says Buber, is the elementary historical barrier at which the basic word of association, I–You, loses its reality, the character of reciprocity.[48]

Buber's personal experiences in Europe and his writings thus attest to his sensitivity to the problem of "unattractive" leadership; clearly, he is not attempting to present a radically antidemocratic and nonliberal conception of community. The paradigmatic figures that Buber has in mind in referring to "builders" of community are those whose personal "turnings" have renewed cultures and transformed prevailing attitudes to being so as to attest to the truth of their experience. These are the "powerful revelations that stand at the beginnings of great communities, at the turning points of human time." The true revolutionaries are not necessarily political leaders. They are the great founders of civilization, those who have established ways of life within which human beings can more fully know themselves, those whose way leads to a radical reevaluation of the meaning and significance of relation. Buber cites examples from the origins of contemporary cultures in the Axial Age. The Buddha, for one, found the way to "confront the undivided mystery undivided."[49] It was from a "relational process that became substance that his deed came, clearly as an answer to the You." Hence the great accomplishment of the Buddha was his generation of a movement that transformed the I–You relation into substance, into that quality of the interpersonal referred to as the Between. Similarly, Socrates knew the "I of infinite conversation." In Buber's terms, Socrates believed that being is intrinsic in each person and sought to address that part of his interlocutor. His interpersonal dialogue was sustained by dialogue with "the world of one truth"; when the "human world [fell] silent for him, he heard his *daimonion* say 'You.' "[50] This twofold attitude to being is what gave Socrates his extraordinary influence over his listeners.[51]

## IMAGES OF THE BUILDER: HASIDISM AND MOSES, COMMUNITY AND COVENANT

Buber's favorite image of a true community established during the modern era is that of the Jewish Hasidim and the *zaddik* (the just person)[52] in their midst. He relates that as a child, "when [he] saw the rabbi striding through the rows of the waiting, [he] felt, 'leader,' and when [he] saw the Hasidim dance with the Torah, [he] felt, 'community' [*Gemeinde, edah*]." Buber suggests that this image represents the "living double kernel of humanity: genuine community and genuine leadership."[53] Note that community and leader are one inseparable "living double kernel." The kernel is one, and within it is a relation. In fact, the impression evoked by this image complements Buber's lifelong search for a solution to the mystery of Adam's having been created in the image of Elohim. We now return to a passage quoted in chapter 4 as an opening to exegesis of Genesis 1:27, which indicated that Adam's being "created in the image of Elohim" is not a mere description, but rather an implication of an active becoming, a task:

> The image out of my childhood, the memory of the *zaddik* and his community, rose upward and illuminated me: I recognized the idea of the fully realized, whole person [*vollkommenen Menschen*]. At the same time I became aware of the summons to proclaim it to the world.[54]

Here, we shall address the last two sentences of the passage, thus complementing our previous discussion of the biblical guiding verse that serves as this passage's opening. Not emphasized by most interpreters of Buber's *social* and *political* thought, this passage clearly indicates that Buber considered the idea of the "fully realized, whole person" central to his work.[55] The implicit connection between the fully realized, whole person and his community, encountered in Buber's recollection of the *zaddik* and his community, is spelled out explicitly when Buber says that in the midst of a true community, such as that of the Hasidim, "stands the *zaddik*, whose function is to help the Hasidim, as persons and as a totality, to authenticate their relation to God in the hallowing of life and just from this starting point to live as brothers with one another."[56] The *zaddik* helps the members of the community "authenticate their relation to God" by considering his encounters with them as opportunities to "[elevate] their need before he satisfies it."[57]

What is the essence of this "need" the *zaddik* sets out to elevate? The *zaddik* seeks to bring his followers to experience the longing for relation that is natural to Adam, yet peripheral to the experience of life that is mediated by ordinary, historical consciousness. This interpretation is corroborated by a quick reference to the book *Tzva'at Ribesh*, cited by Buber as the source of his inspiration regarding the fully realized, whole person. That book quotes the Ba'al Shem as saying that there are two types of just men.[58] The first is concerned only with fulfilling God's commandments; such a *zaddik* is a *zaddik* only to himself. The way of the second type of *zaddik* includes the extra merit of bringing additional persons closer to God, an experience the Ba'al Shem refers to in terms of the Jewish *teshuva*.[59]

*Teshuva* can be translated literally as either "answer" or "turning." In its essential meaning, it is similar to the Greek notion of *periagoge* (or its corollary, *metastrophe*, conversion), most commonly associated with Plato's prisoner in the cave, who "is suddenly compelled to stand up, *turn around*, walk, and look toward the light."[60] In the Jewish context, *teshuva* is associated with the notion of answering the call of Elohim, of effecting a (re)turn to what is (Buber refers to YHVH as He-Who-Is-Here, the Present One).[61] This notion appears as a central theme in Buber's work; he understands it as an inner turning, an opening to a presence previously unnoticed. In fact, *teshuva* may be considered a guiding word that functions in Buber's text as an indication of multiple meanings, similar to the function of the word *lev*. Citing the Jewish prophets, Buber says that the turning is "not a return to an earlier, 'sinless' state; it is the revolution of the whole being—in which process Adam is projected into the way of Elohim."[62]

In Buber's philosophical work we encounter a German rendering of the Hebrew *teshuva* in the concept of *Umkehr*, which means "turning around, reversal."[63] By employing a term devoid of particular religious connotations to denote the experience he considers so important for the fulfillment of a complete human life, Buber seemed to be pursuing his basic goal: to direct modern individuals' attention to "the fundamental separation between the sacred and the profane."[64] The way to overcome this ontological interval is for the person to "find his own self, not the trivial ego of the egoistic individual, but the deeper self of the person living in relationship to the world. And this is . . . contrary to everything we are accustomed to."[65] From this perspective, the "need" of which Buber speaks is the need to seek one's deeper self, the self that is aware of the basic unity underlying the world.

Buber's depiction of Hasidism emphasizes the unique role of the *zaddik* at the center of the transformed community. Indeed, the collections of Hasidic tales that constitute the bulk of his literary works focus on the deeds and lives of the Hasidic masters. Buber portrays the *zaddik* as one who utilizes ordinary daily events and relationships to bring about an immanent experience of incompleteness in the persons he meets; by recognizing this lack, a person is awakened to his or her need. The following story conveys the ordinariness of learning:

> "You can learn from everything," the Rabbi of Sadagora once said to his Hasidim.
>
> "Everything can teach us something, and not only everything that God has created. What man has made has also something to teach us."
>
> "What can we learn from a train?" one Hasid asked dubiously.
>
> "That because of one second one can miss everything."
>
> "And from the telegraph?"
>
> "That every word is counted and charged."
>
> "And the telephone?"
>
> "That what we say here is heard there."[66]

Those whose ordinary needs are elevated to more meaningful ones through meetings such as the one described in this tale join in a fellowship centered on the meeting with the *zaddik* and with one another. These are the Hasidim, " 'the devout,' or more accurately, those who keep faith with the covenant."[67]

While the *zaddik* is clearly the indispensable pole of the relationship, Buber shows him to be as dependent on his followers as the Hasidim are dependent on him. This is the "living double kernel" of community. The wholeness of this relationship is captured in the following image attributed to the Rabbi of Rizhyn:

> Just as the holy letters of the alphabet are voiceless without the vowel signs, and the vowel signs cannot stand without the letters, so *zaddikim* and Hasidim are bound up with one another. The *zaddikim* are the letters and the Hasidim who journey to them are the vowel signs. The Hasidim need the *zaddik*, but he has just as much need of them. *Through them he can be uplifted.* Because of them he can sink—God forbid![68]

The dialogue between the *zaddik* and the Hasid, sealed by the common aspiration to realize higher levels of being,[69] grants Buber's image of the *zaddik* an intrinsically *social* dimension. The dialogue among the members of community is dialectically intertwined with the individual member's dialogue with Elohim. To unveil the deeper self, to come closer to one's being, one needs to enter into meaningful, purposeful, human relationships. To be capable of entering such human relationships, one needs an affinity to the greater reality represented by the idea of God (as both Elohim and YHVH). By serving as a living example of the way to conduct reciprocal relationships in the various circles of community, Buber's *zaddik* exemplifies the paradigmatic conduct of one at the center of a community of persons committed to the fulfillment of this human need. The result of such community is the Between.

This reading of Buber's ideal Hasidic community in the service of his ideal image of the person may shed additional light on the famous controversy regarding his revision of Hasidism and of the biblical sources.[70] Schatz-Uffenheimer criticizes his rendering of Hasidic life on the grounds that

> Buber's realistic, activistic approach—in contrast to Hasidism— ignores the ontic line of thought on such basic problems as God and world, and from the first confines itself to the realm of the *relationships*

of man to God and to his world. The Hasidic sources themselves distinguish between the ontic problem of the world and that of man's relationship to it; thus in Hasidism the problem becomes greatly complicated.[71]

Schatz-Uffenheimer is surely correct in pointing to Buber's selective choice of emphasis; however, in our context, it is interesting to note what Buber *includes* in his revision rather than what he *excludes* from it. Buber emphasizes relationships within the Hasidic community precisely because it is this aspect of human life that he seeks to establish as paradigmatic for the conduct of social life. Moreover, it is not merely relationships that he emphasizes but those of a certain order—between a *zaddik* at the center of a community and his circles of disciples and followers. As a scholar, Buber may deserve poor grades;[72] as a theorist, he is consistent in his attempt to create a new image of community and of the persons at its center.

This reading of Buber's intentions also addresses Gershom Scholem's concerns. For Scholem, Buber's greatest fault is his combining "facts and quotations to suit his purpose, namely to present Hasidism as a spiritual phenomenon and not as a historical one."[73] Scholem's criticism of Buber, like Schatz-Uffenheimer's, is justified on the grounds of his way of reading the past, that is, his claim that Buber distorted the "evidence" of apparent history to serve his own message. What interests us here, however, is that this apparent distortion and the message it serves are extensions of a basic concern guiding *all* Buber's works and that they constitute a central element of his self-conception as a social theorist.[74] Scholem's critique, while justified in terms of his conception of scholarly discourse, does not take into account—or does not consider legitimate—Buber's hidden agenda: to bring the practical implications of the existence of two kinds of history, grounded in two distinct streams of consciousness, into the scope of scholarly and social discourse.

Buber's deep commitment to this mission is evident from a reading of Scholem's account of the last discussion he and Buber conducted on the question of Buber's interpretation of Hasidism. In 1943, Scholem went to Buber "to lay before him the fundamental criticisms of Buber's interpretation of Hasidism which Scholem formed during long years of continuous study of the texts.''[75] Retelling the tale of that meeting, Scholem (in the words of Maurice Friedman) described Buber listening with great earnestness and tension. Buber's response, as recounted by Scholem, is striking in its directness and sense of resignation:

> When I had finished he was silent for a long time. Then [Buber] said slowly and with emphasis on every word: "If what you have said be true, dear Scholem, then I have occupied myself with Hasidism for forty years in vain, for then it would indeed not at all *interest* me." It was the last conversation that I had with Buber over the factual problem of Hasidism. It closed speech for me. I understood that there was nothing more to say.[76]

Although Buber used myths and symbols produced as an integral part of his culture, Buber did not hesitate to transmit them in a new configuration. Criticism of this revision is justified in light of Buber's presenting part of his reflections on Hasidic life in scholarly form; each type of writing presupposes certain rules, and the scholarly format invites scholarly criticism. In this respect, Buber was not entirely forthright in his attempts to refute evidence supplied by critics who claimed that his works lacked a sound scholarly foundation. Nevertheless, if considered a medium for changing people's view of ontology indirectly, a change considered by Buber to be essential for social renewal, these apparent distortions can be measured against the goal they were intended to achieve. Returning to the theme of this book, these legends are part and parcel of Buber's attempt to create an alternative to modern conceptions of man and society. Consequently, scholarly criticism of Buber's use of Hasidic legends and images should be accompanied by evaluation in terms of how it contributed to his goal—that is, to ground the concept of the living center (social philosophy) in a historical metaphor (the founding of the Hasidic community) by casting his portrayal of an ideal social revolutionary (the Ba'al Shem and other *zaddikim*) in the mold of his ideal image (the builder of genuine community).[77]

An additional, most striking example of Buber's scholarly research supporting his goals as a political theorist is his analysis of the life of Moses. At this juncture, I shall show how Buber's *Moses: The Revelation and the Covenant* further supports the reading of Buber as a social theorist who used his literary and scholarly skills to transform existing myths and legends in the course of transmitting them. Buber's analysis depicts Moses as one who serves as the intermediary bond uniting person, community, social renewal, and revelation: the archetypical "originating" founder.[78] As such, Moses serves as a paradigmatic example of one at the center of true community. Moses, says Buber, perceived the necessity of establishing a *social* framework that would let the Israelites emerge as a *holy* people, bearers of a sacred teaching. He established the covenant as a response to the condition and prevailing attitudes of the people he was destined to lead. They were not holy, not prepared to assume the responsibilities accompanying their selection as the people of YHVH. The covenant "shall simultaneously unite the tribes into a people and bind the people to their God; not merely religiously but in their living substance."[79] Consistent with the basic assumptions guiding *I and Thou*, and equally consistent with Buber's rendering of the great founders, Buber again emphasizes the role of the covenant in fostering the quality of relationships that create the Between as the sphere of the interpersonal.

The covenant is a dual conception. That is to say, the covenant between the tribes and YHVH is also a covenant among the tribes, who "become Israel only when they become partners in the Covenant of the God."[80] This conception is presumably a source of Buber's proposition in *I and Thou* that a true community comes into being as a union of those bound in a living reciprocal relationship to one another and concurrently, bound in a relationship to a single, living center.[81] Thus, it is possible that his interpretation of the deeds of Moses, published in 1946, over twenty years after *I and Thou*, came as a later confirmation of his earlier insight.[82] From the perspective of our reading, *Moses* and *I and Thou* complement one another. At bottom, Buber's Moses represents an attempt to unite the tribes into a people and simultaneously bind them to their God. YHVH is the *divine* center, yet Moses is the one who creates the necessary social conditions without which the communities cannot experience the bond with YHVH or join with one another. Moses is thus the *living* center, the binding joint.[83] Buber refers to this combination as the "theopolitical" idea. The relation between YHVH and the people is *political* in its realistic, historical character; it is *religious* insofar as it is guided by the attempt to face the totality of being, the meeting with YHVH, a goal that is not fixed in time or place.[84]

Buber claims that Moses understood himself as a guide; he did not stand between YHVH and man, nor did he shoulder responsibility for the choices of others. The covenant he introduced was intended to create a bond transcending the merely ritual aspect of religion and to introduce the spiritual into the substance of everyday life.[85] Moses did not retreat into some metaphysical, detached realm of being but was firmly established in human society. The unifying force he brought into the life of the community stemmed from the conception of a divine force above him that flowed through him. Hence Buber's interpretation of the episode of the crossing of the Red Sea. For Buber, this story points to Moses' decisive act as creating social conditions that enabled the Israelites to experience extraordinary events, such as the crossing of the Red Sea, in a new way, as a miracle, "which does not mean that they interpreted it as a miracle, *but that they experienced it as such, that as such they perceived it. This perception at the fateful hour, which is assuredly to be attributed largely to the personal influence of Moses,* had a decisive influence on the coming into being of what is called 'Israel' in the history of the spirit."[86] Emphasis is placed not on the "objective" event but rather on Moses' crucial role in transforming the peoples' *perception* of it. Moses led them to perceive reality in a new, fuller way. This turning to reality is the key to their *experiencing* the event as a miracle. Moses led his people to an ontological shift, to a new understanding of reality that included a sacred dimension. For those whose perception was thus transformed, this newfound understanding came into being by virtue of the opening of the body to its function as an organ that serves the human being as a receptive vessel.[87] Buber's ontology, emphasizing the relation that transpires both in social contexts and in relation to other spheres of being, thus supplements the Kabbalah's teachings of the reciprocal relations among the ten spheres of creation with a dialogical interpretation of the nature of relations among social beings within the social sphere.

In terms of Buber's theory of community, the lesson to be learned from Moses concerns the relationship between personal and social transformation. Moses sought to prepare for the overcoming of the dualistic ontology that prevented human beings from experiencing that part of their selves that was attuned to the essential unity of creation. His actions, Buber notes approvingly, sought to "prepare [for the future of a 'holy people'] within history."[88] Moses, like the *zaddikim* of the first generations following the Ba'al Shem, sought to use historical circumstances as an opportunity to experience the psychological dissonance between the way the people are and the way they may be.[89] Hence, regardless of the degree of success with which Moses' actions met, Buber maintains, Moses sets an example on the personal level:

> Moses wished for an entire, undivided human life, as the right answer to mankind, and the right answer to the Divine revelation. But [fragmentation] is the historical way of mankind, and the [unified] persons cannot do anything more than raise man to a higher level on which he may therefore follow his course, as long as he is bound by the law of his history.[90]

Like the way of the second type of *zaddik* mentioned in the *Tzva'at Ribesh*, that of the living center of community entails elevating his contemporaries' level of being. While guided by a desire for unification with the "eternal You," the living center aspires to remain within the realities and needs of the "law of his history," an indirect reference to the hidden history privy to those attentive to the hermeneutic allusions embedded in the text. The goal of raising mankind to a higher level is attained indirectly, by elevating individual persons' needs. Yet this goal can be attained only within the context of communities oriented towards the realities of social and historical existence, guided by the conception of a divine order of the universe.

Buber's rendition of Moses' exemplary life indirectly points to his understanding of the ultimate telos of society and politics: to create and support forms of communal life whose members share the goal of developing, individually and communally, a twofold relation to being within the constraints of particular historical conditions. Thus, for Buber, personal and social are dialectically related.

## THE PHILOSOPHY OF DIALOGUE AS RELIGIOUS SOCIALISM

Buber's social philosophy is usually referred to as "utopian socialism," after ideas that Buber explored in *Paths in Utopia*, first published in 1947. The seeds of "utopian socialism" can be found in embryonic form in three succinct theses on "religious socialism" articulated in an earlier, shorter essay.[91] "Religion" and "socialism," commonplace words with common meanings, are presented as conveyors of hidden meaning, and this hidden meaning is presented as the real reason for the words' appearance at this time in political and philosophical discourse. An examination of this short text again points to Buber's assumptions regarding the transformational potential of words, given appropriate sensitivity on the part of writer and reader alike.

The first of Buber's three theses claims that true socialism is religious socialism and that religion and socialism are essentially directed towards one another:

> *Each of them needs the covenant with the other for the fulfillment of its own essence. Religio*, that is the human person's binding of himself to God, can only attain its full reality in the will for a community of the human race, out of which alone God can prepare his kingdom. *Socialitas*, that is mankind's becoming a fellowship, man's becoming a fellow to man, cannot develop otherwise than out of a common relation to the divine center, even if this be again and still nameless.[92]

Buber uses quick reference to the etymology of the words "religion" and "socialism" (*religio* and *socialitas*) in support of his thesis. This form of reference, although common in the midrashic discourse of the Hebraic tradition, is less prevalent as a form of persuasion in modern political discourse and may be one reason for the lack of impact this essay has on readers who are not well versed in the variety of language games that coexist in Buber's writings. This thesis clearly spells out the interdependence of faith and social action. The meeting with Elohim is dependent on the quality of interpersonal relationships generated in the social sphere. One may note that Buber's emphasis on socialism as becoming a fellowship is, in effect, an effort to redefine its aim: Buber considered the loss of community (not the loss of direct relation to the means of production) and the subsequent intensification of human solitude (rather than the intensification of alienation) to be the problems socialism is to resolve.[93] At the same time, however, the practice of socialism is dependent on a common relation to a divine center, to God (or whatever the conception of the divine may be). The two movements, towards Elohim and towards fellow persons, are dialectically related. In fact, if considered a reflection of the twofold attitude to being that Buber postulates as the basic determinant of the "world" ("The world is twofold for man in accordance with his twofold attitude"[94]), the two movements are united, a unity sustained by the person's attitude, which although twofold is in itself one.

The second thesis suggests that modern religious forms, institutions, and societies have lost all relation to reality. However, modern persons are largely unaware that most forms of organized religion substitute mere ritual for true *religio*. They therefore continue to relate to these counterfeit replications of religion as if they served true human needs. Buber does not claim that this has always been the case, that organized religion has always been a false representation of spiritual needs. Buber thinks that most modern religious forms do derive from an original stage when they served as bearers of real *religio* (the human person's binding himself to God). However, in modern times they merely exist alongside actual *religio* or, even worse, by claiming to represent *religio*, they conceal the movement away from real *religio* into the realm of fictitious religion. The second thesis also examines the apparent dissonance between real *socialitas* (with the emphasis on *socialitas* as fellowship) and the socialism propagated by socialist political parties. Buber accordingly divides representations of socialism into "real" or "fictitious" according to the extent to which they serve as guides to real fellowship or, conversely, merely exist alongside, or even conceal the movement away from real *socialitas*.

The distinctions drawn in the second thesis illuminate the enigmatic and, perhaps, paradoxical nature of Buber's conception of reality, as well as the larger issue of his use of language. Most people would consider religious institutions and political parties as participating in the "real" world. Consequently, it would be expected that a movement away from reality implies retreat from concrete institutions and political practices into a less tangible and, perhaps, more idealistic conception of "reality." For Buber, however, a movement away from reality is mediated by the false representations of religion and socialism propagated by religious institutions and political parties. His analysis of the etymological origins of the concepts of religion and socialism clearly suggests that he considers these terms representations of a hidden, truer reality that the institutional form conceals. Hence his distrust of both institutionalized forms of spiritual activity and political or religious programs that promise salvation in exchange for obedience.

It follows that Buber detects, in prevailing religious forms, a movement that has entered the realm of the fictitious, and in prevailing social-ist programs, a tendency that has not yet emerged from the fictitious. This is a unique moment, when both sources of social renewal, *religio* and *socialitas*, are submerged in a fictitious world circumscribed by the boundaries of a modern ontology that recognizes only a material real-ity.[95] However, Buber considers the movements of *religio* and *socialitas* to be dynamic and subject to the following dialectic: religion is in constant decline, adapting itself to, and increasingly reflecting, the "reality" en-countered through the limits of modern ontology; socialism, in contrast, is moving in the opposite direction. Although misconceived as an instru-ment of political power at its inception, socialism (as Buber defines it) stands a chance of emerging from the "realm of the fictitious" and thereby representing true *socialitas*. Hence Buber's critique of Marx and his followers in *Paths in Utopia*.[96] Buber's primary complaint is that Marx moved away from his early conception of socialism as directed towards the renewal of society to a later emphasis on the political means of attain-ing social power; this shift in emphasis led to a movement away from the true goals of socialism. The second thesis on religious socialism therefore points to an energizing force latent in socialism, awaiting a moment of emergence from the fictitious to the real.

The third thesis indicates the relevance, for the life of the particular person, of the general considerations spelled out in the first two theses. The point where religion and socialism meet is the real person, who by assuming an appropriate attitude to being—and thus generating a finer quality of interpersonal relationships—enables this meeting to material-ize. Just as the truth of religion does not consist of dogma or prescribed ritual but means entering into a real reciprocal relation with the mystery of God, "so socialism in its truth is not doctrine and tactics but standing and withstanding in the . . . real reciprocal relation with the mystery of man."[97] This idea is expressed very clearly in a later essay: "The human person [is] the irremovable central place of the struggle between the movement of the world away from Elohim and its movement to Elohim. This struggle takes place to an uncannily large extent in the realm of public life; yet the decisive battles of this realm too are fought in the depths of the person.[98]

It follows from the third thesis that Buber opposes those who turn away from history, politics and the world. Admittedly, one begins with self-examination, by "pointing to . . . the relation of the individual to his own self."⁹⁹ Yet if in the course of examining relationships within society, one encounters distorted conceptions or corrupt practices of politics and political power, this encounter should not confuse the person and turn him away from politics.¹⁰⁰ As exemplified in Buber's presentation of the images and deeds of Moses and of the *zaddik*, misunderstandings regarding interpersonal relationships that stem from incomplete notions of history (and from the form of consciousness that grants power and domination such a central role in the conduct of human affairs) should be countered by establishing an alternative community that exemplifies how to release unfulfilled human potential.

The ultimate goal of societal relations is the transformation of the person so that he or she may participate in the meeting of fellowship and spirituality, a meeting expressed by conventional concepts—religion and socialism—that are infused with new meaning. Only communities established with this goal in mind stand a chance of developing into real expressions of human fellowship. Buber refers to the distinction between foundings inspired by spiritual sensitivities and those adhering to mere dogma in *Paths in Utopia*, claiming that a cooperative settlement can withstand pressures threatening its existence only when at the moment of origin it comes into being as an expression of "real religious exaltation, and not merely as a precarious substitute for religion."¹⁰¹ This form of political association comports with Buber's convictions regarding the necessity of effecting personal "turnings" within new, innovative forms of community that ought to emerge on a global scale, as alternatives to existing forms of social and political order in the obsolete nation-state. Accordingly, the goal of the "body politic" is to realize "in its genuine formations persons' turning to one another in the context of creation. The false formations distort but they cannot eliminate the eternal origin."¹⁰² The original political community thus aims at creating social conditions conducive to the goal of "persons' turning to one another."¹⁰³ These personal and the social "turnings," although aiming at a unity with the eternal source, are inextricably interwoven with politics and political action.¹⁰⁴

## BUBER AS A THEORIST OF THE
## DIALOGICAL COMMUNITY

To conclude this chapter, we may suggest that while Buber was not an originator of the kind he depicts in his writings (he did not himself become a center of a clearly bounded community), he was a theorist who attempted to present a universally valid image of the fully present dialogical person. This presentation is accomplished indirectly, through the multiple forms described above. Attention to this dimension of Buber's work is an indispensable element of any reading of his work.

For example, consider the essay "China and Us," in which Buber justifies his mode of communicating ideas by observing that the distinctive world views (*Weltanschauung*)[105] generated by the originators of great cultures and societies are always represented by "universally valid images" of the person. Images of this kind can be intuitively recognized as representative of the best of unfulfilled human potential. Buber asserts that such images are "invisible and yet living in the imagination of all individuals. . . . the imitation of them out of the material of the person is the educating, the forming of man." He considered the lack of such a basic unifying symbol of the person to be a troubling characteristic of modern Western culture. The "typical modern Western man" is guided by images of the fully realized life that uphold erroneous notions of fulfillment. In keeping with Buber's conception of the ontology underpinning apparent history, Buber writes that modern persons are presented with images of historical success, of men who have set goals for themselves, accumulated the necessary means of power, and "succeeded." Yet these historical figures are divorced from the primary reality of man, from an understanding of "the original being of the human substance." Consequently, "upon the real mastering of [a universally valid image of the person] depends whether this epoch will fulfill its meaning or not."[106] In "China and Us," Buber does not mention that the meaning to be fulfilled by the present epoch is related to his discussion of the hidden history. A reader who is unaware of Buber's inner code ("apparent" versus "hidden" history, as well as the Between as signifier of the "substance" created through the release of entrapped attention) will find the essay difficult to fathom if read separately from his other works.

Buber appears to have been aware of the problematic nature of a theory of community predicated on (1) a sensitive reader who is aware of the transformed nature of the language Buber presents in the form of ordinary discourse and (2) Buber's success in communicating effectively an image of a fully realized, whole person at the center of the new form of community he envisions. His explicitly political works (those that examine issues properly considered political, such as alienation and universal mistrust, socialism, Zionism and the Jewish-Arab conflict) include only obscure references to the living centers of community;[107] they do not explicitly attempt to explain how the living center is to come about. Such explanations are indirectly communicated through Buber's *a*political works, primarily those that deal with tales of the Hasidic masters, biblical interpretation, the origin and meaning of Hasidism, and dialogue and dialogical persons.

These nonpolitical works are instances of indirect teaching; if the reader is attracted to the ideas or images of human perfection they convey, Buber has brought his reader closer to the perceptual transformation that is the necessary foundation of the social revolution he aspires to initiate. Such a text has then fulfilled its function in relation to its reader in a manner commensurate with Umberto Eco's proposition that "a text is a device in order to produce its model reader."[108] In this case, the reader is one whose reading causes him to act in certain ways in the sphere of interpersonal relationships. Accordingly, the text fulfills its intention when the reader acts. As such, Buber produces a kind of text that fulfills its function if it leads its reader to action predicated on the understanding revealed through the act of reading. This kind of interaction between reader and text also illustrates Stanley Fish's "self-consuming artifacts": by conveying the reader from rational understanding to a point at which he is beyond the aid that discursive or rational forms can offer, such a dialectical presentation "becomes the vehicle of its own abandonment."[109]

When community is imagined as an organic unit predicated on a certain quality of relationships, relationships that generate the Between, a particular set of insights as to the nature of that community is then made available. The image Buber presents provides an elementary sense of what the political community is like, of how physically distinct and solitary individuals are joined together.[110] In times like our own, says Buber, a genuine community begins "with the discovery of the meta-psychic character of reality and rests upon the belief in this reality. . . . Community in a time like ours can only happen out of breakthrough, out of *turning*."[111] Thus we return to the Archimedean point of Buber's social thought presented in our earlier summary of his social and political theory: A new form of community originates in a group of persons' newfound perception of the nature of being. It originates with human beings who are more finely attuned to their responsibilities as parts of a world of manifold forms of life linked together in an interactive web of reciprocal relations. These persons attempt to include others in their circle by bringing those others face-to-face with their true needs; like the original *zaddikim*, members of Buberian communities "elevate [the] needs [of others]" before they satisfy them.

Initially, what brings members of a Buberian community together is a common yearning, a longing deep inside every human being, which Buber associates with the innate You. At the center of such communities are those who can transform that yearning from an intangible, purposeless sensation into a living response to the as yet unknown object of that yearning: being itself. Hence, consideration of Buber's theory as either metasociological or metapolitical is inaccurate and incomplete. His theory is oriented towards supporting active discovery of the essential nature of created being.

Michael Walzer comments that the creative genius in political thought is not a man who invents new symbols. "He is rather a man . . . who elaborates old symbols with a new fullness and eloquence, or . . . who explores the meaning of symbols just emerging in the thought and activity of his immediate predecessors and his contemporaries."[112] Buber is certainly a thinker of the first variety, one who elaborates old symbols with a new fullness and eloquence; whether he also meets the criteria of the second is still unclear. As suggested by Bernard Susser, Buber's vision may evoke an "ineffable meta-political ideal" that cannot animate any real political program and thus will remain, as he claims Buber admits, "a utopian vision."[113] Yet perhaps Buber has seen what others have not, a shift within modern societies in the perception of contemporary conventions regarding relation to self and to cosmos. This newfound relation is commensurate with his understanding of the "fully realized, whole" human life. If so, Buber's voice may also represent Walzer's second kind of creative genius, who "explores the meanings of symbols just emerging in the thought . . . of his immediate predecessors and his contemporaries." To appreciate the originality of this second possibility, the English-speaking reader should bear in mind that Buber wrote decades before the cultural upheavals of the 1960s and the search for innovative forms of community that followed in their wake.

Whatever Buber's eventual contribution to the history of Western political thought may be, the dialogical center of community on which he builds his system is a symbolic figure for emulation. Buber describes persons whose relation to what is creates a quality of relationships that would enable others to reach full self-realization. These persons are no longer alienated individuals of the alienating modern society, no longer passive objects of the impersonal state's control, no longer persons whose actions are devoid of any relation to the cosmos. Instead, such persons are part of fellowship, supported by a symbolic world that assigns them a specific task and a promise for self-realization; the persons' movements, determined by a newfound self-knowledge, are attuned to the callings of the twofold nature of being; these persons create in the course of their everyday relationships the substance from which order is perceived. This is Buber's "Torah on one foot."[114] However, in these concluding comments, we again encounter the paradox inherent in Buber's works: like the teaching of the Tao ("the name that can be named is not the name"),[115] the relation that can be spoken of is not the relation.

Are we then left without concrete guidance as to the way to establish a community commensurate with the vision Buber presents in his writings? Consideration of this question leads us to Buber's commitments as a member of an actual community that was undergoing dramatic transformations in his lifetime. We therefore turn to an examination of the way Buber related to Zionism and to the return of the Jews to the land of their dreams, Israel.

# 7

# DIALOGUE AS POLITICS: ZIONISM AND THE (MIS)MEETING OF BIBLE, HISTORY, PHILOSOPHY, AND POLITICS

B uber's penchant for indirect allusion and for mythical thinking becomes a liability when he seeks *political* solutions to the difficulties
created by Jewish migration to Palestine. The image of the Zionist *halutz*
(the common idiom connoting the socialist "pioneer"),[1] for example,
whom Buber idealized in his writings about the Jewish immigration to
Palestine, does not accord appropriate consideration to the self-conception of these very real persons, who largely were oblivious to the intentions Buber attributed to them. This creates an intrinsic paradox: when
reflecting on the Zionist undertaking, Buber depicts the socialist *halutz*
as a living embodiment of the fulfillment of the spiritual mission of Judaism in the land of Israel;[2] yet at the same time, Buber saw in the *halutzim*
only a future possibility. Buber thus portrays the *halutz* as both the living
embodiment of the "new type" of person and one who might, under
certain conditions, become such a person. From the latter perspective,
the communal kibbutz movement and its *halutzim* had only the *potential*
to become the social basis for the emergence of a "new type."

These and other contradictions in Buber's works can be traced to
his concern with bringing the mythical image of the central, fully realized dialogical person, the linchpin of the social system he envisions, to
historical life.[3] This chapter thus advances an internal critique of Buber's
mode of theorizing, criticizing it in terms of its own logic and presuppositions. At bottom, the closing proposition will claim that Buber's attempt to translate the "secret" of Judaism into direct political practice

179

was an experiment that did not succeed.[4] His vision of a dialogical community of persons who are aware of the magnitude of the self- and
communal transformation they must undergo, could not materialize
through the deeds of political actors who were merely unconscious (and
unwitting) participants in the realization of the teaching and testimony
of the Hebrew tradition.

We begin this critique with an overview of Buber's Zionism.


## ZIONISM: THE BUBERIAN VISION

Buber considered Zionism to be a political expression of the deep
yearning for spiritual renewal that for him was the heart and "secret" of
Judaism. Translated into a social vision, the return to the land was to be
a turn toward a radically transformed form of social association, one that
would establish exemplary communal units of the yet-to-be civilization
of dialogue. By interpreting the political program and policies of Zionism in terms of their commensurability with this spiritual goal, Buber
attempted to introduce a view into the discourse of the emerging Jewish
political entity that the statist and secular leadership of the Zionist movement found incommensurate with the realities of power politics and of
historical contingencies. Zionism as politics was Buber's "hope for this
hour"[5] because he saw in it the potential to translate the desire for national liberation into a radically novel form of association that would
demonstrate in deeds the possibility of bringing back to common experience the enchanting and empowering sensation of trust in life itself. To
trust life is to trust its forms, beginning with the most familiar form of
life, the human being.

Thus, for over sixty years (1898–1965), during a period spanning
the entire prestate period of Zionism and continuing into the first decades of the independent Jewish state, Buber advocated unpopular positions within the Zionist movement, consistently advising restraint in its
advocacy of mass immigration of Jews to Palestine, preferring immigration of Jews whose return to the land was motivated by the intention to
realize a personal need for greater self-fulfillment. After the Holocaust,
the masses of refugees and survivors made this position absolutely im-
practical. Thus, Buber commented at the time that "harassed, tormented
masses crowded into Palestine. Unlike the *halutzim*, for whom no sacri-

fice toward building the land of Jewish rebirth was too great, they saw in this land merely safety and security."[6] Buber expressed similar views in face of the mass immigration of Oriental Jews in the first years of the establishment of the state.[7] Yet he was aware that the dream had to accommodate reality; "who would have taken it upon himself to obstruct this onrush of the homeless in the name of the continuation of the selective method!"[8] In addition, he consistently urged against violence as the first resort in the growing friction with the Arab populace of Palestine, cautioning against the establishment of a separate Jewish state and advocating instead the creation of a Jewish-Arab federation.[9] From early on (see his famous speech at the 1921 Zionist congress),[10] Buber considered the Zionist movement's attitude to the Arabs in Palestine the ultimate test of Zionism's ability to practice what he thought that Jewish tradition sought to create—true dialogical communities in a world torn asunder by violence and lack of trust. Zionism—as a political expression of a spiritual phenomenon, was to show the way to solve the peculiarly modern crisis of trust.

On the face of it, this seems to be a rather strange proposition: Why should a newfound sensation of trust emerge, of all places, in the context of Jewish migration to a land inhabited by an indigenous population that perceived the Zionist enterprise as a colonialist challenge to their physical and cultural existence? Buber's response was formulated in terms of the inner, subterranean history of Judaism; the role of each Jewish generation that decides to attempt a return to the land is to decipher the mystery (*sod*) of its return and then create a historically particular social form commensurate with the realities and difficulties of its historical circumstances.[11]

Buber's discussion of the relation between the secret of the return to Zion and settlement in the ancient land of Israel can be illuminated through a quick reminder of his presentation of the image and mission of Abraham (discussed in chapter 4). The secret of the return to Zion and of the mission of the first Hebrew, Abraham, are juxtaposed by virtue of their common focus on the question of the purpose of Israel's transformation into a nation.

Like Abraham's new beginning in the aftermath of Babel, modern Zionism's new beginning takes place in the context of difficult and irreversible historical circumstances. Abraham's mission was to take place within a world of nations, created in the aftermath of Babel. This condition is analogous to the modern Zionist's return to a land occupied by an indigenous population that is hostile to Jewish migration. Both Abraham and the modern Jew had to find ways of existing as a nation among nations that would nonetheless render them paradigms of spiritual unification in the midst of historical division, using the national form to subvert itself and become a nation unlike other nations. Buber's portrayal of Abraham seems to be written with modern concerns in mind: "His goal can no longer be anymore a humanity without divisions but only a humanity that overcomes its divisions and transcends them, a unification of peoples into humanity, as a people of many peoples."[12]

Buber apparently addresses the historical and political realities of modern Zionism from within this worldview. The twentieth century posed a most daunting task for the true Zionist, who was charged with finding a way of returning to the land without adversely affecting its indigenous population. For Buber, this implied a historical challenge worthy of the people who for generations had retained a memory of the justice and ethics embodied in the ancient teaching and testimony. If the Zionist movement would consider the relation to the Arab inhabitants of the land a test of their commitment to the prophetic heritage, wrote Buber, then a truly new form of human community might come into being. He addressed this concern in unequivocal terms: "If we are able to withstand the challenge, this will be the beginning of a new kind of human togetherness. Indeed, it seems that every time [that the Jewish people attempt to resettle the land] the role becomes more difficult. . . . It is more difficult when the return has to take into account the presence of another people on the land."[13]

Buber added the significant comment: "This fact of life should not be removed from the mission."[14] Simply stated, Buber considered the presence of Palestinian Arabs in the land essential for the fulfillment of Israel's mission: to demonstrate how mistrust may be overcome in a context that appears destined to create the opposite result. If the Jews create a community based on a dialogical relation in its inner relationships as well as in relations with neighboring communities (thereby engendering the I–You quality in interpersonal relationships that gives rise to the Between), their success will serve as a living testament to human ability to overcome the presupposition that conflict and division are "natural" elements of human existence.

Yet to understand Buber's vision and its relation to the political concerns of his day necessitates reflection upon, and acceptance of, his novel relation to history ("hidden" and "apparent") and acceptance of his assumption regarding the relation between social structures and revolutionizing people's view of ontology. Such acceptance did not materialize among the members of Buber's generation, his good intentions notwithstanding.

In explaining this disparity between intention and effect, I shall show that Buber's relation to Zion is too complex for it to be easily translated into an effective kind of political discourse. Very few people who supported his political stance were aware of its roots in the worldview uncovered in this book. These were primarily from the very refined intellectual elite of Jerusalem, some of whom had developed their initial understanding of Zionism under the influence of their meeting Buber in Europe prior to their immigration to Palestine.[15] These were a select few. Unaware of the magnitude of the transformation that Buber envisioned and equally inattentive to the deep-rooted implications of his biblical studies for the apparently secular discourse of his utopian socialism, many of Buber's other admirers (not to mention his many more detractors) found him too naive in his response to the practical demands of political "realities."

Buber may have been mistaken in his attempts to insert oblique references (guiding words and phrases) into his political statements. These served to confuse his listeners and readers more than to guide them. As such, Buber may have been an unwitting example of Rousseau's sage, one who "insist[s] on speaking in [his] own language to the vulgar instead of in the vulgar language." Such a sage, warned Rousseau, "will not be understood."[16] This was apparently the fate of Buber's political writings on Zionism and on its most original contributions to socialist practice, the *halutz* (pioneer) and the kibbutz (the communal form created by the socialist pioneers). In political practice, one reacts to the external form, not to the inner light; to easily digestible statements, not to slowly filtering words.

There are many concrete examples of Buber's unpopular positions vis-à-vis Zionism's political goals and practices. Some of the most telling have been collected by Paul Mendes-Flohr in the volume *A Land of Two Peoples*.[17] However, rather than deal with a particular controversy, I would like to consider an anecdote that raises the question of the practicality of Buber's way of addressing the contingencies and leaders of his times and points to the apparent dissonance between the vision and tongue of a "sage" and the perspective and discourse of a "statesman." The anecdote I have in mind is an exchange between Buber and David Ben-Gurion, the political founder, master statesman, and first prime minister of the State of Israel.

In 1949, Buber was one of a small group of intellectuals who met with the prime minister. In the meeting, Buber noted that politicians used the Hebrew word for "redemption" (*geula*) to create politically effective slogans such as "redemption of the land," "redemption of Hebrew labor," or "redemption of the person in Israel." Most of those who used this word in the service of political slogans, added Buber, did not contemplate its meaning. This comment implied that taken out of its context in traditional discourse, the word "redemption" becomes a rhetorical cue in the war of words of a modern political debate. For example, when using the word "redemption" in relation to the soil, the implied political meaning is not "to redeem the land" (whatever that may mean for tradition, in itself the subject of countless discussions throughout the ages of exile) but rather "to make it our own." "To make it our own" in the political sense is to make sure that Jewish ownership of the land is manifestly evident, through the land's being settled, tilled, and defended by Jews. The political issue at stake is who owns the land? Buber charged that the use of "redemption" was an attempt to obfuscate the thorny question of political sovereignty and the yet more difficult ethical questions that came with the Jewish–Arab conflict over ownership of the land. By enveloping the purely political question of ownership in an appeal to past dreams of redemption and promises of salvation, the mythical discourse of *geula* became intertwined with modern political questions of sovereignty and national rights. Secularization of an ancient idiom by politicians deprived it of its messianic and redemptive overtones, and infused it instead with Hobbesian notions of "mine or thine."

Note that in this analysis, what Buber really cares about was to retain the purity of *geula* as a term that would vibrate with appropriate intensity in the souls of those who understood what redemption was all about. Unlike political actors, who use such words in order to evoke superficial emotions, Buber wanted to keep this notion alive in its original meaning. Pressing this point yet further, Buber asked, "Jewish land— for what purpose?" Ben-Gurion could not contain his exasperation, and responded: "To bring bread from the earth!" "For what end?" "To eat!" "For what end?" "Enough!" Buber persisted:

> I ask: for what purpose do we eat? I ask, for what purpose do we live? It is not sufficient merely to live. We all know that in the life of the individual person, this is not enough. The individual knows that merely to live is not enough, and that there has to be a life "for" [a higher telos]. But when we talk about groups, about a people, the discourse immediately changes. We say, a people lives for itself. I reject this response. I also reject it when uttered in the discourse of other peoples, but I do not have the authority to speak on their behalf. Whatever be the case, [I reject this response] in the case of Israel.[18]

Politicians—even statesmen of Ben-Gurion's stature—want to ensure that there is bread to eat before asking, "why eat?" They want to ensure physical existence before asking, "why exist?" To ask, "why? for what ultimate purpose?" before inquiring, "what should be done and by what means?" is contrary to the way politics is conducted in the modern nation-state. In politics, results are given precedence over questions, just as discernible deeds are given preference over invisible intentions. Yet for Buber, exchanges with political practitioners were opportunities to expose the absence of a firm understanding of the higher purposes of life that social and political institutions ought to support. He represented the view upheld by both philosophers and prophets that ethical imperatives and spiritual development cannot, and should not, be disregarded when one enters the sphere of politics or society.[19] In this respect, Buber is a participant in the ongoing debate within Western philosophy about the tension between philosophy and politics, a question that has been present in Western political thought since the challenge posed by Socrates and Plato to the Athenian city, its Sophists, and its statesmen.

This is but one of many examples of the way Buber's political vision fell on deaf ears. The political implications of Buber's worldview isolated him from the mainstream of his own people. As a political actor, Buber was considered ineffective. Historical events seemed to overshadow his presence and to "marginalize" him. How did a thinker so sensitive both to history and to social renewal become ineffective precisely during his own community's age of epochal transformation? It seems that the answer lies in the disparity between Buber's understanding of the goal of

Zionism and the understanding of the overwhelming majority of Zionists. In contrast to Theodor Herzl, the founder of mainstream political Zionism, who (in Buber's words) considered Zionism to be "a road that is paved between an inferior present and its improved continuity," Buber imagined it as "a rope strung between the secret of a distant past and the secret of an immediate or distant future."[20] For Buber, Zionism was not an incremental improvement of existing conditions or a wholesale importation of existing social practices. It was a revelation of the "secret." As such, consideration of Buber's "failure" as a politician enables us to contemplate the relation between his insight, his indirect way of writing about his insight, his theory of dialogical community, and his vision of a global civilization of dialogue that would emerge from the changes in views of ontology prevailing in, and creating the devastating history of, the twentieth century. These themes are intertwined in the next section.

## ZIONISM AND THE "SECRET" OF JUDAISM

As he matured in years and understanding, Buber maintained that the realization in one's life of the teaching transmitted in the Jewish tradition is the most important deed a person can undertake. He wrote that to discover and relate the existence of the "secret" is the proper role of those who write. Against those whose work constituted an effort to relate to the "secret," Buber posited "the wretchedness of that typical person of our generation, who is blind to the secret yet is willing to testify that what we refer to in its name [i.e., "secret," *sod*] exists only in speech."[21]

The notion of *sod* is central to Buber's discussion of Abraham's mission—the mythical reality that guided his political thinking—as it is to his discussion of the "creation" assigned to Adam. Hence his otherwise obscure comment that "[what] is given to him to create, is shrouded in mystery [*atoof besod*]."[22] The mystery, we have seen, is explored first and foremost by the individual, in his or her attempt to attain inclusive self-knowledge. The mending of the world begins with the mending of self.[23]

Buber's retelling of Hasidic tales, his studies of the Hebrew Bible, and his presentation of the hidden communities of prophets and of the apparent communities of Hasidim were surely written with this under-standing of the word *sod* in mind. That is why he writes that he at-tempted to transmit the *torah* of the realization, of the absolute service, both *directly*, by recounting tales from the lives of those persons whose hidden deeds exemplify the nature of the service, and *indirectly*, "by in-terpretation of that *torah*, from the perspective of the predicament of humanity and of Israel at this hour."[24] Buber mentions the predicaments of humanity and of Judaism in the same breath because the "hidden" secret transmitted by Judaism addresses the human being regardless of religious or other distinctions. Gershom Scholem has referred to this aspect of the writer's vocation as sensitivity to the " 'mystery' that dwells in the midst of life"[25]—*all* life, not only Jewish life.

However, when mentioning the "secret" that is present in the de-sire of this particular people (Jews) to settle in this particular land (the "land of Israel"), Buber refuses to elaborate the precise implication of attaining the unity of this particular people with this particular piece of territory, claiming that this level of interpretation "is and will remain a secret—what has happened, what happens, and what will happen be-tween the two."[26] Here we begin to sense the problematic of using guiding words in the context of concrete political contingencies. A Jew-ish Zionist of the pre-Holocaust period needed concrete responses to the following questions: Why not continue the pattern of immigration established by my persecuted ancestors and go to whatever country is willing to accept me and my family—for example, the United States or Australia? Why should I struggle to liberate myself and my people in Palestine? Why not accept Uganda or some other tract of land offered to me by the colonial powers? Why accept the response that Palestine is my place on the basis of the statement that "there is a secret" one needs to acknowledge prior to making the choice to immigrate to that particu-lar place?

Buber's answers are inadequate, if considered in the context of the hypothetical questions raised above. They are formulated in terms of a critique of the predominant conceptions held by the political leadership of the Zionist movement. As such they are not infused with positive instruction that can serve as an alternative to the worldview that Buber so eloquently rejects. He writes that in the process of accepting Zionism as the unifying concept for their movement of national liberation, the politically oriented leadership of the Zionist movement inadvertently inherited the "secret" embedded in this idea. However, Buber says, oblivious to the implications that the esoteric dimensions of the idea of "Zion" had for a thorough understanding of the unique mission of Israel that they inherited, these predominantly secular leaders attempted to eliminate traces of the "secret." Buber posits that among these secular leaders of the Zionist movement, to mention a "secret" or "mystery" of Zion was to resort to the Jewish past, to the idiom of an unnecessary relic of an obsolete religion. "The secular element within Zionism was arrayed also [i.e., not only against the religious establishment of Judaism but also] against the secret of Zion," writes Buber, adding: "A people like all peoples, a land like all lands, a national movement like all national movements—this is proclaimed in the name of national common sense, against every 'mystery.' "[27] Leaving the exact meaning of the "secret" and "mystery" unclear, Buber attempts to draw attention to their enigmatic presence in the shadows of historical developments by criticizing what he considers the political establishment's disregard of this background.

In his introduction to his book on the idea of Zion, *Between a People and its Land*, Buber, having stated his case against the secular leadership of the Zionist movement, concludes with a statement comprehensible and meaningful only when assessed in terms of the perspectives we have previously pointed out: "This book calls the certainty of the generations of Israel to witness that [these ideas of the secular Zionists] are not sufficient. . . . If we give up the secret, we then give up reality itself. National forms, without the eternal spirit from which they were born, imply the end of the unique fertility of Israel."[28] There is no doubt in my mind that an average socialist pioneer (and an ordinary bourgeois, too), even one relatively well versed in the Jewish sources, would consider inadequate, and perhaps incomprehensible, justifications for his actions couched in terms of such an oblique reference to the secret immanent in the meeting of person and land.

Aware of the difficulty of communicating his vision and translating it into political practice, Buber deployed numerous literary strategies to overcome resistance to his veiws. His novel way of deciphering the Hebrew Bible's hermeneutics, his recasting of Jewish history in terms of apparent and hidden "doers," and his presentation of communal events (such as Hasidism) in terms of their contribution to the renewal of Judaism from within were oriented to establishing a narrative that would posit the present in terms of a past hitherto not conceived in "historical" terms. In this respect, he is not different from other Zionist leaders, who envisioned the future in terms of a reconstructed past. His uniqueness lies in his attempt to consider Zionism as a direct continuity with the Jewish heritage. This was in diametric opposition to the dominant perception of the secular-socialist Zionists, whose self-conception included both a radical break from the passive exilic past and a notion of themselves as a new Jewish order based on the ideals and values of the Enlightenment.[29]

We shall continue to attend to these vexing questions: How can the meeting of biblical and Zionist imagery take place in political reality? Can the secret embedded in hermeneutics turn into practical politics? In the following sections, we shall consider Buber's way of casting the historical present in terms of the legendary past, showing how this mixture of tongues, while coherent to readers of this book, must have been incomprehensible to the political actors of his stormy times.

## THE INDIVIDUAL PIONEER: A. D. GORDON AS A HISTORICAL METAPHOR OF THE DIALOGICAL LEADER

Buber presents A. D. Gordon (1856–1922), already a towering figure in his own lifetime, as the historical metaphor of Buber's dialogical image. Gordon emigrated to Palestine at age forty eight, transplanting his intellectual existence from the seclusion of his study in Russia to the orchards and vineyards of the land of Israel. During the last ten years of his life, spent in Deganya (the first and most influential kibbutz of the time), Gordon became a legendary figure, renowned for his unshakable conviction that Judaism would be renewed only through direct cultivation of the soil and the communal organization of Jewish settlements.[30] Buber's close associate, Ernst Simon, writes that prior to meeting Franz Rosenzweig, Buber did not admire any living man more than he did Gordon. Buber's veneration of Gordon, adds Simon, was mingled with a trace of jealousy; Gordon realized his life mission fully, embodying in his deeds the idea he was called on to present. Buber, torn as he was between his Jewish and other callings, did not devote himself fully to one mission as Gordon did so successfully.[31] To Buber, Gordon exemplified the ideal *halutz*, the revolutionary pioneer of the Jewish socialist movement.[32]

Buber writes that Gordon's great achievement was his perception and realization of the demand that every human being live in true accord with nature, associating "directly with the powers of nature." Buber understands this to constitute a relation with both the natural environment and the cosmos.[33] He clarified the presence of an all-encompassing conception of cosmos in Gordon's thought by comparing Gordon to Thoreau, a thinker who manifested a largely similar affinity with nature: "When I read in Thoreau that the chief thing is to see man as an inhabitant, or a parcel of nature, rather than a member of society, I hear the voice of Gordon. But for these Americans nature is nevertheless still fundamentally the landscape, it is not so really and truly the Cosmos as for Gordon. In their words I see the trees more clearly than the stars."[34] What Buber seems to imply is that compared with Gordon, Thoreau was more attuned to the immediate natural environment than to the interconnection of the landscape and this planet with all creation.

A new type of man, Buber contends, is not created in the imagination of a poet or in the fantasy of a romantic. Such a type is a factual, historical entity, a human life that enters historical reality and is summoned to address the challenges and conditions of the realities it encounters. By comparing Gordon with Walt Whitman as well as with Thoreau, Buber attempts to show how Gordon's life was intertwined with the destiny of his community. According to Buber, Gordon became what Walt Whitman was not and could not be because of the circumstances of his historical situation. Whitman the poet says that the ambitious thought of his song is to further the forming of "a great aggregate nature." Whitman the man, however, was not confronted by historical circumstances that unequivocally challenged him to embody in his life a way commensurate with the goal he articulated in his poetry. Gordon, in contrast, although less articulate, was ordered by his life circumstances to do what Whitman could only talk about; Gordon became "the pioneer of his people on the way to a renewed participation in the life of the Cosmos."[35]

Gordon's brand of socialism, based as it was on a combination of return to the land, life in agricultural communes, and the ideal of self-labor (i.e., not employing wage laborers in the communes), was guided by his striving to unite with the cosmic. Buber sees Gordon's primary contribution to the renewal of Jewish life in Palestine in Gordon's contention (in contradistinction to the dominant, "political" stream of Zionism) that the problem of Jews was to be sought in their fall not from political self-determination but from the cosmos: "The men sent by a newly arising Israel to work on the soil of its land represent its reunion, not merely with the earth but with the Cosmos."[36]

That Gordon's influence stemmed from his deeds, from his way of life, was for Buber a source of lasting admiration. Gordon chose to live in Palestine because it was there and only there that he felt it was possible to translate his contemplation of nature into a direct, organic participation in the life of the land among his own people. Gordon was above all one who acted; he did not venture to speculate about transcendence: "he wants to make a statement not about Being itself but merely about the experience of Being." It is precisely this experience that Buber wished myths and legends to transmit and evoke and persons attracted to these writings to explore and experience. Through examples such as those set by (Buber's depiction of) the life of Gordon, the new Jewish settlements might find their way: "Israel will restore the wholeness of human nature through the work of its people in the natural world of the countryside."[37]

Judged by the standards of organized religion, Gordon was surely a nonbeliever, yet Buber considered him deeply religious in the real sense of the word. Buber quotes him as saying that the main idea is to establish a new "relationship to the mystery of existence and life" for the Jews.[38] In the Jewish setting, Gordon exemplified the life of one who strives to establish a dialogue with the entire range of existence, both the historical and the eternal. For Buber, Gordon's deeds thus manifested one practical expression of the way of true *socialitas* developed in relation to the goals of true *religio*,[39] each attuned to experiencing the mystery of existence in ordinary life situations.

## THE COMMUNAL KIBBUTZ: BETWEEN HASIDISM AS *SOCIALITAS* AND ZIONISM AS *RELIGIO*

Buber was surely aware that the *halutzim* were largely atheists, who hardly represented *religious* socialism, and were similarly divorced from a conscious relation to ancient Judaism's conception of social justice. They were simply emancipated, late-nineteenth-century socialists whose role models were Marx, Lenin, Bucharin, Luxemburg—the entire melange of modern socialist radicals. In fact, it was precisely these heroes that Buber sought to supplant in his portrayal of A. D. Gordon as the ideal *halutz* and in *Paths in Utopia*'s reading of the deeds of major figures in the history of the international socialist movement. It was for the *halutzim*—these emancipated, idealistic young Jews that Buber sought to reinterpret the tradition that—in its ossified form of Orthodox community and culture—they wholeheartedly rejected.[40]

In historical reality, the Jewishness of the *halutzim* was not a religious identity but a national one, marked by signs of nineteenth-century national self-identity. Most of the *halutzim* would have accepted without reservation Marx's contention that a "realm of God" separate from a "realm of man" exists only in the imagination and that speculations about these supposed "realms" is but a "learned pastime . . . [and] theoretical bubble-blowing."[41] In itself, this prevalent attitude to religion did not conflict with Buber's. His second thesis on religious socialism attests to Buber's sharing with the *halutzim* a rejection of that aspect of Judaism that is mere ritual or homiletics. However, unlike most *halutzim*, Buber did not reject—and indeed hoped to revive—a sense of true *religio* inaccessible to modern persons in general and to the *halutzim* in particular. He therefore postulated, in terms reminiscent of his essay on religious socialism, that "a Jewish nation cannot exist without religion any more than a Jewish religious community without nationality. Our only salvation is to become Israel again, to become a whole, the unique whole of a people and a religious community: a renewed people, a renewed religion, and the renewed unity of both."[42]

Buber attempted to transform the attitude of the *halutzim* in more than one way. We have already discussed his presentation of a person in their midst, A. D. Gordon, in terms that emphasized Buber's portrayal of Zionism and his ideal of leadership. In chapters 4, 5, and 6 we noted Buber's revision of Jewish myths and legends as an indirect means of transforming his audience's self-perception. This revision, although drawing on Jewish sources, was not directed exclusively at the *halutzim*. When writing for or addressing the *halutzim* directly, Buber used their socialist idioms, in an attempt to teach them the connection between socialism and the Jewish heritage by establishing a direct historical link, underscoring the continuity between the kibbutz and previous social movements within Judaism and illuminating selected aspects of Judaism that he thought the *halutzim* were, or should have been, reviving.

Thus, Buber refers to the *halutzim* as a specifically Jewish phenomenon (and not as a local branch of a European ideology), realizing in their lives Judaism's age-old goal of establishing a community in the land of Israel that exemplifies social justice.[43] The attempt to establish such a paradigmatic community is a goal shared by socialism and Hasidism. In this respect, Buber presents the Hasidim as historical forerunners of the *halutzim*: "Following the tragic end of the great Hasidic endeavor to create a fellowship of persons, the Jewish striving to realize a yearning that has not been satisfied again emerges and creates for itself a new human type."[44] Accordingly, Buber sees in Jewish socialism an attempt to create, under modern conditions, a community that would satisfy the age-old Jewish "yearning" for the establishment of a "fellowship of persons."

In Buber's allusion to the Hasidic forerunners, he emphasizes the Hasidic role in establishing, or renewing, a quality of fellowship that is always in danger of disappearing from humanity's experience. Furthermore, Buber portrays the Hasidic community as a model of a social pattern that progresses from the relationships between the living center and his disciples to family, neighborhood, settlement, and community.[45] This is a positive form of interdependence, a specifically Jewish form of community that gives rise to the communion of *religio* and *socialitas*.

Having established the Hasidic precedent as an archetype, Buber goes on to consider the renewal of Jewish community by the *halutzim* in analogous terms. He refers to the establishment of the socialist communes and the spread of the spirit of fellowship that these communes generate as a gradual movement outward, through the layers of society, from the core to the periphery.[46] Consequently, he tells the *halutzim* not to be disheartened by the resistance they may encounter. The *halutzim* were opposed by persons adhering to the goals of capitalism, a segment of society Buber refers to as "degenerative elements." It is precisely the challenge of creating a just community in the face of such opposition, encountered in ordinary (and not in detached, "utopian") conditions of life, that they, like their Hasidic predecessors, are called to address. Although neat, this analogy draws our attention to a critical tension in Buber's thinking and writing.

In chapter 6, Buber's revision of Hasidic history and legends was shown to be guided by the goal of portraying the early Hasidic community as a paradigm of social conduct, marked by the commitment of the living center, the *zaddik*, to his own, his fellows', and his community's "turning" to true being. This "turning" was manifested in the Ba'al Shem's attempt to create in apparent history a form of social life that would serve as a living reminder of possibilities of human perfection transmitted in the teaching and testimony of hidden history. Hence Buber's emphasis on the fellowship dimension of the early Hasidic community. This depiction of Hasidic life is a *mythical, legendary reality*, developed in the context of Buber's very careful and indirect mention of hidden history. The centrality of the fellowship dimension of Hasidism is Buber's mythical revision of apparent history, a revision constructed so as to better serve his social vision.

When turning to the *halutzim* and the early kibbutz, Buber situates their historical reality in the context of the mythical reality of Hasidism. In other words, Buber blurs, and at times disregards the distinction between myth and history. He uses the same language to portray hidden and apparent historical "realities," forgoing the careful choice of words characteristic of his nonpolitical writings. Having combined the two realities and considered them as one, Buber goes on to depict the kibbutz as a link in an ongoing *historical* effort. Instead of leaving the mythical image to "stand above the heads of men,"[47] Buber begins to speak of the mythical construct as if it were actual history.

Buber's apparent disregard of historical facts, a propensity that serves him well in his endeavor to articulate a clear worldview, now has the opposite effect; it confuses, rather than clarifies, his ideas and intentions. The *zaddik*'s primary motivation and goal is cleaving to God, while the *halutz*'s primary motivation is the creation of a new social form; the *zaddik* attempts to renew Jewish *faith*, while the *halutz* is out to renew Jewish *society*. Each endeavor represents one pole of the opposites Buber seeks to reconcile in his notion of religious socialism. It is only he, Buber, who would like to have the *zaddik* pay more attention to *socialitas* and the *halutz* to *religio*. This departure from both traditions grants Buber's work its originality and explains, in part, why he attracts those who are dissatisfied with either or both traditions. Yet in his attempt to reconcile the opposites, Buber confuses historical and mythical reality; he seems to forget that the revised representation of reality he constructs as a vehicle for transforming modern ontology is a radical departure from the standard depiction of both Hasidism and socialism.

This indiscriminate mixture of mythical and historical realities is also evident in Buber's assertion that the goal of the Zionist enterprise, manifested in the deeds of its socialist vanguard, is to overcome the "lack of faith of present-day humanity, its inability truly to believe in God."[48] This assertion is based on Buber's discernment of a spirit of fellowship emerging in the socialist communes in Palestine. According to his *theory*, such a spirit can emerge only as a result of a cleaving to true *religio*. Yet the contradiction is evident. If true fellowship arises only as a result of open-ended dialogue with both God and man, then the *halutz* cannot be creating a spirit of true fellowship, as the *halutz* explicitly disavows any relation to religion or to God. Buber himself writes that the typical *halutz* rejects *all* of religion as mere ritual or sermons.[49]

Buber could have resolved these contradictions by reinterpreting reality and conceding that the interpersonal relationships characterizing the kibbutz were not as yet expressions of true *socialitas*. Alternatively, he could have revised the theory, arguing that the spirit of fellowship did indeed arise in the kibbutz but seeking its origins in a source other than the link between the turning to other persons and the turning to God. Buber would then have had to accept the possibility of establishing real fellowship without turning to God or to some other divine entity. An additional possibility would have been to argue, as he did in portraying A. D. Gordon, that the *halutz is* religious in the true sense despite his apparent secularism.

Buber seems to have chosen a different route. To bridge the apparent dissonance between the *halutz*'s avowed rejection of all religious forms and Buber's image of the *halutz* as the new type of human being who introduces to the world a quality of interpersonal relationships[50] conducive to the inclusion of the spirit in modern societies, Buber resorted to the claim that the *halutz* is a revolutionary who is unconscious of the magnitude and implications of his actions. Buber asserted that the desire to create a new form of communal life "did not come to the *halutz* from within, from his historical period, or from the West. Whether conscious of it or not, whether he likes it or not, [the *halutz*] has been attracted to the age-old yearning of the Jew to realize a true fellowship of persons."[51]

This depiction of the *halutz* as one guided by an attraction to an "age-old yearning" of which he is unconscious is at odds with the archetype the *halutz* embodies. Buber's dialogical person, of which the *halutz* is ostensibly a living embodiment, is characterized by his success in regenerating his "stunted [*verkummerten*] personal center."[52] This regeneration is the result of a "turning" to the greater reality hidden from ordinary perception; the "turning" is a *conscious* inner movement that creates an opening to, and a sensation of, that higher "reality." Yet in Buber's depiction of the *halutz*, the conscious experience central to the image of the dialogical person is replaced by a portrayal of one whose actions result from an *unconscious* attraction to a "yearning" he does not consciously acknowledge.[53] Buber's sincere desire to witness the confluence of hidden and apparent history in the political return to Zion in his lifetime appears to have led him to see the actions of others through the mediating filter of the messianic mystery.

A final twist on this confusion of tongues is illustrated through a comparison of a passage from a letter Buber wrote to the Mahatma Gandhi with a passage from Buber's *The Prophetic Faith*. Both were written in the same period, 1938–1939. In the letter to Gandhi, asking him to reconsider his criticism of Zionism for settling a land inhabited by an indigenous Arab population, Buber claims that the migration of the Jewish people to the "land of Israel" (a symbolic frame of reference) should not be judged adversely merely because some participants in the Zionist endeavor are ignorant of the magnitude of the Zionist task. The Jewish community in Palestine (a political and geographical frame of reference) will fulfill its mission at the appropriate moment, when guided by the right human type:

> At its side will stand faithful persons, persons who neither direct nor demand, neither urge nor preach, but who rather take an active part in its life, who help, wait, and are ready for the moment when they will be called upon to give the true answer to those who question. This is the more inner reality of the land; it may harbor importance not only for the solution of the crisis in Jewish faith but also for that of the crisis of faith of the entire humankind. The contact of this people with this land is not only a matter of sacred ancient history; we sense [in the meeting with our land] a secret not yet revealed.[54]

This passage indicates clearly that Buber did not consider the return to Zion to be a national movement structured along the goals and premises of late-nineteenth-century European nationalism. The return is, or should be, a solution of "the crisis of faith of the entire humankind." There is a "secret not yet revealed" in this return. I suggest that this secret has to do with my interpretation of Buber's understanding of the Bible's hidden dialogue, as discussed in chapter 3. This suggestion is substantiated by reference to a passage from *The Prophetic Faith*, written in the same year. The juxtaposition of this passage with the one from the letter to Gandhi comes to mind immediately if one is attuned to the kind of hermeneutics that we have explored in this book. As we have seen in chapter 3, this refers to the mission of Isaiah's *limmudim*, who will wait patiently for those who, in a time of severe crisis, will turn to them as the only way out of the darkness of their lives and times.

> [The *limmudim*] should wait—thus addresses them Isaiah—until at a certain time, in a time of "distress and darkness" (Isaiah 8:22), the crowd will come . . . running toward you, you who wait patiently, who are now perceived as knowing, and will entreat you, as beg those who know no dawn. . . . Then the hour will arrive: "To *torah*! To *te'udah*!" Then you shall remove the seal and unravel the bind of the scroll that is in your hearts, then you shall respond: "The people who have walked in darkness have seen a great light"(Isaiah 9:1).[55]

Comparison of the two passages reveals an unmistakable affinity in linguistic structure and latent assumptions. The emergence of the *limmudim* from the hidden shadows of the hidden history of the prophetic teaching is the symbolic reality that the appropriate leadership of the Zionist pioneers will (or should) embody. Like the biblical *limmudim*, who exist as living but concealed testimony to the *torah*, the true pioneers (*halutzim*) wait patiently, ready to transmit the teaching to those who seek it. Buber suggests that until they are addressed in those terms, the *limmudim* be active in their attempts to assist those receptive to the teaching to orient their hearts towards the hidden truth.[56]

We thus see that in Buber's writings, the *halutz* and the *limmud* represent images of the Hebrew way initiated by Abraham. Yet for the myth to become reality, real persons are needed. This is where the weakness of Buber's idealization of the pioneers comes into the fore, exemplified in his reading of the kibbutz movement as a fulfillment of Jewish destiny.

## SQUARING THE CIRCLE:
## THE INTERMEDIARY ROLE OF THE EDUCATOR

The confusion of mythical and historical reality does not end at this point. One eventuality that Buber contemplated was that the *halutz* might indeed be attracted to the relevance of Judaism and its ancient truths. What should the *halutz* then do? Buber suggests that he turn to the "genuine educator" for further guidance and direction.[57] The transition from the discovery of the truths encapsulated in the image of the ideal *halutz* to concrete social action thus seems to necessitate additional mediation. The *halutz* is to seek out one who is aware of the stakes and the complexity of the phenomenon that the *halutz* embodies.

For Buber, the educator facilitates contact with the hidden aspect of being by leading the *halutz* to realize that a relation to the sacred is an experience, not merely an idea.[58] First, he helps the *halutz* develop latent attitudes that make plausible the existence of the larger reality to which he could be introduced. Among these attitudes are a "healthy" attitude to tradition, an openness to the sacred that implies freedom from fixed preconceptions about "religion," and respect for the secrets of nature and life.[59] In an even broader context, the educator cultivates attitudes receptive to the universal dimensions of a Jewish nationalism that would enable the people of Israel to realize the transnational norms inherent in their particular national movement.[60] An education developed along these lines would call for review and study of the origins of the Jewish nation, inevitably pointing to the real roots of the people in the original meeting with the spirit.[61] Perhaps Buber hoped that through study of the hidden dimensions of the Hebrew sources, the educator would experience the shock of self-recognition suggested as part of the Buberian *therapia*. The educator would also assist the *halutz* by expanding his educational activities to the general community, to the outer circles of the *halutz*'s society. The educator's task, according to Buber, is to bring to those who are not part of the community of *halutzim*, such as urban youth, a taste of the spirit that has given rise to the *halutz*, creating the basis for communication and interaction among the various circles of society. In this context, Buber emphasizes the importance of conveying to non*halutzim* the spirit of fellowship that stems from a positive kind of naivete—a defining feature of the *halutz*.

The crucial role of education and of the "genuine educator" as links between living persons and the traits of the dialogical person they are to emulate is not limited to Buber's writings on the *halutz* and Judaism. The "educator" is also a salient feature of Buber's socialist works. Buber devotes a chapter of *Paths in Utopia* to several major failed attempts to establish cooperative settlements. Such failures, he claims, result from the very egoism that is the malady of the modern civilization that knows no You, that is far removed from the person-orientation. Part of the cure for this malady is the "educative force . . . [that] could assure to the communal will a lasting victory over the residue of egoism that inevitably goes with [this experiment in renewing social life] or rather raise this egoism to a higher form."[62] What is the source and the precise meaning of this mysterious "educative force"? Buber offers no direct answers. One thing seems certain. Directing the reader or listener to intrinsic, hidden hermeneutics would be irrelevant, serving no apparent purpose, as real education is presence, not hermeneutic theory.

Inclusion of the "genuine educator" and the "educative force" as crucial facilitators of the transition from ideal image to practical action is confusing, to say the least. The obliviousness of the *halutzim* to the magnitude of what Buber takes to be their mission necessitates such intermediaries. But now we have two ideal images, the *halutz* (or in Buber's more general social theory, the "ideal revolutionary")[63] and the educator, fulfilling tasks that according to his social theory, are to be carried out by exemplary centers of community. We may recall that in contradistinction to this portrayal of the *halutz*, the builder and the *zaddikim* are "living centers" of community whose direct *un*mediated relationships with their community and with being are the basic virtue that sets them apart from ordinary persons. Having found the way to develop the correct attitude to the twofold nature of being, these living centers create social environments that help others to find the way. Their attitude to community and interpersonal relations is not dependent on the development of any additional latent qualities. The *halutzim*, in contrast, are unaware of their transmission of an ancient teaching and need the guidance of others to learn the true meaning of their actions.

Buber's response to the question "who is to educate the educators?" is the least satisfactory of all. The educator of the *halutz*, says Buber, undergoes "self-education" in a way that is "somehow granted to us." Buber is similarly vague when he suggests:

> The education of men by men means the selection of the effective
> world by a person and in him. The educator gathers in the construc-
> tive forces of the world. He distinguishes, rejects, and confirms in
> himself, in his self which is filled with the world. The constructive
> forces are eternally the same: they are the world bound up in commu-
> nity, turned to God. The educator educates himself to be their ve-
> hicle.[64]

These are platitudes, not concrete explanations. By obscuring the issue
at this critical juncture, Buber leads one to suspect that he does not
know how to effect the transformation he so clearly desires. He can
"bring before his pupils the image of a great character" yet cannot show
how this image is realized, how the educator or his student actually go
about attaining a "rebirth of personal unity."[65] Buber's penchant for
mythical thought, which serves him well in setting up the vision and the
theory, gets in the way of his addressing concrete social reality. The
"genuine educator" is just as abstract an image as the "ideal *halutz*."

In short, Buber's commitment to a form of religious socialism ordered around a living center of community—in itself a layer of thinking
that represents a deep understanding of the origins and goals of the Hebraic tradition—led him to portray in myth and legend the person whose
virtues bring into existence such a form of communal interdependence.
The concrete inspiration for the dialogical, fully realized person is
molded out of the material of Jewish legend, drawing on presumed char-
acteristics of mythologized figures such as the prophet and the *zaddik*.
Contrary to historical evidence, Buber portrays the Hasidic community
as oriented primarily towards creation of new forms of interpersonal
relationships. We have noted that this revision is understandable in terms
of Buber's endeavor to portray Hasidism's and the Ba'al Shem's practical
way of presenting modern society with a radically transformed vision of
community. However, by viewing his immediate reality in terms derived
from the mythical entity he created in the service of his social vision,
Buber stretches the myth too far and misrepresents reality.

This point may be considered from a different perspective. Unlike
the *zaddikim*, the *halutzim* were not mythical figures from the past; they
were living persons who addressed one another as *halutz* and would not
redefine their self-perception simply because of Buber's interpretation
of their hidden purpose. Similarities notwithstanding, Buber's attempt

to redefine the *halutz*'s self-awareness cannot be likened to Marx's endeavor to transform worker consciousness by creating the category of proletarian. Marx invented this classification and attempted to introduce it into socialist discourse,[66] whereas the term *halutz* was already established as part of ordinary discourse in Palestine, primarily connoting a socialist pioneer who establishes the social underpinnings for a new way of life for the predominantly urban, bourgeois Jews returning to their promised land. The *Halutzim's* was a secular, socialist way of life. To attain the kind of transforming impact that Marx sought to effect by calling the worker to consider himself in terms of a new idiom, Buber would have had to replace the notion of *halutz*, associated with a particular form of socialism, with a different concept. However, Buber chose to address the Jewish socialists in their own idiom, retaining the concept but attributing a meaning to it that others did not fully realize or understand. We are aware that this method is characteristic of Buber's use of the written word. Consider his assumption regarding the inner meaning of "socialism" as *socialitas*: when he uses the word in ordinary contexts, the meaning he assumes to be shared is absent. The statements he makes are thus inevitably open to misunderstanding.

This is the political theorist's perennial dilemma: if he speaks the language of his audience, he cannot revise their assumptions; if he eschews that language, he cannot communicate with them. Instead of enlightening his audience, Buber at times confuses—and even irritates—them. Having read Buber's essay "The *Halutz* and His World," one of Buber's followers, a member of a kibbutz, commented disparagingly: "I often ask myself: 'is that really spoken seriously in the face of the reality such as I have come to know it in the last years?' "[67]

## THE DIALOGICAL MYTH
## AND THE JEWISH–ARAB CONFLICT

Another of Buber's misguided attempts to apply his conceptions to concrete reality is his 1947 suggestion that the Jews and Arabs living in Palestine establish a joint supreme council comprising representatives from both communities. At the center of this council, mediating between the warring factions, are to be "several members of [a] circle of impartial men." These are to be persons "of impartial mind . . . who have not fallen prey to, or become entangled in, the war of all against all for dominion and possession."[68] This suggestion, we note, came at a time when it was clear that Palestine was to be partitioned and that the exact boundaries of the two states would probably be determined by the outcome of an inevitable war. Averting war would have required more than an expression of hope that some unidentified "impartial men" take it upon themselves to mediate between the factions. While the substance of this suggestion reflects Buber's preoccupation with the idea of the central, fully realized dialogical person and with Zionism's responsibility to manifest a transformed attitude to politics and to political power—and thus again points to the inner unity this idea grants to his thought—its timing calls his political judgment seriously into question.[69]

The "impartial persons" to whom Buber refers in his call for Jewish–Arab reconciliation seem to be the same ones he envisions as struggling for the future of humanity along a "front—*only seldom perceived by those who compose it*—that cuts across all the fronts of the hour, both the external and the internal." Buber depicts these persons as unconscious constituents of a movement underway in diverse social and cultural settings, a movement of which he is an approving witness: "There they stand, ranged side by side, the men of real conviction who are found in all groups, all parties, all peoples, *yet who know little or nothing of one another from group to group, from party to party, from people to people. As different as the goals are in one place and in another, it is still one front, for they are all engaged in the one fight for human truth.*"[70]

This portrayal may appeal to the imagination and may even project a noteworthy vision of the future global community of communities coming into being as part of a civilization of dialogue. However, once again, as in the case of the *halutz*, we see a group of persons who, according to Buber, transform the world towards spirituality without being aware of the process of which they are a part.[71] In this respect and for these reasons, we must join those who criticize Buber for not providing any clear direction for concrete social action.[72]

## THE NAZI RISE TO POWER AND THE HOLOCAUST: BETWEEN EDUCATION AND DEED

A final example of the difficulty encountered by members of Buber's generation in fathoming the meaning of his words is exemplified in his relation to the Holocaust. The goal Buber considered most urgent and immediate in the face of the Nazi rise to power was to effect a spiritual renewal of Judaism by establishing centers of adult education and learning. In June 1934, he wrote that by creating a network of Jewish centers for adult education, he did not intend to provide students with mere knowledge but meant to "arm [them] . . . for survival." Jewish human beings (as all human beings), wrote Buber, must educate themselves not only to ensure physical survival but "to acquire the essence of their being."[73] Buber recognized in Nazism a crisis of humanity, not only a German event that occurred in isolation from the development of modern man. To him, it represented a crisis in man's self-knowledge, manifest in the deeds of Nazi Germany. Hitler was a historical metaphor for extreme evil, for a civilization ruled by one whose attitude to being is that of monologism become diabolical.

This approach met with mixed responses. Some members of the Jewish community in Germany who were privy to Buber's undertaking of adult education testify that this activity was indeed "a form of spiritual resistance."[74] But many others were skeptical of the importance of spirituality in the face of violence and prejudice. One may imagine many persecuted persons asking then, as we may continue to ask today: "What is the concrete response expected of us? What is the use of 'spirituality' in the face of violence, cruelty and evil? Of what use is my spirituality when my children are being killed and my community destroyed?"[75] Buber's response was not easy to accept and certainly was not popular. It can be divided into three different layers of understanding, addressed to three different ways of asking these questions: (1) What should the Jews of Palestine, in whose midst Buber lived, do? (2) What should the Jews in Europe do? (3) What should Martin Buber do?

### The Jews Living in Palestine

First, one may address the response to the question as asked by Jews living at the time in Palestine: Whatever we do, said Buber, we should never allow our actions to be tainted by the attitude to being that guides the deeds of a Hitler. Speaking in 1939 before a meeting of Jewish writers in Palestine, Buber said that "whoever will do a 'Hitler deed' will be devoured together with him [עמו ביחד יבלע, *yeevalah beyachad eemoh*]."[76] He had in mind acts of violence perpetrated against Arabs by Jews (and he used biblical terminology describing the incident of Korach and his group, who were swallowed into the ground in the presence of the community of Israel [Numbers 16:30–32]). He insisted that evil should be countered by yet greater justice, not by injustice. (Of course, Buber did not equate the two forms of violence; he simply pointed out that one should not turn to the deranged leadership of the Third Reich as a paradigm of appropriate political conduct.) This position led him to repeatedly rebuke the political leadership of the Jewish Yishuv[77] for insufficient attention to Jewish violence directed against the Arab inhabitants of Palestine.[78] Buber's position was unshakable, and he held it steadfastly throughout his later years, in debates leading to the establishment of the Jewish state and in his subsequent responses to the attitude of the Jewish majority to the Arab minority in the Israeli state.

Relating to the Yishuv in the context of the Holocaust, Buber rejected any rhetoric that sought to link the tragedy of European Jewry to the goal of establishing a sovereign Jewish state in Palestine. He consistently advocated refraining from the tendency to capitalize on the suffering of the victims of Nazi persecution in the service of a political goal or—even worse—petty intraparty competition. In a long-term perspective, said Buber, the nature of the Zionist movement would be determined by the quality of relations established within the Jewish community and toward its non-Jewish neighbors and not (as was the predominant opinion) by the numbers of immigrants, settlements, or other apparent political gains. This political position was a direct reflection of Buber's philosophy, with its emphasis on the crucial importance of overcoming the crisis of humanity by founding radically new forms of dialogical community. An exemplary community, not a sovereign state, was for Buber Zionism's primary justification. To be an ordinary nation-state, creating a bourgeois society that adopted the norms, practices, and forms of spiritual alienation characteristic of European nation-states seemed to him misguided and contrary to the vision that had sustained Jewish life in the long period of exile.

Buber's difficulty in communicating his growing understanding of the roots of the crisis of humanity and of Zionism's role in pointing the way to resolving the crisis is evident in a revealing draft of a letter he wrote in 1943 to Professor Fishel Shneorson, in response to the latter's urging that he become more active in presenting to the world the calamity underway in Europe.[79] Whoever wishes to act in a time like this, wrote Buber, must do so in a way that is truly effective. This, he adds, is not the way of propaganda, of replacing one rigid mode of thinking with another. The action must be practical, beginning with the self: "If there is at all a way ahead of us, in my opinion it is different from all ways of persuasion and propaganda. It is the way of the single one, a way of self-sacrifice. But I do not dare speak of it."[80] Buber did not include the last two sentences in the letter that he eventually sent to Shneorson. Dinah Porat comments that they are puzzling sentences. Did Buber mean to suggest sending paratroopers to Europe, she asks? Did he decide to censor this suggestion because at the age of 65 he thought it improper to recommend an action that he himself could not undertake?[81]

I believe that the response to Porat's puzzlement is not to be sought in Buber's rejection of military action but rather elsewhere—by taking the notion of "a way of self-sacrifice" with the utmost seriousness that Buber attributed to it and by seeking to understand what it implies. Buber seemed to imply that accurate responses to the demands of the historical hour necessitated "sacrifice" of deeply ingrained patterns of thought and the consequent notions of "self." For him, this "sacrifice" implied a turn inward, to seek greater clarity of the way of man as intimated by the purpose and mystery of Judaism. Aware that his use of the notion of "self-sacrifice" was difficult to understand, Buber deleted it from the final version of the letter. His decision not to disclose his real reasons for maintaining a distance from ordinary propaganda led to his being criticized for apparent "inaction." I assume that he found comfort in the words of the ancient midrash: "It is written: 'And Abel, he also brought.' The 'he' is what he brought: he brought himself. Only when a man brings himself, too, is his sacrifice valid."[82] Such sacrifice is "action" but of a kind unnoticed by historical consciousness.

It is important to add that Buber's call for a newfound relation to self as the Jewish response to the crisis of humanity stemmed from his understanding that the deeds of the Nazis did not represent a break from human practice. What was unprecedented was the scale and scope of the Nazi violence and cruelty. Speaking after the Holocaust, Buber presented this (unconventional) perspective in the following terms:

> I do not think any basic change took place in the human race when
> the Nazis came into power. . . . It is a matter of proportion, not of

basic content. The Nazi massacres were so horrifying because they were on such unprecedented mass scale. But similar brutalities have occurred before in history. It is not essentially a new phenomenon. And it is certainly not a reason to lose faith and despair of the human race.[83]

As events leading to the establishment of an independent Jewish state unfolded, Buber became increasingly critical of the political venture, fearing that emphasis on the creation of a centralized state would be detrimental to his vision of establishing in the land of Israel (Palestine) a community of communities, Jewish and Arab, related to one another in a binational federative framework of governance. He attempted to influence political discourse and decisions by participating in Brit Shalom and Ichud, political movements that advocated Jewish-Arab dialogue. Although supported by prominent intellectuals and socialists from within the Jewish community, these two movements represented only a small fraction of the Yishuv members and overall were ineffective politically. Once the Jewish state was established, Buber accepted it as a historical fact and continued to express his political views within it. Still, the circumstances seemed to him unfortunate; the historical return to Israel, he commented in 1959, had gone "through the wrong gate."[84] He considered reliance on the physical security afforded by the state to be immoderate, lacking appropriate balance with a more deep-rooted reliance on the sources of the soul. As he aged, Buber became resigned to his inability to influence his own generation in the sphere of practical politics. This, it seems, released a certain burden of thought from his writings and evinced a corresponding deepening of his understanding of the processes that give rise to history, to modern forms of political organization, and to the manner in which these social forms perpetuate human ignorance regarding the essential questions of life.

Buber was aware of the personal price he was to pay for the unpopular positions he advocated and the isolation it would impose on him within his own community. The seriousness with which he weighed his words at this stage of his life is poignantly described in the recollections of a participant who witnessed Buber's 1944 address on the relationship between the Holocaust and political circumstances in Palestine: "The old philosopher . . . who had sat closed eyed, listening to the words of his colleague, stood up to say his own words. He seemed to be raising each word from the depths and weighing it as if it were in his hand, examining it carefully to see if it included all of his intended meaning, before delivering it to those present."[85]

## The Jews Living in Europe

Second, one should consider Buber's response to those Jews living in Europe who questioned the appropriate response to evil as they directly suffered the burdens of war and deprivation. In 1941, Buber published an essay entitled "The Question of 'Job's' Generation" (note the single quotes surrounding the word 'Job' in the original essay, indicating the metaphorical nature of the discussion).[86] It opens with the following sentence:

> When it is revealed that the national catastrophe [השואה הלאומית, *hashoah haleumit*] will indeed transpire, according to external decree and to internal necessity, and in particular when [the catastrophe] has moved from potentiality to actuality, this becomes, as does every great affliction, a creative force in the religious sense; that is, it begins to become a source of new questions, and a reason to deepen old questions.[87]

Although he used the word that was to become in due course a metaphor for the national calamity, *shoah*, at the time of writing Buber was (as were all other members of the Yishuv) unaware of the systematic destruction of European Jewry. Still, he knew that the events were unprecedented in scope and magnitude. The impending disaster, said Buber in 1941, should push the person deeper toward the inner place of perception that knows what question should be addressed to the particular historical moment. The lesson of Job is essentially one of *how* to question catastrophe. *How* to question precedes *what* to question. When Job turns to question the crumbling world that surrounds him, his voice is not that of mere complaint or of angry rejection or denial. It is a voice of total wondering and incomprehension. *Such* questioning—which faces historical reality from the depths of existence—does not remain unanswered. Accordingly, the very fact that Elohim responds constitutes for Buber the central moment of the story of Job. That the hidden Elohim, the silent Elohim, the eclipsed Elohim should suddenly reappear and sound his voice is the decisive fact emerging from Job's relation to the events confronting him. Not what Elohim says, but that Job has found an opening for the voice to be heard is—for Buber—the relation that grants Job his way, his life.[88]

When the awful extent of the Holocaust became known, Buber returned to Job. "In this our own time," he wrote in 1951,

> it is questioned and again questioned: is there still a place for Jewish life after an "Auschwitz deed" (מעשׂה אוֹשׁוויץ)? I would like to modify the question: is there still a place for life with Elohim in a time in which there is an Auschwitz? The place that can withstand horror and terror has overflown, and the hiddenness of Elohim has deepened its secret to a place that cannot be explored. We can still "believe" in Elohim, who enabled these deeds to happen, but can we still speak to him? Can we still call out to him? And can we dare say to the remnants of Auschwitz, to this Job of the gas chambers: "Give thanks unto YHVH, for he is good; for his mercy endureth forever" (Psalm 106:1)?[89]

Once again, Buber returns to his enduring conviction: by turning to Elohim with all his being, Job creates an opening to the possibility of hearing the absent presence. The Hebrew tradition, says Buber, is not a Greek tragedy where the hero must accept the blind dictate of fate. "We do not accept the servitude of earthly existence," continues Buber. "We face [the hidden] Elohim and yearn for the sound of his voice, be it from the storm or from the stillness that follows it."[90]

Elohim responds to Job's faithful address by turning distance into relation. In Elohim's actual words, no explanation is granted, no question directly answered, no apologies offered, no excuses brought forth. Injustice is not transformed into justice, and cruelty does not transpire into mercy. But the person can *hear*, if he will but eliminate the barrier between listening and voice. Here biblical discourse is inseparable from philosophical inquiry. In both areas of Buber's thought, the goal is one: to seek a way to remove the barrier that prevents the individual person from experiencing reality directly through his or her own immediate presence. "Each of us is encased in an armor which we soon, out of familiarity, no longer notice," wrote Buber in 1929;[91] during the years of the Second World War and in their aftermath, this perspective became the focal point of his writing and the root of his understanding.

The events of 1938–1945 taught Buber with greater clarity that the immediate task of every person is to face the "armor": to know it and eliminate it. To turn to "Elohim" implies, practically, to turn to oneself. One must turn "within" if one is to respond with precision and sensitivity to the events "without." "The essential thing," said Buber in a series of radio broadcasts in 1946, "is to begin with oneself, and at this moment a man has nothing in the world to care about more than this beginning." To eliminate violence, man must make peace with himself; the source of all conflict between man and man is a fundamental distortion of the capacities of the mind to contemplate and to think. Modern persons do not realize that "[they] do not say what [they] mean, and that [they] do not do what [they] say."[92] Hence, whoever seeks to comprehend the mystery of historical events by subjecting it to the explanatory powers of the thinking subject will not find adequate responses there, for thought itself, as a capability, is misused and misunderstood.

### Remembering the Hidden Voice

Buber's third response to the question of violence in a man–made world intent on self-destruction was to explore with greater conviction ways of addressing the "hidden voice" ordinarily unnoticed. This is manifest in his extraordinarily prolific writings during and after the Second World War. One must remember that Buber was first and foremost a writer, his political and social activism notwithstanding. It was in his writings that he explored the questions of his troubled times. In these manifold works, one sees different approaches to discovering and communicating the extraordinary understandings that he seems to have discovered. Thus, we have seen how in *The Prophetic Faith*, published in Hebrew in 1942, Buber included hermeneutic clues that point *indirectly* to hidden events that guide historical developments. Our references to *Gog Umagog* (translated as *For the Sake of Heaven*), first published in late 1941, have suggested that Buber used the form of a legendary chronicle of Hasidic reactions to the Napoleonic wars to explore possible responses to historical catastrophes. Our discussion of Buber's 1945 writings about Hasidism, *Bepardes Hahasiduth* (translated into English as *The Origin and Meaning of Hasidism*) has identified this work as a meditation on an epoch characterized by philosophy and faith gone astray, as well as an exploration of ways to overcome the growing distance between man and his essential being. Similarly, our references to the 1945 *Between a People and Its Land: The Essential Development of an Idea* (published in English as *On Zion*) have delineated Buber's growing concern with political Zionism's disregard of the "mystery" and "secret" of Zionism as spiritual renewal. Apparently, therefore, works properly considered studies in social or political theory, such as *Paths in Utopia* (1947), cannot be fully appreciated if not read as secondary writing rooted in the primary search for understanding that takes place in texts such as the aforementioned.

## THE ULTIMATE DILEMMA

Unlike an influential member of his generation, Rabbi A. I. Kook,[93] Buber has not been associated with any political form of modern Israeli messianic discourse, either in his own time or at present. However, his problematic mixing of symbolic categories and political discourse in his relation to the land of Israel has been noted. As Uriel Tal points out, Buber elevates the relationship between Israel and its land to a special degree of absoluteness.[94] This is a problematic dimension of Buber's writings because his positive intentions notwithstanding, his justifications for the settling of the land of Israel are open to the entire gamut of interpretations present in the messianic discourse that has developed in Israel after the founding of the Jewish state, most strikingly in political interpretations of the teachings of Rabbi Kook (whose students and later interpreters formed the hard core of the post-1967 Jewish settlement movement in the West Bank). Buber's writings have been spared the fate of Rabbi Kook's by virtue of insufficient attention to the messianic dimension of his thinking. In fact, the messianic dimension of Buber's thought has been deconstructed and reinterpreted in the context of modern socialist theories rather than in the manner suggested by the logic of the present interpretation of his works.[95] In the process, the unmistakable influence of the messianic mystery on Buber's thinking and politics was not sufficiently explored. In this respect, it seems that Buber acted in a responsible manner in deciding to use the power of messianic imagery carefully and to present it in an indirect manner.

Buber seems to have assumed that his writings would convince his readers that they could, and should, relate to one another (and in the case of Zionism, to a particular land) as metaphors of a higher symbolic reality. Yet myths, symbols, and esoteric writing convey meaning and communicate events that cannot be readily conceptualized or given concrete form. The meaning a symbol conveys is, by neccessity, difficult to grasp by thought and to express discursively or by direct indication.[96] If a symbol is reduced to a direct form of representation, it becomes useless and loses its true meaning. Buber attempted to achieve too much with a form of communication that is limited to indirect instruction. In his eagerness to transform the *halutz* into the living embodiment of the universal image of the dialogical person, Buber confused mythical and historical reality to the extent that his entire project is called into question. By attempting to point to "living myths" in whom the myth actualizes itself, Buber deprived the myths and the ideas they transmit of their ability to change the reader's or listener's view of ontology indirectly.

According to his own teachings, a change of ontology of the magnitude that Buber envisions requires the direct presence and guidance of persons whose deeds can exemplify what such a perception actually means: "For educating characters you do not need a moral genius, but you do need a person who is wholly alive and able to communicate himself directly to his fellow beings. His aliveness streams out to them and affects them most strongly and purely when he has no thought of affecting them."[97] Rather than represent such "aliveness" in terms of exemplary political leadership, Buber introduced the exemplary deeds of people like Gordon, perhaps to compensate for his own inadequacy.

Our analysis leads us to conclude that Buber failed where he most wanted to succeed: in applying his ideas to the actual founding of a concrete community.[98] His mode of theorizing called for a distinct separation between the language for articulating his social vision and the language for addressing immediate political reality. This is particularly grievous because whenever able to participate in events, Buber was bound, by the logic and foundation of his entire life's work, to provide concrete guidance through personal example.

It may be that Buber's extraordinary mastery of words and symbols, the source of his intellectual influence, was also the source of his political inefficacy (and perhaps of a tragic element in his biography). The words streamed from his pen and affected his readers, yet the man himself could not direct others towards a unification of word and deed through direct, immediate example. He thus exposed his entire teaching to the charge of constituting yet another utopian fantasy. Indeed, by characterizing the socialist *halutz* in terms of a new type who corresponded to the universally valid image of the dialogical person, Buber may have weakened the power of his original image to communicate the inclusive perspective of human evolution central to his ontology. Buber consequently exposed the ideas at the heart of his thinking and experience, the very ideas for which he considered himself a filter,[99] to misinterpretation and misunderstanding. Buber's teaching, as he himself insisted, called for either personal example or silence.

These limitations notwithstanding, Buber's lasting achievement was his bringing to light and transmitting the remembrance of the original "teaching" and "testimony." This teaching is inseparable from social philosophy, for it assumes that every person—regardless of cultural and historical background—is equally responsible for fulfilling "natural Adam's" innate potential to create a refined quality of "social space," an invisible, yet vital, essence that Buber called the Between. Such self-fulfillment can be attained only by a total shift in the sensation of self— from self as a subject, whose existence is determined by the extent that "I" succeed in distinguishing myself in opposition to others, to self as a unique expression and participant in the creative flow of life.

Buber's careful transmission of the raison d'etre of the Hebraic tradition along these lines may be untranslatable into political discourse and therefore may appear strange or irrelevant when encountered through that mode of discourse. However, for a reader who is committed to serious and hopeful contemplation of the ends of life, Buber offers fruitful food for thought. In a period of accelerated changes in human self-knowledge, changes that often reflect opposing and warring directions, Buber reminds us to ask the timeless questions: Where do I come from? Where am I going? What will judge my deeds at the end of my days?

If Buber has anything at all to teach us, it is to begin our investigations with a wholehearted attempt to understand the overall context of our existence. It is only when we are satisfied that this examination has yielded substantial understanding that we should turn to the political or social application of the intellectual fruits of that understanding. In this respect, Socrates' parting words to Callicles in the dialogue *Gorgias* come to mind as an appropriate ending to this exposition:

> Now perhaps all this seems to you like an old wife's tale and you
> despise it, and there would be nothing strange in despising it if our

searches could discover anywhere a better and truer account. . . . [Before] all things a man should study not to seem but to be good, whether in private or in public life . . . and we should avoid every form of flattery, whether to ourselves or to others, whether to a few or to many. . . . [And] you may let anyone despise you as a fool and do you outrage, if he wishes, yes, and you may cheerfully let him strike you with that humiliating blow, for you will suffer no harm thereby if you really are a good man and an honorable [one], and pursue virtue.[100]

# ABBREVIATIONS OF BUBER'S
# WORKS CITED IN NOTES

ABH           *A Believing Humanism: My Testament, 1902–1965.* New
              York: Simon and Schuster, 1967.

BAL           *Beyn Am Leartzo* (Between a People and Its Land). Tel
              Aviv: Schocken, 1945.

BH            *Bepardes Hahasidut* (In the Orchard of Hasidism). Jerusa-
              lem: Bialik, 1963.

BMAM          *Between Man and Man.* New York: Collier, 1965.

BS            *Besod Siach* (In the Secret of Dialogue). Jerusalem: Bialik,
              1980.

DSA           *Darkoh Shel Adam Al-Pee Torat Hahasidut* (The Way of
              Adam according to the Teachings of Hasidism). Jerusa-
              lem: Bialik, 1964.

DSM           *Darko Shel Mikrah* (The Way of Scripture). Jerusalem: Bi-
              alik, 1978.

EC            *Ecstatic Confessions.* Translated by Esther Cameron. San
              Francisco: Harper and Row, 1985.

ELA           *Eretz Leshnei Amim* (A Land for Two Peoples). Edited by
              Paul Mendes-Flohr. Tel Aviv: Schocken, 1988.

EOG           *Eclipse of God: Studies in the Relation between Religion and
              Philosophy.* New York: Harper Torchbooks, 1957.

FSH           *For the Sake of Heaven: A Chronicle.* Translated by Ludwig
              Lewisohn. New York: Atheneum, 1986.

GAE           *Good and Evil: Two Interpretations.* New York: Charles
              Scribner's Sons, 1953.

GOG           *Gog Umagog: Megilat Yamim* (Gog and Magog: A Chroni-
              cle). Tel Aviv: Am Oved, 1967.

HAMM          *Hasidism and Modern Man.* Edited and translated by

|  | Maurice Friedman. Atlantic Highlands, N.J.: Humanities Press International, 1988. |
|---|---|
| *Hasidism* | *Hasidism*. New York: Philosophical Library, 1948. |
| *I and Thou* | *I and Thou*. Translated by Walter Kaufmann. New York: Charles Scribner's Sons, 1970. |
| *IATW* | *Israel and the World: Essays in a Time of Crisis*. New York: Schocken, 1963. |
| *ICC* | *On Intersubjectivity and Cultural Creativity*. Edited by S. N. Eisenstadt. Chicago: University of Chicago Press, 1992. |
| *KOG* | *Kingship of God*. Translated by Richard Scheinmann. London: Allen and Unwin, 1967. |
| *LTP* | *A Land of Two Peoples: Martin Buber on Jews and Arabs*. Edited by Paul Mendes-Flohr. New York: Oxford University Press, 1983. |
| *MS* | *Malchut Shamayim* (Kingship of the Heavens). Jerusalem: Bialik, 1965. |
| *Moses* | *Moses: The Revelation and the Covenant*. Atlantic Highlands, N.J.: Humanities Press International, 1988. |
| *NB* | *Netivot Beutopia* (Paths in Utopia). Edited by Avraham Shapira. Tel Aviv: Am Oved, 1983. |
| *OH* | *Or Haganooz: Seepoorim Hasidiim* (The Light of the Hidden: Hasidic Tales). Tel Aviv: Schocken, 1976. |
| *OJ* | *On Judaism*. Edited by Nachum N. Glatzer. New York: Schocken, 1972. |
| *OMH* | *The Origin and Meaning of Hasidism*. Edited and translated by Maurice Friedman. Atlantic Highlands, N.J.: Humanities Press International, 1988. |
| *OTB* | *On the Bible*. Edited by Nachum N. Glatzer. New York: Schocken, 1982. |
| *OZ* | *On Zion: The History of an Idea*. New York, Schocken, 1973. |
| *PA* | *Pnei Adam* (The Faces of Adam). Jerusalem: Bialik, 1962. |
| *PIU* | *Paths in Utopia*. Translated by R. F. C. Hull. Boston: Beacon Press, 1958. |
| *PTW* | *Pointing the Way*. Edited and translated by Maurice Friedman. New York: Harper Torchbooks, 1963. |
| *SAT* | *Scripture and Translation*. Translated by Laurence Rosen- |

|       |                                                                                                                                                                              |
| ----- | ---------------------------------------------------------------------------------------------------------------------------------------------------------------------------- |
|       | wald with Everett Fox. Bloomington: Indiana University Press, 1994.                                                                                                           |
| *TKM*   | *The Knowledge of Man: A Philosophy of the Interhuman.* New York: Harper and Row, 1965.                                                                                       |
| *TLZ*   | *Tikvah Lesha'ah Zo* (Hope for the Present Hour). Tel Aviv: Am Oved, 1992.                                                                                                     |
| *TMM*   | "The Messianic Mystery (*Isaiah* 53)." In Theodore Drey-fus, "Martin Buber: Hameestoreen Hameesheechee (The Messianic Mystery)." *Da'at,* no. 5 (Summer 1980): 127–33.        |
| *TN*    | *Torat Hanevi'im* (The Prophetic Teaching). Tel-Aviv: Dvir, 1950.                                                                                                             |
| *TPF*   | *The Prophetic Faith.* New York: Harper and Row, 1949.                                                                                                                        |
| *TR*    | *Ten Rungs: Hasidic Sayings.* Translated by Olga Marx. New York: Schocken, 1947.                                                                                              |
| *TTF*   | *Two Types of Faith.* Translated by Norman P. Goldhawk. New York: Collier, 1951.                                                                                              |
| *TTM*   | *Tales of the Masters.* 2 vols. Translated by Olga Marx. New York: Schocken, 1947–48.                                                                                         |
| *TV*    | *Te'udah Veyeud* (Testimony and Mission). 2 vols. Jerusa-lem: Zionist Library, 1984.                                                                                          |
| *Werke* | *Werke.* 3 vols. Munich: Kosel-Verlag und Verlag Lambert Schneider, 1962.                                                                                                     |

# NOTES

## CHAPTER 1: INTRODUCTION

1. S. H. Bergman, *Hogay Hador* (Contemporary Thinkers) (Jerusalem: Magnes, 1970), 181–82.

2. Martin Buber, "Replies to My Critics." In *The Philosophy of Martin Buber*, edited by Paul A. Schilpp and Maurice Friedman (La Salle, Illinois: Open Court, 1967), 693. Almost identical language appears twenty years earlier, in Buber's response to criticism of his "novel" *Gog Umagog* (translated into English as *For the Sake of Heaven*). See "Le'enyan 'Gog Umagog,'" *Ha'aretz*, 8 December 1944, republished in *TLZ*, 140–41.

3. Throughout the discussion, the use of italics when using derivatives of the words "*to see*" and "*to listen*" is my own. This includes passages from Buber's works, like the one that follows.

4. Introduction to *PA*, first page, no number.

5. "My Way to Hasidism," in *HAMM*, 59.

6. *TR*, 65–66.

7. I am referring here to the sequence in which the collected Hebrew editions of Buber's works were published, *not* to the sequence in which Buber wrote the texts that these collections include. My emphasis is on the symbolic significance of the order of publication of the final retrospective: the last collection focuses on the individual man; the one that precedes it on human community; and the one before that, *TV* (to be mentioned shortly), on the Jewish heritage.

8. Introduction to *BS*, 47–48.

9. Introduction to *BS*, 48.

10. "The Two Foci of the Jewish Soul," *IATW*, 30–31.

11. For example, Michael Walzer notes that Buber's most important work of political theory, *Paths in Utopia*, is a "strikingly secular defense of communitarian socialism, with an epilogue on the kibbutz. Curiously, its arguments play little

part in his Zionist criticism." Michael Walzer, "On Buber," in *Tikkun* 3, no. 3 (March–April 1988): 128.

12. For the meaning of "refined" self-knowledge see my " 'Know Thyself': Socratic Companionship and Platonic Community," *Political Theory* 23, no. 2 (May 1995): 306–08.

13. Laurence J. Silberstein in his *Martin Buber's Social and Religious Thought: Alienation and the Quest for Meaning* (New York: New York University Press, 1989) has analyzed Buber's concern with the modern estrangement of self. Donald Berry has focused on Buber's relation to nature. Donald L. Berry, *Mutuality: The Vision of Martin Buber* (Albany: State University of New York, 1985).

14. Buber suggests that the artistic and philosophical vocations converge at this juncture, where both are concerned with the creation of images and symbols. This similarity overrides differences generated by the disparate concerns, or objects, of these creative activities. When engaged in the figuration of symbols, the two vocations share an attempt to express the unmediated relation to being: "The artist does not hold a fragment of being up to the light; he receives from his contact with being and brings forth what has never before existed. It is the same with the genuine philosopher." "Bergson's Concept of Intuition," in *PTW*, 64. See also "Man and His Image Work," *TKM*, 149–65. Considered in this light, Buber may be described as a social thinker whose primary vocation is the creation of social and political symbols and images through literary forms that indirectly subvert conventional notions of the appropriate social order worthy of a well-balanced human life.

15. This proposition is developed in Steven Kepnes' notion of "dialogical hermeneutics" in his *The Text as Thou: Martin Buber's Dialogical Hermeneutics and Narrative Theology* (Bloomington: Indiana University Press, 1992).

16. "Audacious" connotes both "boldness, confidence, daring" and "unrestrained by, or setting at defiance, the principles of morality and decorum." It thus refers to conduct that may be interpreted as either bold or impudent. See *The Compact Edition of the Oxford English Dictionary*, volume I, 140, "audacious."

17. This notion will be explained in detail in chapter 6.

18. Karl Jaspers, *The Origin and Goal of History* (New Haven: Yale University Press, 1953). See also the essays collected in *Daedalus* 104:2 (Spring 1975) and in S. N. Eisenstadt, ed., *The Origins and Diversity of Axial Age Civilizations* (New York: State University of New York, 1986).

19. Having mentioned the word "postmodern," I hasten to add that this book is neither an exercise in endless deconstruction nor a claim that every text can be interpreted according to the whims of the reader. On the contrary, I shall present a clear interpretation of intentions immanent in texts written by Buber, guided by hermeneutic principles of reading that Buber himself established. This is no guesswork but rather careful scholarship. I write these words with Stanley

Rosen's wry critique of Derrida's deconstruction of Plato in mind: "The blind postmodernist listens for the voice of Being; he hears nothing but the rustling of texts turning their own pages." Stanley Rosen, *Hermeneutics as Politics* (New York: Oxford University Press, 1987), 86.

20. Abraham Joshua Heschel, *Theology of Ancient Judaism* (in Hebrew), vol. 1 (London: Soncino Press, 1962), i–iii.

21. Gerald L. Bruns, *Hermeneutics Ancient and Modern* (New Haven: Yale University Press, 1992), 72.

22. Moshe Idel, *Language, Torah, and Hermeneutics in Abraham Abulafia* (in Hebrew) (Tel Aviv: Schocken, 1994), 14–15.

23. Moshe Idel, *Kabbalah: New Perspectives* (in Hebrew) (Tel Aviv: Schocken, 1993), 264.

24. See Umberto Eco's discussion in his *The Limits of Interpretation* (Bloomington: Indiana University Press, 1990), especially at 24–25.

25. Umberto Eco, *Interpretation and Overinterpretation* (Cambridge: Cambridge University Press, 1992), 64.

26. See Eco's reference to Dante, who also created limits to possible interpretations of his texts by providing hermeneutic keys for reading the intentions of his texts. *Interpretation and Overinterpretation*, 64.

27. Buber, "Replies to My Critics," 739. See also p. 730. In these and additional pages Buber refers the critic to verses from the Book of Isaiah that he uses in his writings as conveyors of ideas that he found difficult to express directly. I have called such verses "guiding verses," and I explain their function and meaning in chapters 3 and 4.

28. See chapter 4.

29. I feel uncomfortable using the word "smart," but its use in Eco's theory of interpretation is sound. This is a case not of hubris but rather of using categories supplied by somebody else as a way of explaining my method of reading.

30. Eco, *The Limits of Interpretation*, 77.

31. Eco, *The Limits of Interpretation*, 58–59.

32. Bruns, *Hermeneutics Ancient and Modern*.

33. This article appears as "Bergson and the Intuition" in *PA*, 417–33. An abridged version of it has been translated into English as "Bergson's Concept of Intuition," in *PTW*, 81–86. Buber wrote it in 1943 as an introduction to a Hebrew translation of Bergson's essays on "spiritual energy." See Maurice Friedman, *Martin Buber's Life and Work: The Middle Years, 1923–1945* (Detroit: Wayne State University Press, 1988), 281–82.

34. "Bergson and the Intuition," in *PA*, 420.

35. Martin Buber, *The Way of Man according to the Teachings of Hasidism.* (New York: Carol, 1995).

## CHAPTER 2: BIOGRAPHY: FROM MYSTICISM TO DIALOGUE TO ATTENTIVE SILENCE

1. Avraham Shapira, "Meetings with Buber" (in Hebrew), *Amot* 3, no. 6 (June–July 1965): 16. Shapira summarizes this exchange with the terse comment, apparently Buber's: "The form does not oppress the content but rather supplants it."

2. Akivah Ernst Simon, Introduction to *Cheeloofay Egrot* (Exchange of Letters), by Martin Buber, vol.1 (Jerusalem: Bialik, 1983), 8.

3. Maurice Friedman, *Martin Buber's Life and Work: The Later Years, 1945–1965* (Detroit: Wayne State University, 1988), 186.

4. Simon, Introduction to *Cheeloofay Egrot*, 8. See also the condensed English translation in Ernst Simon, "Preface to the German Edition," in *The Letters of Martin Buber*, edited by Nahum N. Glatzer and Paul Mendes-Flohr (New York: Schocken Books, 1991), xi.

5. See Haim Gordon, *The Other Martin Buber: Recollections of His Contemporaries* (Ohio University Press, 1988) for Buber's vices: pride (pages 66, 75), sweet tooth (92, 146), stinginess (69, 123–24). One might add that excessive pride is often the mark of great political theorists. See Norman Jacobson, *Pride and Solace: The Limits and Functions of Political Theory* (Berkeley: University of California Press, 1978).

6. Friedman, *The Later Years*, 187. Additional evidence relating to Buber's aversion to psychoanalytic interpretations of one's life is in Gordon, *The Other Martin Buber*, 71–72, where one of his mature students (Yochanan Bloch) tells of Buber's disapproval of his turn to psychoanalysis.

7. Nevertheless, some critics choose to focus on trivial details of Buber's mannerisms or on his all-too-human weaknesses. The most prominent examples are in Gordon, *The Other Martin Buber,* and his "Martin Buber: Sippur Ishi," *Hadashot* (weekend magazine), 23 September, 1988, 33–37. See Gershon Schocken's response, "Merachlim al Buber" (Gossiping about Buber), *Ha'aretz*, 30 September, 1988, 5.

8. Gordon, *The Other Martin Buber*, 92.

9. Buber, "Autobiographical Fragments," in *The Philosophy of Martin Buber*, edited by Paul Arthur Schilpp and Maurice Friedman (La Salle, Illinois: Open Court, 1967), 105, 110.

10. Buber, "Autobiographical Fragments," 77–78, 84, 105, 110.

11. S. Y. Agnon, " Zichronot al Martin Buber" (Memories of Martin Buber), *Ha'aretz*, 13 June 1975.

12. For Buber's account of the impact of his mother's absence, see Martin Buber, "Autobiographical Fragments," 3–4, and Friedman, *The Later Years*, 186–87.

13. Buber, "Autobiographical Fragments," 3.

14. Buber, "Autobiographical Fragments," 3–4.

15. Friedman, *The Later Years*, 187.

16. Pamela Vermes, *Buber* (London: Peter Halban, 1988), 1–9.

17. Buber, "Autobiographical Fragments," 4–5.

18. Akivah Ernst Simon, *Aims-Junctures-Paths: The Thinking of Martin Buber* (in Hebrew) (Tel Aviv: Sifriat Hapoalim, 1985), 11.

19. See Steven Kepnes, *The Text as Thou: Martin Buber's Dialogical Hermeneutics and Narrative Theology* (Bloomington: Indiana University Press, 1992), 6–18; Grete Schaeder, *The Hebrew Humanism of Martin Buber*, translated by Noah Jacobs (Detroit: Wayne State University Press, 1973), especially 40–53; Paul Mendes-Flohr, *From Mysticism to Dialogue: Martin Buber's Transformation of German Social Thought* (Detroit: Wayne State University Press, 1989).

20. Schaeder, *The Hebrew Humanism*, 58.

21. *I and Thou*, 53.

22. Paul Mendes-Flohr, "Nationalism as Spiritual Sensibility: The Philosophical Suppositions of Buber's Hebrew Humanism," *The Journal of Religion* 69, no. 2 (April 1989): 164.

23. See Buber's account of his row with Herzl in "Autobiographical Fragments," 16–19.

24. Simon, *Aims-Junctures-Paths*, 146.

25. Gershom Scholem writes that prior to Buber's work on Hasidism, this movement was unnoticed by scholars of religion. Scholem attributes his curious oblivion to the impact of the Enlightenment on Jewish scholars, who considered Hasidism a rather primitive, emotional form of mysticism that lacked the rational elements that make religion respectable and relevant to modern sensibilities. Gershom Scholem, *Devarim be-Go*, vol. 2 (Tel Aviv: Am Oved, 1982), 361.

26. See S. N. Eisenstadt, Introduction to *ICC*, 4–5.

27. The English translations of these lectures, known as "Three Addresses on Judaism," are in *OJ*, 11–55.

28. "Judaism and the Jews," in *OJ*, 21. See Simon, *Aims-Junctures-Paths*, 148.

29. "Herut: On Youth and Religion," in *OJ*, 155.

30. Simon, *Aims-Junctures-Paths*, 148–49.

31. For additional references to Buber's impact on the Bar Cochba group, see Paul Mendes-Flohr, *Divided Passions: Jewish Intellectuals and the Experience of Modernity* (Detroit: Wayne State University Press, 1991), and Vermes, *Buber*, 31–33.

32. Glatzer and Mendes-Flohr, *The Letters of Martin Buber*, 160.

33. See Arthur A. Cohen, "Martin Buber and *Der Jude*," *Midstream* 26:6 (June-July 1980): 31–32. See also Pamela Vermes, *Buber on God and the Perfect Man* (London: Littman Library of Jewish Civilization, 1994), 20–22.

34. Foreword to *PTW*, ix.

35. For Buber's essays and speeches on the political aspects of Zionism, see *LTP*.

36. "The How and Why of Our Bible Translation," in *SAT*, 213, and in *DSM*, 351. Buber writes that Rosenzweig could not speak and "could only indicate, with great effort and uncertain fingers, the essential letters on an alphabetical chart, which letters his wife filled out into words."

37. Martin Buber, "Justice and Renewal," *Haolam*, 21 April, 1934. This is a Hebrew translation of an article that Buber published in Polish on the eve of Yom Kippur, 1933 (original source not available). I thank Amnon Sadowski for drawing my attention to this article in his unpublished research paper, "On 'Adam' and his attitude to 'Being': Martin Buber on the Eve of the Nazi Rise to Power in Germany, 1932–1933." (Hebrew) (Jerusalem: The Hebrew University of Jerusalem, May 1994).

38. Buber had toyed with idea of emigrating to Palestine from the 1920s. His indecision exasperated some of his supporters and followers. For a brief summary of this issue, see Vermes, *Buber on God*, 32–37.

39. See, for example, Buber's letter to S. H. Bergman, sent on June 26, 1933, in which Buber writes in response to an article written in the journal *Hahed*: "I am surprised by [the author's] confidence in his assumption that my behavior is based solely on egoistic motives, fueled by the need to advance my self-interest. . . . I received this 'greeting' from the land of Israel at a difficult period, when my attempt to set up a system of Jewish education worthy of its name—the reason for my staying [in Germany] at this time—has drawn me into serious conflicts with a number of official representatives of German Jewry." In *Hahed* (September 1933): 14. Reprinted (with slight changes) in Martin Buber, *Cheeloofay Egrot* (Exchange of Letters), vol. 2, 447.

40. The vision and plan for a Jewish university, *Eine Judische Hochschule*, was written jointly by Martin Buber, Berthold Feiwel, and Haim Weitzman (later to become the first president of the State of Israel) and was published in 1902 by the Judischer Verlag, the publishing house founded by Buber and Feiwel. It has been republished in Hebrew as *Beit Sefer Gavoha Yehudi* (A Jewish School of Higher Education), translated from the German by Shaul Esh (Jerusalem: Magnes Press, 1968).

41. S. Y. Agnon to Martin Buber, December 1938, published in *Ha'aretz*, September 15, 1985, section b, 1. Agnon was referring to "The Spirit of Israel and the World of Today," in *OJ*, 179–90.

42. See chapter 7 for a review of additional works not mentioned in this chapter.

43. "What Is Man?" in *BMAM*, 118–205.

44. For Buber's positions on the Jewish-Arab conflict, see *LTP*.

45. See Aubrey Hodes, *Martin Buber: An Intimate Portrait* (New York: Viking, 1971), 121.

46. S. N. Eisenstadt, Introduction to *ICC*, 16.

47. In 1951, Buber was awarded the Hanseatic Goethe Prize in Hamburg; in 1953 the Peace Prize of the German book trade in Frankfurt.

48. Hodes, *An Intimate Portrait*, 65–66.

49. Friedman, *The Later Years*, 357–64.

50. Hodes, *An Intimate Portrait*, and Shapira, "Meetings with Buber," 11–17.

51. Shapira, "Meetings with Buber," 11–17.

52. Hodes, *An Intimate Portrait*, 83.

53. Buber's life has been documented at length and in great detail, and the efforts of others will not be repeated here. The most extensive biography of Buber's life is Maurice Friedman, *Martin Buber's Life and Work*, in three volumes: *The Early Years, 1878–1923*; *The Middle Years, 1923–1945*; and *The Later Years, 1945–1965* (New York: E. P. Dutton, 1981–1983; Reprint, Detroit: Wayne State University Press, 1988). For Buber's own account of experiences he considers of particular significance, see Martin Buber, *Meetings* (La Salle, Illinois: Open Court, 1973). A good introduction to Buber's life, intertwined with reference to his major works, is Vermes, *Buber on God*, 3–75. For intellectual biographies, see Maurice Friedman, *Martin Buber: The Life of Dialogue* (New York: Harper Torchbooks, 1955); Schaeder, *The Hebrew Humanism*; and Paul Mendes-Flohr, *From Mysticism to Dialogue*. The division I employ parallels that of Friedman, although I define the later, most intellectually mature period of Buber's development as beginning in 1938, on Buber's move to Palestine and his attempt to comprehend the events of the Second World War and the establishment of a Jewish state in Israel.

54. Dan Avnon, "The 'Central Person' in Martin Buber's Political Theory (Doctoral dissertation, University of California at Berkeley, 1990), 3–5.

55. *EOG*, 129.

56. The division of Buber's work into a pre-1919 (or pre-1923) period and the rest of his life (he died in 1965) is common among Buber's biographers. Buber himself treated *I and Thou* as a turning point in his life. The choice of the precise watershed year varies between 1919 (or perhaps as early as 1916) and 1923. Scholars debate the exact date by proposing various suggestions for the decisive factor or relationship influencing Buber's "turning." All, however, agree that Buber's mature period is officially inaugurated with the publication of *I and Thou*. See "The History of the Dialogical Principle," in *BMAM*, 209–24; Rivkah Horowitz, "Discoveries Pertaining to the Coming into Being of Martin Buber's Book *I and Thou*" in *Divray Haakademia Hayisraelit* (Annals of the Israeli Academy) 5, no. 8, (1972): 161–87. An enlarged English version of Horowitz's study has been published as *Buber's Way to* I and Thou: *The Development of Martin*

*Buber's Thought and His "Religion as Presence" Lectures* (Philadelphia: Jewish Publication Society, 1988). See also Paul R. Flohr "The Road to I and Thou," in *Texts and Responses: Studies Presented to Nachum N. Glatzer On the Occasion of His Seventieth Birthday By His Students*, edited by Michael A. Fishbane and Paul Mendes-Flohr (Leiden: E. J. Brill, 1975), 201–25.

57. Encounter (*Begegnung*) is a central concept in Buber's terminology. It connotes the event, or the situation, within which relation (*Beziehung*) occurs. It signifies something temporal and temporary. Relation, while occurring within an encounter, may remain present after the end of the circumscribed event. Accordingly, as summarized succinctly by Pamela Vermes, "relation can exist without encounter. But encounter cannot occur except from a state of relation." For a full discussion of these two concepts see Vermes, *Buber on God*, 195–98.

58. Nahum N. Glatzer, postscript to *OJ*, 241–42.

59. *EC*, xvi–xvii, 9.

60. *EC*, 6.

61. Cited in Paul Mendes-Flohr, Introduction to *EC*, xvii–xviii.

62. See "Myth in Judaism," in *OJ*, 95–107.

63. *I and Thou*, 56.

64. This, says Buber, can be perceived through the study of the Chinese teaching of the Tao, the Indian teaching of liberation, and the Jewish and early Christian teaching of the Kingdom of God. When speaking of the Jewish and early Christian teachings, Buber had in mind the living communities that bore them: for example, the Rechabites (Jeremiah 35) and the Essenes. Both are cited in "The Teaching of the Tao," in *PTW*, 38–39.

65. "Dialogue," in *BMAM*, 13–14; Maurice Friedman, *Martin Buber's Life and Work: The Early Years* (Detroit: Wayne State University Press: 1988), 187–90.

66. Paul Mendes-Flohr, "From Kulturmystik to Dialogue. An Inquiry into the Formation of Martin Buber's Philosophy of I and Thou" (doctoral dissertation, Department of Near Eastern and Judaic Studies, Brandeis University, June 1973), 10. A revised version of this dissertation has been published as Paul Mendes-Flohr, *From Mysticism to Dialogue*. See also Eugene Lunn's account of this exchange in his *Prophet of Community: The Romantic Socialism of Gustav Landauer* (Berkeley: University of California Press, 1973), 245–47.

67. For a concise statement about the meaning of *Erlebnis* philosophy see an essay by Wilhelm Dilthey, "Draft for a Critique of Historical Reason," in *The Hermeneutics Reader*, edited by Kurt Mueller-Vollmer (Oxford: Basil Blackwell, 1986), 149–52.

68. Susan A. Handelman, *Fragments of Redemptions: Jewish Thought and Literary Theory in Benjamin, Scholem, and Levinas* (Bloomington: Indiana University Press, 1991), 20.

69. Of the two English translations of Buber's *I and Thou*, the first, by Ronald Gregor Smith, translates the German *Du* as "Thou" (Edinburgh: T. & T. Clark, 1937; 2nd ed., New York: Charles Scribner's Sons and T. & T. Clark, 1957) and the second, by Walter Kaufmann, employs "You" in order to avoid the formal and theological connotations of "Thou" (New York: Charles Scribner's Sons, 1970). I follow Kaufmann, whose correction seems to me closer to the intentions of the Buberian text (see Kaufmann's comment on pp. 14–15). However, the title of *I and Thou* was retained in the Kaufmann translation, as it had already become well known by this title before Kaufmann's translation appeared.

70. Martin Buber, quoted in Sydney Rome and Beatrice Rome, eds., *Philosophical Interrogations* (New York: Holt, Rinehart and Winston, 1964), 27.

71. "Basic words do not state something that might exist outside them; by being spoken they establish a mode of existence. Basic words are spoken with one's being. . . . The basic word I–You can only be spoken with one's whole being. The basic word I–It can never be spoken with one's whole being." *I and Thou*, 53–54.

72. This point has often been misunderstood and has led to erroneous presentations of the social significance of Buber's philosophy of dialogue. See Buber's comment in Rome and Rome, *Philosophical Interrogations*, 27.

73. "Distance and Relation," *TKM*, 60.

74. Flohr, "From Kulturmystik to Dialogue," 2.

75. Thus, for example, Buber concluded that in the parable of the master, conveyed in myth, "there already rests in seed all the intoxication of ritual and the madness of dogma. . . . The dissolution [of the teaching] takes place in religion, and is consummated in that perpetuated act of violence that calls itself religion yet holds religiousness in chains." "The Teaching of the Tao," in *PTW*, 35–36.

76. The beginning of this transition is evident in Buber's book from 1913, *Daniel: Dialogues on Realization*, translated by Maurice Friedman (New York: Holt, Rinehart & Winston, 1964), where Daniel's view of myth as focusing on the unique value of the present event anticipates the directness, mutuality and presentness of the I–You relationship. Maurice Friedman suggests that Daniel realizes that the individual, like the community, cannot always live in direct contact with reality; hours of orientation must follow hours of realization. In this respect, *Daniel* forms a clear transition to the alternation between the I–You and the I–It relation that lies at the heart of *I and Thou*. Friedman, *The Early Years*, 150–64.

77. For an illuminating comparison of an original Hasidic legend and Buber's revision, see Pinchas Sadeh, *Sipure Ha-Besht* (Jerusalem: Carta, 1987), 177–81. Sadeh shows that Buber exorcised the original text of any mention of the magical powers associated with the Ba'al Shem or of his wild, emotional, ecstatic,

and at times brutal conduct, instead portraying meetings with the *zaddik* as a "social visit of two academics in the Hebrew University library," 181.

78. *TR*, 80.

79. Introduction to *EC*, 2.

80. "Dialogue," in *BMAM*, 4.

81. "Dialogue," in *BMAM*, 26.

82. "Dialogue," in *BMAM*, 3–4, 9–10, 19, 24–25. See also "The Faith of Israel," in *TV*, 1:191, and in *IATW*, 26–27.

83. "Dialogue," in *BMAM*, 16.

84. "The Dialogue between Heaven and Earth," in *OJ*, 214–25. See also "Biblical Leadership," in *OTB*, 137–50.

85. "The Dialogue between Heaven and Earth," in *OJ*, 220.

86. Umberto Eco, *The Limits of Interpretation* (Bloomington: Indiana University Press, 1990), 24–25.

87. Susan Handelman suggests that Walter Benjamin's posthumous essay "On Language as Such and on the Language of Man" is, in part, "a refutation of the Buberian position that language cannot communicate the essence of revelatory experiences." In Handelman, *Fragments of Redemptions*, 62.

88. "Al Hanetzah Veharega" (On Eternity and the Moment), in *TLZ*, 125.

89. Martin Buber, "Replies to My Critics," in *The Philosophy of Martin Buber*, edited by Paul A. Schilpp and Maurice Friedman (La Salle, Illinois: Open Court, 1967), 691.

## CHAPTER 3: BIBLE: THE HIDDEN HERMENEUTICS

1. As mentioned by Talmon, it is important to clarify that the words "Bible," "Scripture," and "biblical" all refer in this book (as in Buber's) to the *Hebrew* Bible alone. See Shemaryahu Talmon, "Martin Buber's Ways of Interpreting the Bible," *Journal of Jewish Studies* 27, no.1 (Spring 1976): 195, n. 1.

2. For the notion of intertextuality as an interversal type of hermeneutics, read Moshe Idel, "Midrashic versus Other Forms of Jewish Hermeneutics: Some Comparative Reflections," *The Midrashic Imagination: Jewish Exegesis, Thought, and History*, edited by Michael Fishbane (New York: State University of New York Press, 1993), 50–52, and Daniel Boyarin, *Intertextuality and the Reading of Midrash* (Bloomington: Indiana University Press, 1990), 14. Boyarin writes that to assume that a text is intertextual implies that "every text is constrained by the literary system of which it is a part and that every text is ultimately dialogical in that it cannot but record the traces of its contentions and doubling of earlier discourses." While both Idel and Boyarin write about Midrash, and hence about

a body of literature that developed as an open intergenerational commentary on the closed text of the eternal Hebrew Bible, they assume that the midrashic writings are based on principles of interpretation that guide the reading of the original scripture.

3. Steven Kepnes, *The Text as Thou: Martin Buber's Dialogical Hermeneutics and Narrative Theology* (Bloomington: Indiana University Press, 1992), 48.

4. Michael Fishbane, *The Garments of Torah: Essays in Biblical Hermeneutics* (Bloomington: Indiana University Press, 1989), 88.

5. Franz Rosenzweig, "The Unity of the Bible: A Position Paper vis-à-vis Orthodoxy and Liberalism," in *SAT*, 22–26.

6. "From the Beginnings of Our Bible Translation," in *SAT*, 179.

7. Yehoshua Amir, "Buber K'Parshan HaMiqrah" (Buber as an Interpreter of the Hebrew Bible), *Amot* 4, no. 1 (August–September 1965): 26–27.

8. Yehoshua Amir summarizes a lifelong study of Buber's interpretation of the Bible with the observation that "this effort to pierce beyond the 'what' of revelation toward its 'how,' to listen to the echo of the eternal, foundational phenomena that is behind the 'historical' revelation and insinuated by it [where 'it' refers to the historical manifestation of the hidden reality] is the motivation at the basis of all of Buber's biblical work." "Emunah Veheetgaloot etzel Morde-chai Martin Buber" (Faith and Revelation in the Work of Mordechai Martin Buber), in *Bar-Ilan* 22–23 (1988): 301.

9. See Umberto Eco in *The Limits of Interpretation* (Bloomington: Indiana University Press, 1990), especially 24–25.

10. For good introductions to Buber's translation of the Bible, see Everett Fox, "The Book in Its Contexts," in *SAT*, xii–xxvii; Lawrence Rosenwald, "Buber's and Rosenzweig's Challenge to Translation Theory," in *SAT*, xxix–liv; and Michael Fishbane, *The Garments of Torah*, 81–90, 99–111.

11. An important exception is the brief yet insightful comment by Theodore Dreyfus in "Hasheevoot hamoosag Umkehr l'havanat Haguto Shel M. Buber" (The Importance of the Concept *Umkehr* for Understanding M. Buber's Thought), *De'ot* 9 (Summer 1982): 71–74.

12. Rosenzweig, "The Unity of the Bible," in *SAT*, 23.

13. Quoted in Kepnes, *The Text as Thou*, 45.

14. Abraham Korman, *Introduction to Written and Oral Torah* (in Hebrew) (Tel Aviv: private edition, 1980). Korman offers an excellent synthesis of diverse sources regarding the sources of the Torah. One tradition relates that Moses received the Torah after he received the Ten Commandments. He first read the Torah to his brother Aharon, then to Aharon's two sons (in the presence of Aharon), and then to the elders (in the presence of Aharon and his sons). The fourth time Moses read the Torah was to the entire congregation of Israel. After this reading, Moses left, and the people heard the Torah an additional four times,

by way of Aharon, his sons, and the elders. Thus, every person in that generation heard the Torah at least four times. According to this tradition, the oral Torah began its parallel course of development as Moses answered questions addressed to him in the course of these readings. See 42–54.

15. "The How and Why of Our Bible Translation," in *SAT*, 211.

16. Franz Rosenzweig, "Habonim (The Builders)," *Naharayim* (Two Rivers: Collected Essays) (Jerusalem: Bialik, 1960), 80–93.

17. Franz Rosenzweig, "The Unity of the Bible" (in Hebrew), in *Naharayim*, 24.

18. "From the Beginnings of Our Bible Translation," in *SAT*, 179.

19. Fishbane, *The Garments of Torah*, 94; Kepnes, *The Text as Thou*, 45.

20. Translators' note 9 in *SAT*, 208.

21. "The How and Why of Our Bible Translation," in *SAT*, 208.

22. "The How and Why of Our Bible Translation," in *SAT*, 219.

23. Karl-Johan Illman, "Buber and the Bible." Written in 1991, this essay will appear in *Martin Buber: A Contemporary Perspective*, edited by Paul Mendes-Flohr (Jerusalem: Israel Academy of Humanities and Sciences, forthcoming). This citation is from p. 3 of Illman's manuscript.

24. Franz Rosenzweig, "Scripture and Word," in *SAT*, 42.

25. "From the Beginnings of Our Bible Translation," in *SAT*, 180–81.

26. "The How and Why of Our Bible Translation," in *SAT*, 218.

27. David Stern reminds us of the traditional sayings that the Torah has seventy aspects and/or the additional tradition that Moses was instructed on Mount Sinai in all seventy aspects of the seventy languages of the Torah. David Stern, "Midrash and Indeterminacy," *Critical Inquiry* 15 (Autumn 1988): 136–37.

28. Shemaryahu Talmon comments that Buber's work "lacked any precisely defined instructions as to how his method could be transmitted from teacher to pupil, how anyone could teach and learn his technique without having been blessed with Buber's masterly ability to attain an instinctive understanding of the Bible text." Talmon, "Martin Buber's Ways of Interpreting the Bible," 201. This apparent lack is, in fact, commensurate with the Hebrew tradition of oral, communal study. On this point, see Eliezer Schweid, "Martin Buber k'parshan Filosophi Shel Hamiqra' " (Martin Buber as Philosophical Interpreter of the Bible), *Jerusalem Studies in Jewish Thought* 2, no. 4 (1983): 594.

29. "The How and Why of Our Bible Translation," in *SAT*, 181.

30. David Stern has called the multiple meanings present in any scriptural passage "Scriptural polysomy," indicating that presentation of multiple interpretations is probably the Scripture's most ubiquitous feature. Stern, "Midrash and Indeterminacy," 137. Stern discusses Midrash, yet his comments regarding the multiplicity of interpretations assume that the interpreted text—the Hebrew Bible—is written in a manner that invites such multiplicity.

31. Buber's most important essays on the theoretical underpinnings of his biblical hermeneutics are included in *DSM* and in *SAT*. Yehoshua Amir, the translator into Hebrew of essays Buber wrote in German, has written two excellent commentaries on Buber's interpretation of the Bible: "Buber K'Parshan HaMiqra" (Buber as an Interpreter of the Hebrew Bible), and "Darko Shel Miqra Al-pee Buber" (The Way of the Bible according to Buber), *Beth Miqra* 12, no. 2 (March 1967): 116–20. In English, the following are the best introductions: Talmon, "Martin Buber's Ways of Interpreting the Bible"; Michael Fishbane, "Martin Buber as an Interpreter of the Bible," *Judaism* 27 (1978), 184–95; Ulrich E. Simon, "Martin Buber and the Interpretation of the Prophets," in *Israel's Prophetic Tradition*, edited by Richard Coggins et al. (Cambridge: Cambridge University Press, 1982), 250–61; Benyamin Uffenheimer, "Buber and Modern Biblical Scholarship," in *Martin Buber: A Centenary Volume*, edited by H. Gordon and J. Bloch (New York: Ktav and Ben-Gurion University, 1984), 163–211.

32. Illman, "Buber and the Bible," 4.

33. "People Today and the Jewish Bible," in *SAT* 4–21. The English translators struggled with the wording of of the essay's title. An earlier, inferior rendition, "The Man of Today and the Jewish Bible," translated the word *Mensch* (in *Der Mensch von heute*) as "man." Rosenwald and Fox comment that this adds sexist terminology where not intended in the original (the German *Mensch* refers equally to men and women). In *SAT* 4, translators' note 1, they explain why *Mensch* should be translated as person or human being. I agree with this approach, especially in view of the fact that in many English translations of Buber's work, one encounters frequent use of "man," which connotes a sexist approach I do not think characteristic of Buber's philosophy. See also Laurence J. Silberstein, "Note on Gender and Language," in *Martin Buber's Social and Religious Thought: Alienation and The Quest for Meaning* (New York: New York University Press, 1989), xvii–xviii. The same essay was translated by Buber from German into Hebrew as "A Member of Our Generation and the *Miqra*' (the Hebrew Bible)" (בן דורנו והמקרא), *DSM*, 41–64. Passages quoted in this book are my own translation of the Hebrew version, though I do include parallel references to the English translations in *SAT* and (where possible) *IATW*. Because the translation in *IATW* is of an abridged form of the essay, many of the passages cited here do not appear in *IATW*.

34. *DSM*, 47. There are four different uses of the verb *Patach* in the Hebrew edition, all indicating a form of "opening." *IATW* does not use derivatives of the verb stem p\t\ch in translating this passage. See "The Man of Today and the Jewish Bible," in *IATW*, 97. In "People Today and the Jewish Bible," in *SAT*, 10, the translation is more faithful to Buber's original intention. However, since Rosenwald and Fox translate from the German version, not all of the Hebrew

derivatives appear in their translation. We do read in their translation "openness to belief" and "opening oneself up" as translations of what I render as "the opening of the heart to faith" and of "opening the heart." Where Buber writes in Hebrew שער פתוח (open gate) and שנחזור ונפתח (we shall once again open) the Rosenwald translation writes "the way in" and "we begin."

35. *DSM*, 47.

36. "Ben Doraynu Vehamiqra," in *DSM*, 49. This page (49) alone includes seven variations of the root *patach*. The parallel text in "The Man of Today and the Jewish Bible," in *IATW*, 99–100, does not refer to this root at all. In "People Today and the Jewish Bible," in *SAT*, we do find two renditions of "opening" on p. 12: "the reality of revelation opened is opened to people today . . ." and "Where then is the opening to the way into the reality of creation?"

37. *DSM*, 48–49.

38. "Ben Doraynu Vehamiqra," in *DSM*, 49; "People Today and the Jewish Bible," in *SAT*, 12.

39. For example, preconceptions of "religion," notions of valid ways of "knowing," convictions regarding faith as an assumed property of organized religion.

40. "Ben Doraynu Vehamiqra," in *DSM*, 52. This section of the essay is not included in "The Man of Today and the Jewish Bible," in *IATW*. See the sensitive translation in "People Today and the Jewish Bible," in *SAT*, 14.

41. "Ben Doraynu Vehamiqra," *DSM*, 58. Translated as "openness to believe" in "People Today and the Jewish Bible," in *SAT*, 21.

42. The words *miqra b'cheenat m'tseeoot* from a previous passage, in "Ben Doraynu Vehamiqra," are in *DSM*, 46. See "The Man of Today and the Jewish Bible," in *IATW*, 96, and "People Today and the Jewish Bible," in *SAT*, 9.

43. "Ben Doraynu Vehamiqra," in *DSM*, 49; "The Man of Today and the Jewish Bible," in *IATW*, 100; "People Today and the Jewish Bible," in *SAT*, 11–12.

44. Irving Jacobs, *The Midrashic Process* (Cambridge: Cambridge University Press, 1995), 171.

45. *DSM*, 321.

46. This interpretation of the notion of *limmud* is based on my own reading, to be substantiated subsequently in the discussion of Isaiah's and Jeremiah's use of this term. For scholarly perspectives on this difficult notion see H. Gvaryahu, "Limmudim: Talmidim-Sofrim be-Sefer Yesha'ayahu" (*Limmudim*: Student-Scribes in the Book of Isaiah), *Beth Miqra* 16, no. 4 (1971): 438–56. Restricting his analysis to an examination of the historicity of the circles of *limmudim*, Gvaryahu does not address the hidden instruction indicated by this term.

47. Buber apparently considered Isaiah 8:16 of decisive importance for an understanding of the manner in which the secrets of the Bible are to be received

and passed on. Before developing this thought, several references significant in this context should be pointed out. With uncharacteristic emphasis, Buber noted that he and Rosenzweig were in full agreement regarding the interpretation of Isaiah 8:16, the verse that first introduces the notion of *limmud* and is considered by both scholars to be a guiding word that resurfaces in Isaiah 54:13. "He'arot le-Sefer Yesha'ayaho," in *DSM*, 332 n. 4 (this short essay was not translated in *SAT*). Moreover, Rosenzweig's dedication of a major article to Buber opens with a talmudic exposition of verse 8:16: אל תקרא בניך אלא בוניך—ה' ורב שלום בניך וכל בניך למודי ("And all your sons are *limmudei* YHVH and great shall be the peace of your sons"—read not 'your sons' [*banayich*] but rather 'your builders' [*bonayich*]). *Babylonian Talmud*, Tractate Berachot 64a. See Franz Rosenzweig, "Habonim," (The Builders), in *Naharayim*, 80. This rare confluence of Rosenzweig's and Buber's explicit mutual recognition of the importance of the verse that includes this particular guiding word merits contemplation.

48. "Achdut Sefer Yesha'ayahu, Kaytsad?" in *DSM*, 322.

49. "Achdut Sefer Yesha'ayahu, Kaytsad?" in *DSM*, 322–23.

50. As interpreted by Rabbi Eliyahu, the Vilna Gaon, the word "bind" (*tzror*) denotes that the testimony will not be understood, as none are worthy of understanding; the word "sealed" (*hatum*) indicates that only those worthy of hidden knowledge will be privy to it. Cited in Gvaryahu, "*Limmudim*," 441.

51. Isaiah calls such seekers *Beit Ya'akov*. See Genesis 32:28.

52. "I will wait for the LORD, who is hiding his face from the house of Jacob, and I will hope in him." *The New Oxford Annotated Bible: Revised Standard Edition* (New York: Oxford University Press, 1973).

53. *TPF*, 134.

54. *TN*, 125; *TPF*, 134.

55. Buber's essay on Isaiah appears to have been overlooked by Harold Bloom, who comments that in Buber's writings "the reader is left uncertain as to the historical difference between the two Isaiahs." Harold Bloom, Introduction, to *OTB*, xxvii.

56. See S. L. Gordon's introduction to his commentary on the Book of Jeremiah, in the volume *Jeremiah*, in *Torah, Nevi'im, Ketuvim* (Tel Aviv: Masada, no date), i–iii.

57. *DSM*, 323.

58. *The New Oxford Annotated Bible* (New York: Oxford University Press, 1973), 911.

59. Jeremiah 31:33 states: "But this is the covenant which I will make with the house of Israel after these days, says the Lord: I will put my law within them, and I will write it upon their hearts; and I will be their God, and they will be my people." The Hebrew word for "within them" is בקרבם (*b'keerbam*), from the root K\R\B, designating both proximity and inherence.

60. *TN*, 187; *TPF*, 203.

61. Kepnes, *The Text as Thou*, xii, 69.

62. *TPF*. This translation is inattentive to the suggestive power of Buber's choice of biblical Hebrew words. Consequently, certain citations will be otherwise translated and so designated.

63. The word translated is תולדות (*toldot*). See, for example, Genesis 2:4, 5:1, 6:9, 11:10.

64. *TN*, 1. The English translator is not sensitive to the importance of retaining the biblical sense of the Hebrew words Buber chose to use in these important opening comments. Compare the opening paragraph of *TPF*: "The task of this book is to describe a teaching which reached its completion in some of the writing prophets from the last decades of the Northern Kingdom to the return from the Babylonian exile, and to describe it both as regards its historical process and as regards its antecedents. This is the teaching about the relation between the God of Israel and Israel. It did not begin with the first writing prophets. Generally speaking, it is not a new teaching they advance, but they fashion its form to fit the changing historical situations and their different demands, and they perfect a teaching they have received—but where is the beginning of this teaching?"

65. The word *te'udah* appears elsewhere in the Bible only once, in Ruth 4:7.

66. "Comments to the Book of Isaiah," in *DSM*, 326.

67. "Achdut Sefer Yesha'ayhu—Keytsad?" in *DSM*, 321–23.

68. Isaiah 7, 8:1–10. See *TN*, 130–31. Buber's wording echoes Exodus 4:21.

69. *TN*, 131.

70. *TN*, 122.

71. *TN*, 108; *TPF*, 115.

72. *KOG*, 157.

73. *TN*, 59–60. The English translation, on p. 63, is seriously flawed, translating נזירים (*n'zeerim*) as "Nazirites" rather than "hermits."

74. *TN*, 56; *TPF*, 59.

75. *TN*, 99; *TPF*, 105; *DSM*, 256–57. In the east source, Buber presents his case against those who deny either the existence or the importance of groups of prophets whose presence is inseparable from that of the individual prophet.

76. "The Kingship of Saul," in *DSM*, 232–37 and 241–42. In this and other essays in biblical interpretation, Buber's writing is oriented towards scholarly, academic discourse. His discussion of "circles of prophets" that operated in the periphery of the emerging kingship does not address the esoteric significance of their presence but rather supports his claim that they actually existed. Chapter 4 of this book presents Buber's understanding of their role in the development of the "hidden history" of the spirit of Israel (developed implicitly in between the lines of Buber's biblical studies, or explicitly in other studies).

77. *TN*, 60; *TPF*, 63–64; *DSM*, 200–201.

78. *DSM*, 212–13.

79. The name Saul, which may be translated as "loaned," or "secondhand," hints that Saul's spiritual powers were not independent of reliance on external forces. See Buber's discussion in *DSM*, 256–60.

80. *TN*, 102; *TPF*, 108.

81. *TN*, 61; *TPF*, 64; *DSM*, 255.

82. *TN*, 61; *TPF*, 64. The English translation does not capture the play on words related to the verse in Genesis.

83. *TV*, vol. 1: 89. *OJ*, 110–11.

84. *TN*, 186–88.

85. *TN*, 157. For a detailed study of the application of the notion of a hidden God in the Bible, see Samuel E. Balentine, *The Hidden God* (Oxford: Oxford University Press, 1983). Balentine overlooks Buber's discussions of this notion.

86. Quoted in Harold Bloom, Introduction to *OTB*, xxvi. Bloom considers Buber's perspective "astonishing."

87. "Biblical Leadership," in *OTB*, 150.

88. *TN*, 135–6.

89. In this context, Buber cites Isaiah 9:1: "The people who walked in darkness have seen a great light." It is interesting to note that in a different context, Buber refers to a verse by the poet Hölderlin that is strikingly similar to the words of Isaiah: "But alas! Our generation walks in the night, dwells as in Hades, without the divine." Mention of Hölderlin serves Buber's attempt to mark the fundamental difference between himself and Heidegger. See *EOG*, 22–24.

90. *TN*, 136–37.

91. *TN*, 188.

92. A presentation of the extensive literature available on the topic of the "suffering servant" is beyond the scope of this book. For a general idea of the image, see Isaiah 42–44:8.

93. *TN*, 205.

94. See the reference to this state in *TN*, 125–26; and in *TPF*, 135–36.

95. *TN*, 136; *TPF*, 147.

96. *TN*, 214–15; *TPF*, 232–34.

97. *TN*, 211; *TPF*, 230.

98. Martin Buber, "The Messianic Mystery," a lecture delivered in Germany on 6 April 1925 on the occasion of the opening of the Hebrew University. The German original and the Hebrew translation of this most significant lecture are *TMM*. The references in the paragraph of text accompanying this note are to pp. 130–31, 133.

99. *MS*, 80; *KOG*, 92. See also *TN* 120; *TPF* 129.

100. "Mokdei Haneshama Hayehudit," in *TV*, vol. 1: 200. Translated as "The

Two Foci of the Jewish Soul," in *IATW*, 38. See also Buber's comment that "the servant here denotes a person—individual or corporate," *TPF*, 233.

101. *TN*, 200–1, 204–5.

102. For Buber's depiction of the community from which the "dialogical" persons of the Bible emerged, see *TN*, 6, 61, 102, 116, 131; *TPF*, 6, 64, 108–9, 124, 141. See also *KOG*, 157, where Buber alludes to a hidden community from which the judges came forth.

103. In "Martin Buber as Philosophical Interpreter of the Bible," 508, Eliezer Schweid notes: "Buber assumes that in the biblical text there is an interpretive apparatus that guides the reader toward a hidden message." This observation may be applied to our understanding of Buber's intentions as an interpreter of the Bible.

104. "The Messianic Mystery," 133, distinguishes between "apparent" and "hidden" history in the transmission of the "secret" of Judaism. I have translated the term גלויה (*g'luyah*) as "apparent" rather than "revealed," to preclude misguided association with the theological discourse of revelation. Ehud Luz has translated these two streams of history as "overt" and "covert" in "Buber's Hermeneutics: The Road to Revival of the Collective Memory and Religious Faith," *Modern Judaism* 15 (1995): 76–77. However, as "overt" and "covert" may evoke misleading connotations of sinister activity, I have chosen "apparent" (what appears to be) and "hidden" (present but unnoticed).

## CHAPTER 4: HIDDEN HISTORY:
## THE "TWO STREAMS" OF ADAM

1. Aubrey Hodes, *Martin Buber: An Intimate Portrait* (New York: Viking, 1971), 118.

2. "My Way to Hasidism," in *HAMM*, 51; *Werke*, vol. 3:968. For the Hebrew translation, see "Darki El Hahasidut," in *TLZ*, 108. I have changed Maurice Friedman's translation of *vollkommenen Menschen* from "perfected man" to "fully realized, whole person." *Vollkommenen* is difficult to translate; "perfected" does not convey the sense of wholeness and complete realization incorporated in this notion. Hence the choice of "fully realized, whole . . ." (The Hebrew translator has chosen to translate this notion as *shalem*, "whole.") This is not a mere quibble, for the idea of a perfected person has a long history in Christian discourse and thus gives Buber's work a chiliastic slant that I am not certain is actually present. Furthermore, one may note in passing that *Menschen* is not "man" but rather "person" or "human being." In Hebrew, the word used for *Menschen* is *Adam*, which is the exact word Buber intends here, as it is based on the biblical source. (See also chapter 3, note 33.)

3. This is a key passage for those seeking the heart of Buber's teaching. It is thus puzzling that when quoting the same passage, Laurence Silberstein omits the concluding sentence entirely, in which Buber speaks of the idea he feels "summon[ed]" to "proclaim." Silberstein thus overlooks the impact of this idea on the direction and focus of Buber's thought. See Laurence J. Silberstein, *Martin Buber's Social and Religious Thought: Alienation and the Quest for Meaning* (New York: New York University Press, 1989), 47.

4. I use the term Adam rather than "man" or "the first person" in order to be as faithful as possible to the original story, which emphasizes the unity of Adam as a being possessed of a dual nature, male and female. See Genesis 1:26–29, where Elohim consistently addresses the one Adam in the plural: "ברא אותם," "וירדו בדגת הים," "הנה נתתי לכם," "ויברך אותם אלוהים ויאמר להם," "זכר ונקבה." Genesis 1:27 states that Elohim created "the Adam," connoting a general, unindividuated being. Apparently, this choice of wording seeks to present the created being as a species, not as a particular individual. Adam appears as a specific individual only in Genesis 4:25, after the story of Cain and the survey of the generations that came after Cain. It is then that the text stipulates that a particular individual, Adam, "knew his wife again; and she bore a son, and called his name Seth." English translations are not always sensitive to this nuance. In the King James Version, Genesis 4:1 is translated "And Adam knew Eve his wife . . ." whereas the original Hebrew literally states "And *the* Adam knew . . ." See also *The New Oxford Annotated Bible: Revised Standard Edition* (New York: Oxford University Press, 1973).

5. I do not include in this analysis additional possibilities of interpretation available to the reader of this passage. For a further exposition, see Dan Avnon, "The 'Central Person' in Martin Buber's Political Theory" (doctoral dissertation, University of California at Berkeley, 1990), 42–48.

6. See, for example, *Meeshnayot: Masechet Avot* (Tractate Avot) 3:14, interpreted by Pinchas Kehati (Jerusalem: Kontras Yomi, 1983), 63.

7. "Ben Doraynu Vehamiqra," in *DSM*, 57.

8. "Ben Doraynu Vehamiqra," 56, Buber refers to this task as becoming Elohim's partner in the act of creation. In "The Wisdom and Deeds of Women," in *DSM*, 137, Buber writes that compassionate deeds are the realization of the commandment to cleave to Elohim's image, to "realize our being created in *tselem* (image)."

9. See also "The Faith of Israel," in *TV*, vol. 1: 182–83 and "The Two Foci of the Jewish Soul," in *IATW*, 30, where Buber writes, "The Jewish in man seems to me to be the ever renewed rediscernment of *Elohim*."

10. "Imitatio Dei," in *IATW*, 73.

11. "Prophecy and Apocalypse," in *DSM*, 114. The description of Adam's "desire" invites comparison with Platonic eros. See Stanley Rosen, "The Role

of Eros in Plato's *Republic,*" *Review of Metaphysics* 18, no. 3 (March 1965): 452–75, for a preliminary discussion of eros with attention to its implications for public life.

12. "Justice and Injustice according to the Songs of the Book of Psalms," in *DSM*, 142.

13. "Imitatio Dei," in *IATW*, 72–73.

14. "Imitatio Dei," in *IATW*, 66–77.

15. See sources cited in notes 7–9, 11–14, 16, and 24 of this chapter.

16. *TTM*, vol. 2: 117; *OH*, 319.

17. For an additional reference to Genesis 1:26 in Buber's Hasidic tales, see Rabbi Mendel's saying that the task of Adam is to prepare itself for the sacrifice of all the elements that its personality erects as barriers between itself and Elohim. *TTM*, vol. 2: 276–77; *OH*, 433–34.

18. "Justice and Injustice according to the Songs of the Book of Psalms," in *DSM*, 151–53.

19. David Blumenthal, ed., *Understanding Jewish Mysticism* (New York: Ktav, 1978), 154–59. See also Moshe Idel, *Kabbalah: New Perspectives* (in Hebrew) (Tel-Aviv: Schocken, 1993), 279–80.

20. This summary draws on Gershom Scholem's discussion in *Devarim Bego* (Explications and Implications) (Tel Aviv: Am Oved, 1990), 1:206–10. See also Gershom Scholem, *The Messianic Idea in Judaism* (New York: Schocken, 1971), 43–48.

21. Idel, *Kabbalah: New Perspectives*, 279–80.

22. See Rabbi Avraham Itzhak Kook, *Orot Hakodesh* (Jerusalem: Mossad HaRav Kook, 1985) 1:187, 2:302.

23. "Abraham's Mission," in *DSM*, 68–69.

24. This translation is based on *The New Oxford Annotated Bible.*

25. Isaiah 42:2.

26. *TMM*, 126.

27. "Leadership in the Bible," in *DSM*, 127; "Biblical Leadership," in *OTB*, 142.

28. "Leadership in the Bible," in *DSM*, 127; "Biblical Leadership," in *OTB*, 142.

29. Eliezer Schweid has summarized Buber's line of investigation as follows: "Buber dealt with the tension between the idea of a covenant and the idea of kingship. The social-political form of organization was a central axis in Buber's study of the Bible." Eliezer Schweid, "Martin Buber k'parshan Filosophi Shel Hamiqra' " (Martin Buber as Philosophical Interpreter of the Bible), *Jerusalem Studies in Jewish Thought* 2, no. 4 (1983): 596.

30. "Abraham the Seer," in *OTB*, 42–43.

31. Michael Walzer has drawn attention to the significance of Buber's distinc-

tion among peoples, nations, and nationalism: "The first is a matter of common experience, 'a unity of faith'; the second a collective awareness of this unity; the third a heightened or 'overemphasized' awareness in the face of division or oppression. Peoplehood is an impulse, nationality an idea, nationalism a program." In Michael Walzer, "Search for Zion," *Tikkun* 3, no. 3 (March–April 1988), 75. See also Michael Walzer, *The Company of Critics* (New York: Basic Books, 1988), 66–67.

32. "Abraham the Seer," in *OTB*, 28–29.

33. See chapter 6.

34. *Moses*, 127. See my discussion in Dan Avnon, "The 'Living Center' of Martin Buber's Political Theory," *Political Theory* 21, no.1 (February 1993): especially 68–70.

35. "Biblical Leadership," in *OTB*, 146.

36. "Biblical Leadership," in *OTB*, 147.

37. "Biblical Leadership," in *OTB*, 148 (italics added).

38. "Leadership in the Bible," in *DSM*, 132; "Biblical Leadership," in *OTB*, 148.

39. "Leadership in the Bible," in *DSM*, 148.

40. "Biblical Leadership," in *OTB*, 150.

41. "Historia Mitraheshet," in *TV*, vol. 1: 212. An English translation "In the Midst of History," is found in *IATW*, 79.

42. "Tvee'at Ha-Raach ve-Hametseeoot ha-Heestoreet" *TV*, vol. 2: 59–60. Buber wrote this essay in 1938, as part of his inaugural lecture at the Hebrew University of Jerusalem. It has been translated as "The Demand of the Spirit and Historical Reality," in *PTW*, 177–91. However, the key passages that serve the present exegesis are omitted from the English translation.

43. The words *teudah* and *torah* appear on pp. 59–60 of the original Hebrew text in *TV*, vol. 2. This is, of course, significant in terms of the hermeneutics guiding the present interpretation of Buber's intentions. The paragraph that includes these words is absent from the English translation. In addition, the English translation alters the remaining text and is oblivious to the allusions to the biblical text scattered throughout the Hebrew original. As such, it is useless as a guide to the hidden hermeneutics present in Buber's original essay.

44. "The Great Crisis," in *NB*, 265.

45. "Biblical Leadership," in *OTB*, 144; "Leadership in the Bible," in *DSM*, 128–29.

46. Martin Buber, "Replies to My Critics," in Schilpp and Friedman, 739.

47. Harold Bloom, Introduction to *OTB*, ix–xxvi. Bloom is referring to "Leadership in the Bible." It is surprising to note that Bloom devotes attention to "the author J," disregarding Buber's clear and unequivocal rejection of interpretations of the Bible that divide the text into the works of different, competing scribes. See my discussion in chapter 3.

48. Buber writes that the essay was first presented in 1928. Preface to *IATW*, 6–7.

49. "Biblical Leadership," in *OTB*, 150; "Leadership in the Bible," in *DSM*, 133–34.

50. As noted above in the text, Harold Bloom comments that this passage is a misreading of Isaiah's intentions and sounds more like a gnostic or cabalistic point of view than a biblical one. Bloom might revise his criticism (as would Gershom Scholem, whose works inspire Bloom's critique) were he to take into consideration the relation of this passage to Buber's other references to Isaiah's verses. See Bloom, Introduction to *OTB*, xxv–xxvi.

51. *TMM*, 133. This human type is the source of the true history (*die wahre Weltgeschichte*), 127.

52. "Biblical Leadership," in *OTB*, 150; "Leadership in the Bible," in *DSM*, 133–34.

53. "Biblical Leadership," in *OTB*, 142, 144; "Leadership in the Bible," in *DSM*, 128–29.

54. "Leadership in the Bible," in *DSM* 127; "Biblical Leadership," in *OTB*, 142.

55. "Biblical Leadership," in *OTB*, 150.

56. This is implied in "People and Leader," in *TV*, vol. 2: 69–71, in which Buber draws the line between Machiavelli's doctrine (which includes the good of the state as a criterion for the Prince) and that of Hitler and Frank (whose sole criterion is themselves). See *PTW*, 157–58, for an abridged translation of the Hebrew original.

57. "The Demand of the Spirit and the Historical Reality," in *TV*, vol. 2: 53. See also "The Spirit of Israel Facing the Present Reality," in *TV*, vol. 2: 101–2.

58. "Freedom and Destiny," in *TV*, vol. 1: 217.

59. "Biblical Leadership," in *OTB*, 142; "Leadership in the Bible," in *DSM*, 127. See also *TMM*, 133.

60. See the discussion in Michael Fishbane, *The Garments of Torah: Essays in Biblical Hermeneutics* (Bloomington: Indiana University Press, 1989), 33–46. Rabbi Simeon is quoted as saying that "the tales related in the Torah are simply her outer garments, and woe to the man who regards the outer garb as the Torah itself, for such a man will be deprived of a portion in the next world. . . . Just as wine must be in a jar to keep, so the Torah must be contained in an outer garment. That garment is made up of the tales and stories; but we, we are bound to penetrate beyond." *Zohar* 3:152, from G. Scholem, ed., *Zohar: Book of Splendor: Basic Readings from the Kabbalah* (New York: Schocken, 1963), 121–22, cited in Fishbane, *The Garments of the Torah*, 35, 138 n. 1.

61. "Occurring History," in *TV*, vol. 1: 211–14; translated as "In the Midst of History," in *IATW*, 78–82. The guiding verse appears in the Hebrew version on p. 212 and in the English version on p. 79.

62. In this context, see Buber's discussion of the effects of causal thinking on scientific explanations of the world we live in, presented in the second part of *I and Thou*, 100–107; and in *BS*, 39–45.

63. I emphasize "of this kind" because I do not attribute to Buber a nihilistic rejection of all that is "religious" or "scientific." On the contrary, when religion and science are presented within their modest limits, Buber has no quarrel with their assertions.

64. "Occurring History," in *TV*, vol. 1: 211; "In the Midst of History," in *IATW*, 80–82.

65. "Occurring History," in *TV*, vol. 1: 211; "In the Midst of History," in *IATW*, 78.

66. "In the Midst of History," in *IATW*, 78–79; "Occurring History," in *TV*, vol. 1: 211–12.

67. "Spinoza, Sabbatai Zvi, and the Baal-Shem," in *BH*, 19, and in *OMH*, 107.

68. Obviously, Buber is thinking about Weberian analysis of the impact of Christian doctrines on the development of Western ontology in Max Weber, *The Protestant Ethic and the Spirit of Capitalism*, translated by Talcott Parsons (New York: Charles Scribner's Sons, 1958).

69. *I and Thou*, 166.

70. Karl Jaspers, *The Origin and Goal of History* (New Haven: Yale University Press, 1953), 1.

71. *I and Thou*, 103. The context clarifies that Buber is thinking of revolutionary figures such as the Buddha, Socrates, Jesus, and Lao-Tzu.

72. "Biblical Leadership," in *IATW*, 131–32.

73. *I and Thou*, 103. See also "Medinah Ve-Tarbut" (State and Culture) in *TV*, vol. 2: 357–58; "China and Us," in *PTW*, 123. This conception of cultural renewal is strikingly similar to Oswald Spengler's analysis of the cycles of growth and decay of cultures. See John Macquarrie, *Twentieth-Century Religious Thought: The Frontiers of Philosophy and Theology, 1900–1980* (New York: Scribner's Sons, 1981), 125–26.

74. S. N. Eisenstadt, "Intersubjectivity, Dialogue, Discourse, and Cultural Creativity in the Work of Martin Buber," in *ICC*, 8.

75. *TMM*, 114.

76. "Christ, Hasidism, Gnosis," in *OMH*, 250, and in *TLZ*, 120.

77. "Christ, Hasidism, Gnosis," *OMH*, 251. See also "Dialogue," in *BMAM*, 5.

78. Quoted in Akivah Ernst Simon, "Martin Buber," *Jewish Frontier* 15 (February 1948):26.

79. "Christ, Hasidism, Gnosis," in *TLZ*, 120–21, and in *OMH*, 250. See also "Spinoza, Sabbatai Zvi, and the Baal-Shem," in *Hasidism*, 114.

80. "To the Issue of *Gog and Magog*," in *TLZ*, 140.

81. "Christ, Hasidism, Gnosis," in *OMH*, 251, and in *TLZ*, 120.

82. "The Spirit of Israel Facing the Present Reality," in *TV*, vol. 2: 106; "The Spirit of Israel and the World of Today," in *IATW*, 186–87.

83. "Christ, Hasidism, Gnosis," in *OMH*, 251, and in *TLZ*, 120.

84. *FSH*, 231. *Teshuva*, a central theme in Buber's work, can be translated literally as either "answer" or "turning." In the Jewish context, its meaning is associated with the notion of answering the call of God, of effecting a (re)turn to God. Buber says that the prophets of Israel understood this as an inner turning, an opening to a presence previously unnoticed.

85. See also "To the Issue of *Gog and Magog*," in *TLZ*, 140.

86. *TMM*, 133.

87. "Jesus—not, certainly, the actual man Jesus, but the image of Jesus as it entered into the soul of the peoples and transformed it—allows God to be addressed only in conjunction with himself, the Christ." *OMH*, 92.

88. "Spinoza, Sabbatai Zvi, and the Baal-Shem," in *OMH*, 92, and in *BH*, 10.

89. "Hasidism and Modern Man," in *HAMM*, 20.

90. "Spinoza, Sabbatai Zvi, and the Baal-Shem," in *OMH*, 110–11, and in *BH*, 21.

91. "Spinoza, Sabbatai Zvi, and the Baal-Shem," in *OMH*, 107, 111.

92. "The Word That Is Spoken," in *TKM*, 113.

93. "Spinoza, Sabbatai Zvi, and the Baal-Shem," in *OMH*, 93.

94. "Spinoza, Sabbatai Zvi, and the Baal-Shem," in *OMH*, 92, and in *BH*, 10.

95. See, for example, Spinoza's comment: "For as the highest power of Scriptural interpretation belongs to every man, the rule for such interpretation should be nothing but the natural light of reason which is common to all—not any supernatural light or any external authority," in Benedict de Spinoza, *A Theologico-Political Treatise and A Political Treatise* (New York: Dover, 1951), 119.

96. *OMH*, 93.

97. "Spinoza, Sabbatai Zvi, and the Baal-Shem," in *OMH*, 107, and in *OH*, 19.

98. *OMH*, 107–8.

99. *Hasidism*, 17–18.

100. "The Foundation Stone," in *OMH*, 68, and in *BH*, 47.

101. *BH*, 50; *Hasidism*, 46.

102. "Spirit and Body of the Hasidic Movement," in *OMH*, 128, and in *BH*, 67.

103. "Symbolic and Sacramental Existence," in *OMB*, 164–65, and in *BH*, 86.

104. Maurice Friedman, *Martin Buber's Life and Work: The Later Years, 1945–1964* (Detroit: Wayne University Press, 1988), 228.

105. "Hasidism and Modern Man," in *HAMM*, 19.

106. *HAMM*, 34.

107. *BMAM*, 34–35.

## CHAPTER 5: DIALOGICAL PHILOSOPHY: BETWEEN THE WORDS OF TEXTS AND THE CONTENT OF THOUGHT

1. "Judaism and Culture," in *TV*, vol. 1: 234, 257.

2. Hence Buber's exceptional sensitivity to the question of cultural renewal. See the fine collection of his essays dealing with this issue in *ICC*.

3. "Education," in *BMAM*, 92–93, and in *BS*, 249. Eliezer Schweid writes that Buber took upon himself the role of preparing the heart to listen to the scripture and its voice. Eliezer Schweid, "Martin Buber k'parshan Filosophi Shel Hamiqra' " (Martin Buber as Philosophical Interpreter of the Bible), *Jerusalem Studies in Jewish Thought* 2, no. 4 (1983): 606–7. My view that the expedience of *listening* is prior to particular emphasis on the Scripture as the embodiment of the primal "voice" differs from Schweid's reading of Buber's intentions.

4. Stanley Fish, *Self-Consuming Artifacts* (Berkeley: University of California Press, 1972).

5. "The Holy Way," in *OJ*, 143–48.

6. See chapter 4, notes 2–3. See also "The Holy Way," in *OJ*, 136.

7. For the centrality of the theology-versus-philosophy issue in modern political philosophy, see the correspondence between Voeglin and Strauss in P. Emberly and B. Cooper, eds., *Faith and Philosophy: The Correspondence between Leo Strauss and Eric Voeglin, 1934–1964* (University Park: Pennsylvania State University Press, 1993). See also Thomas Pangle, "On the Epistolary Dialogue between Leo Strauss and Eric Voeglin," *Review of Politics* 53, no.1 (Winter 1991):100–124; Ernest L. Fortin and Glenn Hughes, "The Strauss-Voeglin Correspondence: Two Reflections and Two Comments," *Review of Politics* 56, no.2 (Spring 1994): 337–57.

8. Sydney Rome and Beatrice Rome, eds., *Philosophical Interrogations* (New York: Holt, Rinehart and Winston, 1964), 17.

9. For a comprehensive introduction to the basic questions guiding the philosophical quest, see Jacob Needleman and David Appelbaum, *Real Philosophy: An Anthology of the Universal Search for Meaning* (Harmondsworth, England: Penguin Arkana Books, 1990).

10. *OH*, front page, unnumbered. These tales have been translated into English as *TTM*. The story about the hidden light does not appear in the English

version. For a different translation and a sensitive analysis of this midrashic hom-
ily, see Michael Fishbane, *The Garments of Torah: Essays in Biblical Hermeneutics*
(Bloomington: Indiana University Press, 1989), 81–90.

11. This is my translation of *OH*, 218; see the English translation in *TTM*,
vol. 1: 232.

12. This interpretation offers a solution to the philosophical quandary presented by Stanley Rosen, who comments on the direction taken by modern
hermeneutics in the following terms: "If nothing is real, the real is nothing;
there is no difference between the written lines of a text and the blank spaces
between them." Buber's philosophy, absent from the pages of Rosen's text, takes
this quandary into consideration and offers an alternative way of thinking about
this issue. See Stanley Rosen, *Hermeneutics as Politics* (Oxford: Oxford University
Press, 1987), 169.

13. *TTM*, vol. 2: 300; *OH*, 452.

14. *TTM*, vol. 2: 301; *OH*, 453.

15. *TTM*, vol. 2: 301–2; *OH*, 453–54.

16. *TTM*, vol. 1: 104; *OH*, 111.

17. Paul Mendes-Flohr refers to Buber's sociology as "a Heraclitean metasoc-
iology." See Paul Mendes-Flohr, "Havruta Vehidusha" (Society and its Renewal), in *Kan Veachshav*, edited by Shmaryahu Talmon et al., 2nd ed.
(Jerusalem: Martin Buber Center of Hebrew University of Jerusalem and the
Interfaith Community, 1989), 100.

18. Heraclitus, *Fragments*, translated with a commentary by T. M. Robinson
(Toronto: University of Toronto Press, 1987), fragment 50, p. 37. For a discussion of the problematics involved in attributing to Heraclitus one single understanding of Logos, see Robinson's commentary to fragment 1, pp. 74–76.

19. Heraclitus, *Fragments*, fragments 32, 27. Buber's inexact quote of this fragment is in *EOG*, 30. Interpreting this fragment, Buber claims that Heraclitus
"has given philosophical expression to an original relation between philosophy
and religion as that between the meeting with the divine and its objectification
in thought." *EOG*, 30–31.

20. Quoted in Heraclitus, *Fragments*, fragments 46, 33.

21. Leo Strauss, *Liberalism Ancient and Modern* (Ithaca: Cornell University
Press), 233.

22. Leo Strauss, *What Is Political Philosophy?* (Chicago: University of Chicago
Press, 1988), 28–29.

23. See, in this context, Simmel's philosophy of As-If, as summarized in Michael Kaern, "The World as Human Construction," *Georg Simmel and Contemporary Sociology*, edited by Michael Kaern et al. (Dordrecht, Netherlands: Kluwer
Academic Publishers, 1990), 75–98.

24. Strauss, *Liberalism Ancient and Modern*, 235.

25. *EOG*, 30–31.

26. *TTM*, vol. 1: 107.

27. *EOG*, 19.

28. "The Word That Is Spoken," in *TKM*, 113. Steven Kepnes correctly notes that in this essay "Buber shows that he has moved from a focus on the pre-linguistic, immediate relationship between person and world and person and person in *I and Thou* to further develop . . . linguistic notions. . . ." For purposes of this chapter, it is important to note the awareness on Buber's part of the prelinguistic stage of relation as the source of all other linguistic developments. See Kepnes's interesting discussion of "The Word That Is Spoken" in his *The Text as Thou: Martin Buber's Dialogical Hermeneutics and Narrative Theology* (Bloomington: Indiana University Press, 1992), 62–71.

29. "The Word That Is Spoken," in *TKM*, 113. I have substituted the word "stage" for "level," as the latter may be misinterpreted as an indicator of hierarchy or of degree. In fact, the notion of three stages attempts to convey transitions that are not demarcated in terms of height or measurable distance, although the progressive stages do indicate a gradual distancing from the original experience.

30. "The Word That Is Spoken," in *TKM*, 113.

31. This passage is written with the essay "Distance and Relation," in *TKM*, 59–71, in mind.

32. "Abraham the Seer," in *OTB*, 26.

33. "The Word That Is Spoken," in *TKM*, 117.

34. "Abraham the Seer," in *TKM*, 26.

35. "The Word That Is Spoken," in *TKM*, 117.

36. See Jacob Needleman, "Why Philosophy Is Easy," *Review of Metaphysics* 22, no.1 (September 1968): 3–4; Huston Smith, *Beyond the Post-Modern Mind* (Wheaton, Illinois: Quest Books, 1984), 53–54; and Dan Avnon, " 'Know Thyself': Socratic Companionship and Platonic Community," *Political Theory* 23, no. 2 (May 1995), 304–29.

37. Robert E. Cushman, *Therapia: Plato's Conception of Philosophy* (Westport, Conn.: Greenwood Press, 1976), xv.

38. Rene Descartes, "Discourse on the Method of Rightly Conducting the Reason and Seeking Truth in the Field of Science," in *Discourse on Method and Meditations*, translated by Lawrence J. Lafleur (New York: Macmillan, 1988), 24.

39. "Religion and Philosophy," in *EOG*, 39–40, and in *PA*, 249–50.

40. Rene Descartes, "The Meditations concerning First Philosophy," in *Discourse on Method and Meditations*, 84.

41. Descartes, "Discourse on the Method of Rightly Conducting the Reason and Seeking Truth in the Field of Science," 24.

42. See also Rene Descartes, "Principles of Philosophy," in *The Philosophical Writings of Descartes*, translated by John Cottingham, Robert Stoothoff, and Dugald Murdoch (Cambridge: Cambridge University Press, 1985), 1:197–204.

43. For an excellent presentation of Descartes's impact on the development of modern notions of identity, see Charles Taylor, *Sources of the Self: The Making of Modern Identity* (Cambridge: Harvard University Press, 1989).

44. "Religion and Philosophy," in *EOG*, 42–43, and in *PA*, 252–53.

45. "Religion and Philosophy," in *EOG*, 45; *PA*, 252.

46. "Dialogue," *BS*, 118; *BMAM*, 10.

47. "Elohim and the Spirit of Adam," *PA*, 317; *EOG*, 124.

48. "Elohim and the Spirit of Adam," *PA*, 317; *EOG*, 124.

49. "Dialogue," in *BS*, 118–19, and in *BMAM*, 11.

50. This idea is presented in similar terms in relation to Spinoza: "The thinking of our time is characterized by an essentially different aim. It seeks, on the one hand, to preserve the idea of the divine as the true concern of religion, and, on the other hand, to destroy the reality of the idea of God and thereby the reality of our relation to him." "Religion and Reality," in *EOG*, 17, and in *PA*, 229.

51. "Elohim and and the Spirit of Adam," in *PA*, 317, and in *EOG*, 125 [my translation—the last line was omitted in the English version].

52. "Elohim and the Spirit of Adam," *PA*, 317–18, and in *EOG*, 125.

53. "Elements of the Interhuman," in *BS*, 218, 220, and in *TKM*, 77. An unnumbered cover page of *BS* notes that the essay was originally written in Hebrew in 1953. See the faulty English translation in *TKM*, 75–76.

54. "Dialogue," in *BMAM*, 3–4.

55. "Dialogue," in *BMAM*, 19.

56. "Dialogue," in *BMAM*, 31.

57. "Dialogue," in *BMAM*, 10. It is important to note that the Hebrew version of "Dialogue" refers to "awareness" as תשומת לב, *tsoomet lev*, "the knowledge (attention) of the heart." *BS*, 117.

58. See the cover page of *BS* for details about the original language of this essay.

59. *BS*, 231. Smith translates this difficult passage as follows: "And of course I must also be intent to raise into an inner word and then into a spoken word what I have to say at this moment but do not yet possess as speech. To speak is both nature and work, something that grows and something that is made, and where it appears dialogically, in the climate of great faithfulness, it has to fulfill ever anew the unity of the two." By eliminating the place of the heart as the origin of speech, Smith's translation deprives Buber's presentation of its essential intention. *TKM*, 86.

60. "The Word That is Spoken," in *TKM*, 110–20.

61. "Elements of the Interhuman," in *BS*, 230–31.

62. See "Dialogue," in *BS*, 115–17, and in *BMAM*, 8–10.

63. See Buber's discussion in "Who Speaks?" in *BMAM*, 14–15.

64. "Prelude: A Report on Two Talks," in *EOG*, 6–9.

65. *EOG* discusses this characteristic of modern philosophy, analyzing the philosophies of Feuerbach, Hegel, Heidegger, Jaspers, Jung, Kant, Nietzsche, and Sartre, among others.

66. Philosophers who follow Wittgenstein would emphasize that a word gains *actual* meaning only in the context of its *use* in writing, speech, or conversation. Hanna Pitkin, *Wittgenstein and Justice* (Berkeley: University of California Press, 1972), 140–68.

67. *EOG*, 17, 19, 51–52, 54. Buber goes on (pp. 55–61) to show how Herman Cohen realized the incompleteness of his dependence on thought as the place for understanding God. Cohen's subsequent conclusion that the love of human beings for God "is the love of the moral ideal" may be an account of how persons of faith interpret their relation to God, but as Buber points out, "He who loves God only as the moral ideal is bound soon to reach the point of despair at the conduct of the world where, hour after hour, all the principles of moral idealism are apparently contradicted." *EOG*, 59–60.

68. *EOG*, 50.

69. The second commandment includes the following stipulation: "You shall not make for yourself a graven image, or any likeness of anything that is in heaven above, or that is on the earth beneath, or that is in the water under the earth; you shall not bow down to them or serve them." Exodus 20:4.

70. "Therefore take good heed to yourselves. Since you saw no form on the day YHVH spoke to you at Horeb from the midst of the fire, beware lest you act corruptly by making a graven image for yourselves, in the form of any figure, the likeness of male or female . . . lest you forget the covenant of YHVH your Elohim, which he made with you, and make a graven image in the form of anything which YHVH your Elohim has forbidden you." Deuteronomy 4:16, 23.

71. The English translator sometimes uses the words "colloquy" and "soliloquy" to designate "dialogue" and "monologue," respectively. I believe that this is an inappropriate choice, as it ignores Buber's basic terminology. See, for example, *EOG*, 13.

72. *PA*, 236; *EOG*, 24.

73. *PA*, 237; *EOG*, 24.

74. *PA*, 322; *EOG*, 129.

75. "A Philosophy of the Interhuman" is the subtitle of *TKM*.

76. *OH*. For the history of this publication, see Moshe Cattan, *A Bibliography of Martin Buber's Works [1895–1957]* (Jerusalem: Bialik, 1958), 38–39, 82.

77. *GOG*, translated into English as *FSH*. For Scholem's comment, see Gershom Scholem, "Al Peulato Shel Buber Bisdeh Hagasidut," in *Devarim Bego* (Explications and Implications) (Tel Aviv: Am Oved, 1990), 2:453.

78. See Meir Weiss, in "BeSod Siah HaMikra," introduction to *DSM*, 25–26, where Weiss discusses Buber's attempt to bridge the tension he must have experienced between academic discourse and the story he wished to convey.

79. I refer to the essays collected in *TKM*. See Maurice Friedman's note: "Martin Buber is 'old in a young way, knowing how to begin.' His philosophical anthropology represents an exciting new beginning in his thought—begun at the age of seventy-three and completed just after his eighty-fifth birthday!" Maurice Friedman, Foreword to *TKM*, 7.


## CHAPTER 6: DIALOGICAL COMMUNITY: THE THIRD WAY BETWEEN INDIVIDUALISM AND COLLECTIVISM

1. Georg Simmel, "The Problem of Sociology," in *Georg Simmel, 1858–1918*, edited by Kurt H. Wolff (Columbus: Ohio State University Press, 1959), 310–36. Donald Levine succinctly summarizes Simmel's attention to the fabric and texture of the space that is in between persons: "This 'something in reality' is always an interaction of parts. Society, then, for Simmel is neither a collective being nor a fictitious entity; rather, it exists in the processes of interaction among individuals and groups. The principle of interaction is of the greatest importance in all of Simmel's thought." Donald Levine, "The Structure of Simmel's Social Thought," in *Georg Simmel, 1858–1918*, 19–20. Coser adds that this is the reason that Simmel considered association (rather than society) to be the major field of study for the student of society. Lewis A. Coser, ed., *Georg Simmel* (Englewood Cliffs, New Jersey: Prentice-Hall, 1965), 5.

2 For an introductory discussion of the concept *das Zwischenmenschliche*, see Maurice Friedman, Introduction to *TKM*, 25–33.

3. "What Is Man?" in *BMAM*, 204–5.

4. *I and Thou*, 68, 171. On p. 78, Buber writes: "The innate You is realized in the You we encounter."

5. The most important studies of Buber's social and political thought published in English in recent years are Paul Mendes-Flohr, *From Mysticism to Dialogue: Martin Buber's Transformation of German Social Thought* (Detroit: Wayne State University Press, 1989); Laurence J. Silberstein, *Martin Buber's Social and Religious Thought: Alienation and the Quest for Meaning* (New York: New York University Press, 1989); and Bernard Susser, *Existence and Utopia: The Social and Political Thought of Martin Buber* (London: Associated University Presses, 1981).

6. Buber finds that when art and philosophy are engaged in the figuration of symbols, the two vocations share a common attempt to express an unmediated relation to being: "The artist does not hold a fragment of being up to the light; he receives from his contact with being and brings forth what has never before

existed. It is the same with the genuine philosopher." "Bergson's Concept of Intuition," in *PTW*, 64. See, in this context, "Man and His Image Work," in *TKM*, 149–65.

7. Eric Voegelin, *The New Science of Politics* (Chicago: University of Chicago Press, 1987), 28–29.

8. The Between, says Buber elsewhere, "has received no specific attention because, in distinction from the individual soul and its context, it does not exhibit a smooth continuity, but is ever and again re-constituted in accordance with men's meetings with one another." "What Is Man?" in *BMAM*, 203.

9. This point has often been misunderstood, which has led to erroneous presentations of the social significance of Buber's philosophy of dialogue. See Buber's comment in Sydney Rome and Beatrice Rome, eds., *Philosophical Interrogations* (New York: Holt, Rinehart and Winston, 1964), 27.

10. See the exchange between Emmanuel Levinas and Buber in Rome and Rome, *Philosophical Interrogations*, 23–29.

11. A common misconception concerning Martin Buber's social and political theory is that Buber's importance as a theorist of community "resides in his stress upon the indispensable role of God as the center of community, the creator of its conditions, and the agent who calls it into being through his relations with his creatures." Frank G. Kirkpatrick, *Community: A Trinity of Models* (Washington, D.C.: Georgetown University Press, 1986), 142. In light of our contention that Buber considered it incumbent upon philosophers and theorists to rid their discourse of the word God, this claim becomes problematic, pointing to either a contradiction in Buber's thought or a misunderstanding thereof by Frank Kirkpatrick. This chapter assumes the latter proposition to be more accurate.

12. *I and Thou*, 94; *Werke*, 1:108.

13. *I and Thou*, 53.

14. The medium through which Buber's words reach us is the written text about the mystery embedded in other written texts. As such, Buber qualifies as an "ontological hermeneut," whom Stanley Rosen describes as one who treats the text "as indirect evidence of a general doctrine of Being . . . as data to be transformed and hence replaced by a theoretical artifact." Stanley Rosen, *Hermeneutics as Politics* (New York: Oxford University Press, 1987), 167–69.

15. Plato, *Republic*, book 5, 473b4.

16. "Urdistanz und Beziehung," in *Werke*, 1:412; "Distance and Relation," in *TKM*, 60–61. See Maurice Friedman's excellent discussion in the introduction to *TKM*, 21–33.

17. In this context, see Buber's interpretation of the creation story in Genesis 1 as an instance of this dual movement. In *GAE*, 67–80.

18. "Distance and Relation," in *TKM*, 60.

19. *I and Thou*, 113–14.

20. "Wittgenstein's discussion of language games and forms of life suggests that we might think of language as being subdivided into clusters of similar and related concepts, used in similar and related language games." Hanna Pitkin, *Wittgenstein and Justice* (Berkeley: University of California Press, 1972), 140.

21. *I and Thou*, 114–15.

22. *I and Thou*, 115.

23. "The Spirit of Israel and the World of Today," in *IATW*, 186.

24. *I and Thou*, 94; *Werke*, 1:108 (emphasis added). Laurence Silberstein has suggested to me that one may read this passage differently, with emphasis on the latter part of the last sentence as indicating the active agent. Read along these lines, that sentence would imply that the living, active center is the builder, rather than that the builder is the living, active center, as I suggest. This is indeed a possible interpretation. For Silberstein's reading of this passage, see his *Martin Buber's Social and Religious Thought*, 177. I believe that this chapter provides sufficient support for my alternative interpretation of Buber's intentions.

25. See *BMAM*, 31–32; Robert E. Wood, *Martin Buber's Ontology: An Analysis of* I and Thou (Evanston: Northwestern University Press, 1969), 74–75.

26. Kirkpatrick, *Community: A Trinity of Models*, 186. On Buber, see 140–46.

27. In an interview he granted toward the end of his days, Buber repeated this in different words: "By community I understand a connection of men who are so joined in their life with something apportioned to them in common that they are, just thereby, joined with one another in their life." In Rome and Rome, *Philosophical Interrogations*, 20.

28. Paul R. Mendes-Flohr, "Martin Buber's Concept of the Center and Social Renewal," in *Jewish Journal of Sociology* 18, no. 1 (June 1976): 19–20.

29. In *I and Thou*, 103, Buber emphasizes the ongoing nature of the enterprise: "Every great culture that embraces more than one people rests upon some original encounter, an event at the source when a response was made to a You, an essential act of the spirit. Reinforced by the energy of subsequent generations that points in the same direction, this creates a distinctive conception of the cosmos in the spirit; only thus does a human cosmos (*Kosmos des Menschen*) become possible again and again." Hence my reference to the "ones," rather than the "one," at the center.

30. "The Faith of Judaism," in *IATW*, 124.

31. Mendes-Flohr, "Martin Buber's Concept," 20.

32. Buber's remark in *PIU*, 135, that a community need not undergo a founding, is in a different context. There he is analyzing the question of renewal of an existing community, within the broader context of modern socialism.

33. "Al Mahuta shel Tarbut" (The Essence of Culture), in *PA*, 384–86. See S. N. Eisenstadt, "Haguto Ha-Chevratit Shel Martin Buber" (Martin Buber's Social Thought), an essay written on the occasion of the thirtieth day following

Buber's death and published in *Al Professor Mordechai Martin Buber: Devarim She-Neemru Le-Zichro* (About Professor Mordechai Martin Buber: Addresses in his Memory), edited by S. H. Bergman (Jerusalem: Magnes, 1966), 10–12.

34. See "Spirit of the Hasidic Movement," in *Hasidism*, 73–94.

35. "Teaching and Deed," in *IATW*, 139. This depiction of the process of transmission is strikingly similar to the one described by Plato in the Seventh Epistle: "Only after long partnership in a common life devoted to this very thing does truth flash upon the soul, like a flame kindled by a leaping spark, and once it is born there it nourishes itself thereafter." Plato, *Phaedrus and Seventh and Eighth Letters*, translated by Walter Hamilton (Harmondsworth, England: Penguin Books, 1973), 136.

36. "Teaching and Deed," in *IATW*, 139.

37. See the collection of essays in *ICC*.

38. S. N. Eisenstadt, Introduction to *ICC*, 15–16, 21.

39. See the chapter on Landauer in *PIU*, 46–57.

40. *PIU*, 138; *PTW*, 222–23.

41. *PIU*, 138.

42. *I and Thou*, 157–68; "Hope For This Hour," in *PTW*, 220–30.

43. "The Spirit of Israel and the World of Today," in *IATW*, 193–94; "The Holy Way," in *OJ*, 143–48.

44. Paul Mendes-Flohr, for example, joins two separate passages from *I and Thou* and, in the process, omits mention of the builder. This is how he quotes the passage excerpted in the text accompanying note 24 above: "living reciprocal relationship includes feelings but is not derived from them. A community (*eine Gemeinde*) is built upon a living, active center . . . men's relations to their true You, being radii that lead from all I-points to the center, create a circle. That alone assures the genuine existence of a community (*eine Gemeinde*)." Mendes-Flohr, "Martin Buber's Concept," 20. This essay is included in Mendes-Flohr, *From Mysticism to Dialogue*, 121. In a Hebrew version of the essay, Mendes-Flohr corrects the quotation by inserting ellipses to show where he left out the part about the builder. He does not, however, modify his analysis accordingly. See Paul Mendes-Flohr, "Fellowship and Its Renewal: Dialogue as a Metasociological Principle" (in Hebrew), in *Kaan Vechshav*, edited by Shmaryahu Talmon et al., 2nd ed., (Jerusalem: Martin Buber Center of Hebrew University of Jerusalem and the Interfaith Community, 1989), 57. Reading the same passage from *I and Thou*, Bernard Susser says: "This 'center,' community's transcendent archetype, is the generating point of contact; the binding joint that permits the movement of individuals toward each other. Metaphorically speaking, each individual is a spoke off the radiating 'center.'" Susser, *Existence and Utopia*, 52. Laurence Silberstein, too, omits mention of the builder when discussing this passage. Silberstein, *Martin Buber's Social and Religious Thought*, 171–72. Avraham Yassour

follows Mendes-Flohr on this point. Avraham Yassour, *Prakim Behaguto Hache-vratit Shel M. M. Buber* (Tel Aviv: Aleph, 1981), 31.

45. See Dan Avnon, "The 'Living Center'of Martin Buber's Political The-ory," *Political Theory* 21, no. 1 (February 1993): 73 n. 33.

46. Buber calls such leaders *hanhagah ne'ederet torah*, literally translated as "leadership devoid of torah." "Am Vemanheeg," in *TV*, vol. 2: 62. In the abridged English translation this expression has been rendered as "successful leading without teaching." "People and Leader," in *PTW*, 149. I think that this translation misses the richness of the original expression, with its multiple connotations (Buber uses the term torah in its meaning as "instruction," "direc-tion," or a "teaching"; he thus translates *torah* into German as *Weisung*).

47. Although drawing on the sociological definitions of Max Weber, Buber does not explain the difference between his notion of "negative" charisma and other notions of charisma. He assumes a difference and then goes on to refer to examples (Jacob Frank, Adolph Hitler, Mussolini). This is a major flaw in his argument, for without a clear understanding of the element that sets "negative" charisma apart from (true?) charisma, this concept is of little use as a sociological category.

48. *I and Thou*, 117–19.

49. *I and Thou*, 138–39, 166.

50. *PTW*, 115.

51. See Avnon, " 'Know Thyself': Socratic Companionship and Platonic Community," *Political Theory* 23, no. 2 (May 1995): 304–29.

52. *Zedek* is the Hebrew word for justice. *Zaddik* is a term usually translated as "the righteous one" or "the just one." Buber says that it actually refers to "those who stood the test" or "the proven." *TTM*, vol. 1: 1.

53. "My Way To Hasidism," in *HAMM*, 53, in *Werke*, 3:964, and in *TLZ*, 104.

54. *HAMM*, 59.

55. Laurence Silberstein omits the concluding sentence (where Buber speaks of the idea he felt "summon[ed]" to "proclaim") when citing this passage. See Silberstein, *Martin Buber's Social and Religious Thought*, 47. Pamela Vermes does point to the centrality of this idea for Buber's religious thought, yet she does not make the connection between Buber's writings on Jewish matters and his politi-cal and social theory. See Pamela Vermes, *Buber on God and the Perfect Man* (Lon-don: Littman Library of Jewish Civilization, 1994).

56. Rome and Rome, *Philosophical Interrogations*, 68.

57. "My Way to Hasidism," in *HAMM*, 68.

58. *Tzavoas Horivash* (New York: Kehot Publication Society, 1975), sec. 125, pp. 44–45.

59. Buber attributes a similar story, "Two Kinds of *Zaddikim*," to Rabbi Israel of Rizhyn. *TTM*, vol. 2: 53–54.

60. Plato, *Republic*, book 7, 517c7. One should not overemphasize the similarity. In Plato's depiction, the turning around is toward the "puppet-like objects" that are the originals of the shadows and images the prisoner had previously been seeing; in Judaism, the turning is toward a higher and imageless reality.

61. *Moses*, 66.

62. Martin Buber, "The Faith of Judaism," in *IATW*, 21. See also "Prophecy, Apocalyptic, and the Historical Hour," in *PTW*, 196–97, and 206, and in *TTF*, 63–64, 91–92, 155–56. See also a good analysis of Buber's interpretation of this concept in Malcolm Diamond, *Martin Buber: Jewish Existentialist* (New York: Oxford University Press, 1960), 147–49.

63. The incorporation of the notion of *teshuva* into Buber's major philosophical work is not surprising. For Buber, the wholeness of life, the essential seamlessness of all that is, is the other side of the Jewish teaching of the unity of God. See "Two Foci of the Jewish Soul," in *IATW*, 33–34. Walter Kaufmann's translation of *Umkehr* as "return" is inaccurate; *Wiederkehr* would be "return." See Walter Kaufmann, Prologue to *I and Thou*, 35–36.

64. "Hasidism and Modern Man," in *HAMM*, 28.

65. "The Way of Man, According to the Teachings of Hasidism," in *HAMM*, 158–59.

66. *TR*, 65.

67. *TTM*, vol. 2: 2. Elsewhere Buber says that *Hasidut*, the social movement of those called Hasid, is "a word that can be translated into English still far less than the Latin *pietas* that corresponds to it; its meaning might most easily be rendered through a verbal paraphrase: to love the world in God." In "The Baal Shem-Tov's Instruction in Intercourse with God," in *HAMM*, 179.

68. *TTM*, vol. 2: 54 (emphasis added).

69. On the idea of "levels of being," see E. F. Schumacher, *A Guide for the Perplexed* (New York: Harper and Row, 1977), 15–25.

70. A good summary of this debate is found in Maurice Friedman, "Interpreting Hasidism: The Buber-Scholem Controversy," *Leo Baeck Yearbook* 33 (1988): 449–67.

71. Rivkah Schatz-Uffenheimer, "Man's Relation to God and World in Buber's Rendering of the Hasidic Teaching," in *The Philosophy of Martin Buber*, edited by Paul A. Schilpp and Maurice Friedman (La Salle, Illinois, 1967), 404.

72. See Rivkah Schatz-Uffenheimer, *HaHasidut Kemystica* (Quietistic Elements in Eighteenth Century Hasidic Thought) (Jerusalem: Magnes, 1988), 17.

73. Gershom Scholem, "Martin Buber's Interpretation of Hasidism" in *The Messianic Idea in Judaism* (New York: Schocken, 1971), 230. In chapter 2 of *Martin Buber's Social and Religious Thought*, Silberstein presents a thoughtful reading of the Scholem-Buber debate. Silberstein interprets Buber's Hasidic works as examples of (what Harold Bloom calls) a "strong reader" who engages in "creative misreading."

74. For an illuminating comparison of an original Hasidic legend and Buber's revision, see Pinchas Sadeh, *Sipure HaBesht* (Jerusalem: Carta, 1987), 177–81. Sadeh shows that Buber exorcised the original text of any mention of magical powers associated with the Ba'al Shem, of the Ba'al Shem's wild, emotional, ecstatic, and at times brutal conduct. This diluted version, says Sadeh, creates the misleading impression that a meeting with the *zaddik* was as tame as a "social visit of two academics at the Library of the Hebrew University," 181.

75. Friedman, "Interpreting Hasidism," 465.

76. Friedman, "Interpreting Hasidism," 465.

77. Buber's favorite example of a "true" revolutionary is Gustav Landauer. See "Recollection of a Death," an essay devoted to the memory of Gustav Landauer, in *PTW*, 115–20. See also *PTW*, 46–57, and the essays "Landauer and Revolution," "The Hidden Leader," and "Landauer in These Times," in *NB*. For Landauer's influence on Buber, see Grete Schaeder, *The Hebrew Humanism of Martin Buber*, translated by Noah Jacobs (Detroit: Wayne State University Press, 1973), 258–64. See also Robert Weltsch, "Buber's Political Philosophy" in *The Philosophy of Martin Buber*, edited by Schilpp and Friedman, 438–40. For a comprehensive analysis of Landauer, see Eugene Lunn, *Prophet of Community: The Romantic Socialism of Gustav Landauer* (Berkeley: University of California Press, 1973).

78. In 1922 Buber outlined three different plans for additional volumes to follow *I and Thou*, which he was about to complete. One outline, titled "The Primary Forms and Magic," has a volume called "The Person and Community: (1) The Originator, (2) The Priest, (3) The Prophet, (4) The Reformer, (5) The Lonely Man." Shortly thereafter Buber abandoned this plan. What is interesting to note is the unwritten chapter on the originator, mentioned in *I and Thou*, 103; hence my use of this term. See Rivkah Horowitz, *Buber's Way to* I and Thou*: The Development of Martin Buber's Thought and His "Religion as Presence" Lectures* (Philadelphia: Jewish Publication Society, 1988), 188–89.

79. *Moses*, 66.

80. *Moses*, 112.

81. *I and Thou*, 94.

82. See Michael Fishbane's Introduction to *Moses*, 4–10. The question of the relation between *I and Thou* and *Moses* is discussed on pages 9–10.

83. Compare with Susser, *Existence and Utopia*, 52.

84. *Moses*, 101, 115, 186–89.

85. See also "Symbolic and Sacramental Existence," in *OMH*, 151–82.

86. *Moses*, 75 (emphasis added).

87. The quote paraphrases Ulrich E. Simon, "Martin Buber and the Interpretation of the Prophets," 252.

88. *Moses*, 188.

89. The one who prepares a people does so as an inseparable extension (and reflection) of his own personal transformation. Moses hoped that the desert that had once "purified and freed [Moses] from himself" would help his people experience the same liberation. His personal experience, his way to know himself, was therefore a central influence on his conception of the way to renew his people. *Moses*, 69–70. For the spiritual significance of the Hebrew word for desert, *midbar*, see our discussion in chapter 3.

90. *Moses*, 199.

91. "Three Theses of a Religious Socialism," in *PTW*, 112–15 and in *NB*, 180–83. See also "On the Science of Religion," in *ABH*, 127. For the historical background of the movement known in the 1920s as Religious Socialism, see Ephraim Fischoff, Introduction to *PTW*, xvii–xxii. See also the following English-language sources: Richard Falk, *Martin Buber and Paul Tillich: Radical Politics and Religion* (New York: National Council of Protestant Episcopal Churches, 1961); Lunn, *Prophet of Community*; Ruth Link-Salinger, "Friends in Utopia: Martin Buber and Gustav Landauer," *Midstream* 24:1, 67–72; and Charles B. Maurer, *Call to Revolution: The Mystical Anarchism of Gustav Landauer* (Detroit: Wayne State University Press, 1971).

92. *PTW*, 112.

93. See "What Is Man?" in *BMAM*, 157. For a different perspective on Buber's contribution to the discourse of modern socialism, see Susser, *Existence and Utopia*, 78–79.

94. *I and Thou*, 53.

95. This idea reappears in various forms and formulations throughout Buber's work. Buber presents a similar position when he asserts, "We shall accomplish nothing at all if we divide our work and our life into two domains: one in which God's command is paramount, the other governed exclusively by the laws of economics, politics, and the 'simple self-assertion' of the group." "And If Not Now, When?" in *IATW*, 235–36. Elsewhere, Buber justifies this way of thinking in terms of his biblical interpretations, where he writes that unlike modern persons, there is one sin that biblical sinners do not commit: "they do not confine God to a circumscribed space or division of life, to 'religion.' They do not have the insolence to draw boundaries . . . and say to him: 'Up to this point, you are sovereign, but beyond these bounds begins the sovereignty of science or society or the state.' " "Hebrew Humanism," in *IATW*, 247.

96. See *PIU*, 80–99. In addition, see the essays "Society and State" and "The Validity and Limitation of the Political Principle," in *PTW*, 172–76, 214–15.

97. *PTW*, 113, and also "The Question to the Single One," in *BMAM*, 69–70.

98. "On the Ethics of Political Decision," in *ABH*, 20.

99. "The Education of Character," in *BMAM*, 110–11.

100. Mendes-Flohr writes that "Buber's philosophy of the Center and social renewal may be designated as a meta-sociology." This conclusion is based on the premise that the "ontic directness accompanying the I–Thou relation" is a principle formally independent of social life. Mendes-Flohr's analysis suggests that no social agent or context acts as an intermediary facilitating the movement from an attitude of I–It towards an attitude of relation to being, to I–You. Mendes-Flohr, "Martin Buber's Concept," 22–23. Emphasizing the centrality of central persons as social agents, the present book offers a different interpretation of Buber's social theory.

101. "Experiments," in *PIU*, 73. This understanding is formulated yet again when Buber comments, "The individual spiritual spheres which have become influential *unite* when a genuine religious communal life again exists." In "A Believing Humanism," in *IATW*, 133.

102. "The Question to the Single One," in *BMAM*, 60.

103. As we noted in the discussion of Buber's notion of socialism as *socialitas*, here too the conception of political community developed by Buber is idiosyncratic. For comprehensive analysis of the concept and meaning of community in Western political thought, see the essays included in *Community*, edited by Carl J. Friedreich (New York: Liberal Arts Press, 1959). Also published as the 1959 yearbook of *Nomos*.

104. Thus, in "The Validity and Limitation of the Political Principle," in *PTW*, 211, Buber says that human life is bound to separation, to division; it cannot run its course in wholeness.

105. "Education and World-View," in *PTW*, 100.

106. "China and Us," in *PTW*, 121, 123–24.

107. *PIU*, 175, 238. See also "The Validity and Limitation of the Political Principle," in *PTW*, 218; "Afterword: The History of the Dialogical Principle," in *BMAM*, 216–17, and in *LTP* 119, 202.

108. Umberto Eco, *Interpretation and Overinterpretation* (Cambridge: Cambridge University Press, 1992), 64.

109. Stanley Fish, *Self-Consuming Artifacts* (Berkeley: University of California Press, 1972), 3.

110. These concluding comments draw upon, and relate to, Michael Walzer's discussion in "On the Role of Symbolism in Political Thought," in *Political Science Quarterly*, 82, no. 2 (June 1967):191–204.

111. "On the Psychologizing of the World," in *ABH*, 151. See also "Politics Born of Faith," in *ABH*, 174–79.

112. Walzer, "On the Role of Symbolism," 196.

113. Susser, *Existence and Utopia*, 53. Susser does not say where Buber "admits" that community is a "utopian vision." He may be referring to *Paths in Utopia*, 138, where Buber concludes in the final lines, "The picture I have hastily

sketched will doubtless be laid among the documents of 'Utopian Socialism' until the storm turns them up again. . . . I do believe in the meeting of idea and fate in the creative hour." If Susser is indeed thinking about this passage, then I do not find here an admission by Buber that his idea of community is an attempt to translate an "ineffable meta-political idea into a real political program"; what I do see here is a concluding note that points to the importance of the "meeting of idea and fate in the creative hour."

114. "It happened that a certain heathen came before Shammai and said to him, 'convert me on condition that you teach me the entire Torah while I am standing on one foot.' Shammai drove him away with the builder's measuring stick that was in his hand. He then came before Hillel who converted him. Hillel said to him, 'That which is hateful to you, do not do to your neighbor. This is the entire Torah: the rest is commentary—go and learn it.' " *Babylonian Talmud*, Shabbat 31a, quoted in Barry W. Holtz, *Back to the Sources: Reading the Classical Jewish Texts* (New York: Summit Books, 1984), 11.

115. *Tao Te Ching*, 1:1. For a discussion of the influence of Oriental philosophies, and of the Tao in particular, on Buber's work, see Maurice Friedman, *Martin Buber and the Eternal* (New York: Human Sciences Press, 1986), 102–34, and Irene Eber, "Martin Buber and Taoism," in *Monumenta Serica*, 42 (1994): 445–64.

# CHAPTER 7: DIALOGUE AS POLITICS: ZIONISM AND THE (MIS)MEETING OF BIBLE, HISTORY, PHILOSOPHY, AND POLITICS

1. This idiom (*halutz*) is rooted in the Bible. See Joshua 6:7, where as part of the preparations to circle Jericho it is written that *halutzim* (translated as "armed men") would pass before the ark of YHVH.

2. Buber's most succinct presentation of this viewpoint is in "A Letter to Gandhi," in *PTW*, 142–47.

3. My use of the notions of mythical reality and historical metaphor is indebted to Marshal Sahlin's discussion in his *Historical Metaphors and Mythical Realities* (Ann Arbor: University of Michigan Press, 1981). He analyzes the incidents of Captain Cook's life and death in Hawaii as historical metaphors of the Hawaiians' mythical reality.

4. In this comment, I am playing off of Buber's discussion of the way of the kibbutz movement in his essay "An Experiment that Did Not Fail," in *NB*, 145–56.

5. This is an allusion to "Hope for This Hour," in *PTW*, 220–29.

6. "Israel and the Command of the Spirit," in *IATW*, 255.

7. "Lechyot L'Shem Mah? Loh Die Leechyot" (To Live—For What Purpose? It Is Not Enough to Live) in *TLZ*, 31–36.

8. "Israel and the Command of the Spirit," in *IATW*, 255.

9. See Akivah Ernst Simon, *The Line of Demarcation: Nationalism, Zionism and the Jewish-Arab Conflict in Martin Buber's Theory and Action* (in Hebrew) (Givat Haviva: 1973). For a more general discussion of Buber's contribution to the development of the binational idea, see Susan Lee Hattis, *The Bi-National Idea in Palestine during Mandatory Times* (Haifa: Shikmona, 1970).

10. "Nationalism," in *IATW*, 214–26.

11. This perspective guides *BAL*. See Buber's comments in the introduction to *BAL*, "Zionism and National Ideas," 1–6.

12. "Abraham's Mission," in *DSM*, 70. An alternative English translation is found in "Abraham the Seer," in *OTB*, 28.

13. *BAL*, 6.

14. *BAL*, 6.

15. I have in mind intellectual giants such as Gershom Scholem, Akivah Ernst Simon, S. H. Bergman, and others who belonged to the small political movements that Buber joined and supported, Brit Shalom (in the 1930s) and later on Ichud (in the 1940s and 1950s).

16. Jean-Jacques Rousseau, *The Social Contract*, translated by Maurice Cranston (Harmondsworth, England: Penguin Classics, 1968), book 2, chap. 7, p. 86.

17. *LTP*.

18. *TLZ*, 33.

19. See Aubrey Hodes, *Martin Buber: An Intimate Portrait* (New York: Viking, 1971), 72, which states that "a fascinating book could be written about the relationship between [Buber and Ben-Gurion], who continued the Biblical disputes between the prophets and the rulers."

20. Martin Buber, "Eem Herzl haya od bachayim" (If Herzel Had Still Been Alive). *Ha'aretz*, May 17, 1940, quoted in Avraham Shapira, *Between Spirit and Reality: Dual Structures in the Thought of M. M. Buber* (in Hebrew) (Jerusalem: Bialik Institute, 1994), 41.

21. "Haeevaron Lasod Umabah Hasod: Agnon" (Blindness to the Secret and Pronunciation of the Secret: Agnon), *TLZ*, 173.

22. "The Two Foci of the Jewish Soul," in *TV*, vol. 1: 200, and in *IATW*, 37.

23. "The Way of Man according to the Teachings of Hasidism," in *HAMM*, 146–51.

24. "Al Hanetzach Veharegah" (On Eternity and the Moment), in *TLZ*, 125.

25. Gershom Scholem, *On Jews and Judaism in Crisis: Selected Essays*, edited by Werner Dannhauser (New York: Schocken, 1976), 47–48, quoted in Michael Oppenheim, "The Meaning of Hasidut: Martin Buber and Gershom Scholem," *Journal of the American Academy of Religion* 49, no. 3 (September 1981): 419.

26. *BAL*, 5.

27. *BAL*, 5.

28. *BAL*, 5.

29. For a good introduction to the ideals of the predominantly secular Zionist leadership, see Shlomo Avineri, *The Making of Modern Zionism: The Intellectual Origins of the Jewish State* (New York: Basic Books, 1981).

30. E. Silberschlag, introduction to *Selected Essays*, by A. D. Gordon and translated by Frances Burnce (New York: League for Labor Palestine, 1938), xi–xiv.

31. Akivah Ernst Simon, *Aims-Junctures-Paths: The Thinking of Martin Buber* (in Hebrew) (Tel Aviv: Sifriat Hapoalim, 1985), 150.

32. Buber says, "of all the men who came to the land in the period of new settlement the man Aharon David Gordon appears to me to be the most remarkable." "A Man Who Realizes the Idea of Zion: A. D. Gordon," in *OZ*, 154. I do not criticize Buber's presentation of Gordon and his work, for my focus is on Gordon as an illustration of Buber's "myth-making" project. For such a critique, see Eliezer Schweid, "Martin Buber and A. D. Gordon: A Comparison," in *Martin Buber: A Centenary Volume*, edited by Haim Gordon and Jochanan Bloch (New York: Ktav, 1984), 255–69. Schweid attributes the difference between Gordon's and Buber's philosophies to the fact that the former wrote from an experience of realization while the latter wrote out of a literary, idealistic, conception of realization. Thus, says Schweid, the centrality of physical labor in Gordon's works, and the absence of this element from Buber's.

33. *OZ* 154–55; *BAL*, 162–64. For a treatment of Buber's relation to nature see in Donald L. Berry, "A Tree," *Mutuality: The Vision of Martin Buber* (Albany: State University of New York, 1985), 1–38.

34. *OZ*, 156; *BAL*, 164.

35. *OZ*, 157; *BAL*, 165.

36. *OZ*, 155; *BAL*, 165.

37. *OZ*, 156, 158; *BAL*, 165–66.

38. *OZ*, 155; *BAL*, 166.

39. "Three Theses of a Religious Socialism," in *PTW*, 112–15.

40. For an interesting discussion of the secular culture that Zionism created, see Michael Berkowitz, *Zionist Culture and Western European Jewry before the First World War* (Cambridge: Cambridge University Press, 1993).

41. Karl Marx, "The German Ideology," *The Marx-Engels Reader*, edited by Robert C. Tucker (New York: W. W. Norton, 1978), 166.

42. "Hebrew Humanism," in *IATW*, 252.

43. See "Raayonoth al HaChinuch HaLeumi VeHachalutzi" (Thoughts about National and Pioneering Education), in *TV*, vol. 2: 387–97, especially 390. See also "Hebrew Humanism," in *IATW*, 248. According to Buber, the

importance of the mission of Israel—to establish social justice—was attested to by the prophets, who warned that if Israel would not find a way to fulfill the demands of social justice in the period of its national independence, it would have to learn (as it indeed did) in exile, in servitude to others, what is justice and what is not.

44. "Haalutz Veolamo" (The Pioneer and His World), in *TV*, vol. 2: 255.

45. "The Spirit of Israel and the World of Today," in *IATW*, 193–94.

46. "Hitchadshut Chayai Am" (Renewal of the Life of a People), in *TV*, vol. 2: 180–89.

47. "China and Us," in *PTW*, 123.

48. *LTP*, 119.

49. "Hebrew Humanism," in *IATW*, 252.

50. In *PIU*, 143, Buber speaks of the unique "pioneer spirit."

51. "Hahalutz Veolamo," in *TV*, vol. 2: 255.

52. Afterword to *I and Thou*, 179; *Werke*, 1:167. Smith renders *verkummerten* as "anthrophied" in his translation of *I and Thou*, 133. See also "What Is Man?" in *BMAM*, 202.

53. For additional essays analyzing the origins of the *halutz*, see *TV*, vol. 2: 183–86 and 255–57.

54. This is an amended version of the English translation of "An Open Letter to Mahatma Gandhi," in *LTP*, 119. For the Hebrew version, see *TV*, vol. 2: 168.

55. *TN*, 136; *TPF*, 147.

56. "Hearot LeSefer Yesha'ayahu" (Comments about the Book of Isaiah), in *DSM*, 326. See also the discussion in chapters 3 and 4.

57. Afterword to *I and Thou*, 178.

58. I am extrapolating from Buber's essay "The Education of Character," in *BMAM*, 104.

59. *TV*, vol. 2: 397.

60. "Thoughts About National and Pioneering Education," *TV*, vol. 2: 390.

61. The origins of the Jewish nation go beyond nineteenth-century nationalism and are expounded in Buber's notion of Hebrew humanism. "Hebrew Humanism," in *IATW*, 248.

62. *PIU*, 73.

63. Buber's favorite example of a true revolutionary is Gustav Landauer. See *PTW*, 115–20; *PIU*, 46–57. For Landauer's influence on Buber, see Grete Schaeder, *The Hebrew Humanism of Martin Buber*, translated by Noah Jacobs (Detroit: Wayne State University Press, 1973), 258–64.

64. "Education," in *BMAM*, 101.

65. "The Education of Character," in *BMAM*, 116.

66. The concept of a proletariat class was not itself a new one; it derived from the Roman term for lower classes. It was new to *socialist* discourse.

67. Menachem Gerson quoted in Maurice Friedman, *Martin Buber's Life and Work: The Middle Years, 1923–1945* (Detroit: Wayne State University Press, 1988), 246. See also Menachem Dorman, "Martin Buber's Address 'Herut' and Its Influence on the Jewish Youth Movement in Germany," in *A Centenary Volume*, edited by Gordon and Bloch, 233–44. For numerous references to the difficulties many of Buber's listeners encountered trying to follow his discourse, see Haim Gordon, *The Other Martin Buber: Reflections of his Contemporaries* (Ohio State University Press, 1988), 156–57, 159, 161, 165.

68. *LTP*, 202. For mention of this idea in Buber's more general social theory, see his reference to "humanity's spiritual conscience" in *PIU*, 134, and to the "essential We" in "What is Man?" in *BMAM*, 175.

69. In fairness to Buber, I must emphasize that I have singled out for criticism one part of a more elaborate proposal Buber brought forth in April 1947. Buber suggested two primary projects of future cooperation between Jews and Arabs in Palestine. One was a jointly undertaken major irrigation project that, while serving the economic interests of both communities, would also illustrate how the opponents could cooperate in the development of the contested land. The second venture Buber had in mind he called "spiritual-political." Buber hoped to transform the problem of Palestine into "a touchstone by which the world shall be tried. From among all the peoples, men of inspiration must arise, men who are of impartial mind and who have not fallen prey to, or become entangled in, the war of all against all for dominion and possession." *LTP*, 202. For a thorough, sympathetic analysis of Buber's attitude to the Jewish-Arab conflict in Palestine, see Hodes, *An Intimate Portrait*, 89–104, and Simon, *The Line of Demarcation*.

70. "The Validity and Limitation of the Political Principle," in *PTW*, 218 (emphasis added).

71. See "Afterword: The History of the Dialogical Principle," in *BMAM*, 216–17, where Buber speaks of the realization that "in this our time men of different kinds and traditions had devoted themselves to the search for the buried treasure." Gabriel Marcel speaks of this conjunction as a moment of "spiritual convergence" in his essay "I and Thou" in *The Philosophy of Martin Buber*, edited by Paul A. Schilpp and Maurice Friedman (La Salle, Illinois: Open Court, 1967), 41.

72. Haim Gordon, "Existential Guilt and Buber's Social and Political Thought," in *A Centenary Volume*, edited by Gordon and Bloch, 224–31.

73. Martin Buber, "Mittlestelle für Judische Erwachsenenbildung," *Runbrief* (June 1934), 4, quoted in Yehoyakim Cochavi, "Arming for Survival: Martin Buber and Adult Education in Nazi Germany," *Holocaust and Genocide Studies*, 3 (1988):56.

74. Cochavi, "Arming for Survival," 63; Simon, *Aims-Junctures-Paths*, 80.

75. The wording of the questions is mine. They reflect the spirit of many critiques of Buber's activities during and after the Second World War. See, for example, Richard L. Rubenstein's scathing critique of Buber in "Buber and the Holocaust: Some Reconsiderations on the 100th Anniversary of His Birth," *Michigan Quarterly Review* 18, no. 3 (Summer 1979): 382–402.

76. "Them and Us," *Ha'aretz*, 15 November, 1939, quoted in Dinah Porat, "Martin Buber in Eretz Yisrael in the Years of the Holocaust, 1942–1944," *Yad Vashem*, vols. 17–18 (1987): 31–32.

77. Yishuv connotes the Zionist community in Palestine in the period preceding the founding of the State of Israel.

78. See Porat, "Martin Buber in Eretz Yisrael," for an excellent presentation of this aspect of Buber's activities in the years 1942–1944.

79. This important document, dated 12 February 1943, was discovered by Dinah Porat in the Buber Archives at the Hebrew University, in file 699/8. A photocopy is appended to her article "Martin Buber in Eretz Yisrael," 61–63.

80. Porat, "Martin Buber in Eretz Yisrael," 63.

81. Porat, "Martin Buber in Eretz Yisrael," 42.

82. *TR*, 53.

83. Hodes, *An Intimate Portrait*, 127.

84. Quoted in Simon, *Aims-Junctures-Paths*, 338. One may note that in traditional interpretations of the Bible, the Hebrew word for gate (שער) is considered an indication of openings to deeper truth.

85. M. Bar-Yechezkel, *Bema'agal Hasatoom* (Tel Aviv, 1973), 92–93, quoted in Porat, "Martin Buber in Eretz Yisrael," 47.

86. "She'elat Doro Shel 'Eyov' " (The Question of "Job's" Generation), *Moznayim* 13, nos. 1–6 (1941): 321–31. By excerpting a passage from *The Prophetic Faith* rather than presenting the original essay, the English translation has omitted the opening two pages of the original article and has changed the title in a manner that omits the obvious intention that the reference to Job be considered a metaphor for immediate events. See "Job," in *OTB*, 188–98.

87. "She'elat Doro Shel 'Eyov,' " 322.

88. See also "Al Sefer Eyov" (About the Book of Job), in *DSM*, 340–42.

89. This is my translation of "The Dialogue between Elohim and Adam in the Bible," in *TV*, vol. 1: 251–52. Another English translation is presented as "The Dialogue between Heaven and Earth," in *OJ*, 224.

90. *TV*, vol. 1: 252; *OJ*, 225. For a good reader-friendly introduction to the question of Job, see Nahum N. Glatzer, "Baeck-Buber-Rosenzweig Reading the Book of Job," Leo Baeck Memorial Lecture 10 (New York: Leo Baeck Institute, 1966), 3–19.

91. "Dialogue," in *BMAM*, 10–11.

92. These radio talks were published in 1957 as *DSA*. The quotation is from *HAMM*, 150.

93. Together with A. D. Gordon, Rabbi A. I. Kook is singled out for special thanks in the preface to Buber's book about Zion, in *BAL*, viii. Buber writes: "With a feeling of deep gratitude, I acknowledge the influence that two meetings had on the fundamental position of this book. These meetings were with persons who died a number of years ago: with A. D. Gordon in Prague in 1920, and with Rabbi Kook in Jerusalem in 1927."

94. Uriel Tal, *Mitos Vetvunah Beyahadoot Yameynu* (Myth and Reason in Contemporary Judaism) (Tel Aviv: Sifriat Poalim, 1987), 7–8.

95. See Michael Lowy, *Redemption and Utopia: Jewish Libertarian Thought in Central Europe* (Stanford: Stanford University Press, 1988), especially 53–57.

96. See Jacob Needleman, *A Sense of the Cosmos: The Encounter of Modern Science and Ancient Truth* (New York: Doubleday, 1975), 85, for a discussion along similar lines.

97. *BMAM*, 105.

98. The philosopher Hugo Bergman suggests that in the mature period of Buber's work, the social factor in his thought swallowed up the religious one. Hugo Bergman, "Martin Buber and Mysticism," in *The Philosophy of Martin Buber*, edited by Schilpp and Friedman, 302.

99. Martin Buber "Replies to My Critics," in *The Philosophy of Martin Buber*, edited by Schilpp and Friedman, 731. See also Gordon, *The Other Martin Buber*, 74.

100. Plato, *Gorgias*, 527b–d.

# INDEX

# ABOUT THE AUTHOR

**Dan Avnon** is senior lecturer of political science at The Hebrew University of Jerusalem. The author of numerous essays in political theory and in comparative politics, he has also edited a number of books, including *Squaring the Circle: Liberalism and Its Practice* (with Avner deShalit).